W9-ASX-722

INHERIT THE LAND

To Betsy –
Cheers,
Gene Stowe
7-7-06

Gene Stowe

Illustrated by Carl A. Sergio

UNIVERSITY PRESS OF MISSISSIPPI / JACKSON

INHERIT THE LAND

Jim Crow Meets Miss Maggie's Will

www.upress.state.ms.us

The University Press of Mississippi is a member of the
Association of American University Presses.

First edition 2006
∞
Library of Congress Cataloging-in-Publication Data

Stowe, Gene.
Inherit the land : Jim Crow meets Miss Maggie's will / Gene Stowe ;
Illustrated by Carl A. Sergio.— 1st ed.
p. cm.
Includes bibliographical references and index.
ISBN 1-57806-864-9 (cloth : alk. paper) 1. Union County (N.C.)—Race relations—History—20th century. 2. Ross, Maggie, d. 1920—Will. 3. African Americans—Segregation—North Carolina—Union County—History—20th century. 4. Inheritance and succession—Social aspects—North Carolina—Union County. 5. Racism—North Carolina—Union County—History—20th century. 6. Union County (N.C.)—Biography. 7. Ross, Maggie, d. 1920—Family. 8. Ross family. I. Title.
F262.U5S76 2006
305.8009756'755—dc22

2005032820

British Library Cataloging-in-Publication Data available

To my father

Justice, justice shall you pursue, in order that
you may live and inherit the land which
the Lord your God is giving to you.

—DEUTERONOMY 16:20

CONTENTS

PREFACE

My father told me they should know better, those good folks in Monroe who proclaimed "niggers don't have souls" and hounded him for allowing a black student to sing in the First Presbyterian Church choir in the late 1960s, when I was in high school. He was right. Their stance was that they were preserving a "way of life" passed on by ancestors who were "products of their times." That argument fails. Fortunately, most people in Monroe had adopted a new way of life, producing more harmonious times, when I went back in the early 1980s as a reporter for the *Charlotte Observer*. P. E. Bazemore, a city council member for more than twenty years and mayor pro tem, cites his first election in 1981 as a mark of the change. He won the office while he was the lead plaintiff in a court case that charged the state agriculture department with racism—and the local paper was calling the class-action suit "Bazemore's case."

"Since that time, I would say they've moved progressively forward," said Bazemore, who kept getting elected, often leading the ticket, after the Supreme Court ruled for his side in *Bazemore v. Friday* in 1986. "People who were not as strong racially began to step forward. You always had quality people in Monroe and some in the county as well. They weren't the die-hard racists. They were silent in the trouble days. They're not silent any more."

They should have known better all along. Nearly one hundred years before I was in high school, on a plantation at the edge of their county, three white women knew better. Susan Ross took Bob Ross as a black apprentice in her home and, with her spinster daughters Maggie and Sallie, raised him as an equal member of the family. When he married and had a daughter, Mittie Bell, they brought her up the same way. The black people were so fully family that the women bequeathed them their homeplace, only to have the will challenged by more than one hundred cousins after Maggie died in 1920.

These antebellum women, no less "products of their times" than their cousins, fashioned a way of life in black-and-white contrast to the world around them. They came to terms with that society—Mittie Bell tied up her hair and waited table when formal visitors came—but they lived a different life on their fifteen-hundred-acre "little empire" of black and white tenants. They made an apprentice an heir at a time when other white Southern masters were using the law to maintain an abusive order barely distinguishable from slavery. They built houses and a church for black people at a time when other whites were burning buildings to terrorize the race. They left eight hundred acres to a black man and his daughter at a time when other Southern whites were lynching black people in order to steal their land.

Moreover, their sheer goodness—their faith, hope, and charity, their simple affection, their guileless generosity—shielded the family from any reprisal during their lifetime or after and made mutual respect a matter of course for many in their community. No matter how odd their life—and odd it was in the stifling days of Reconstruction, Jim Crow, and the Klan—the content of their character won acceptance in the churches, stores, and homes around them.

"Mom used to speak very highly of the Ross women," said Lavinia Kell, whose mother, uncles, and cousin testified for Maggie. "People talked about them because they raised the colored boy. They saw this child needed help, so they took him in and raised him. Nobody had done such a thing back in that day. I guess they thought they were helping that family. They were more integrated than anybody else. Color didn't matter to them."

They knew better.

ACKNOWLEDGMENTS

In the past twelve years, dozens of people have added their own bits to this story, which began as a set of newspaper articles, detoured into an attempted novel for eight years, and wound up as history when the North Carolina Supreme Court Library found the long-forgotten trial transcript. Cliff Harrington, my editor at the *Charlotte Observer*'s *Union Observer* office, was there at the beginning in 1993. Rev. Henrico White is still pastor of Marvin AME Zion Church. My friend John Banks, who has read at least ten versions since the first fiction attempt, rightly calls it "a true story based on a novel." Robert Houston, who gave me the first glimpse of the story, and Lavinia Kell, who told me what her mother said about the Ross women, have died.

Many who helped are longtime friends: Virginia Kendrick Bjorlin, Sis Dillon, and the others at the Heritage Room of Union County; Julie Hampton Ganis and Frances Small of the Carolinas Genealogical Society; Union County Sheriff Frank McGuirt; Union County Clerk of Superior Court Nola McCollum; Monroe Mayor Lewis Fisher; Linda Blackwelder; and Joe Kerr.

Many are descendants of people in the story: Cornelia Plyler and Margaret Butler, Frank Crane's granddaughters; Pearl Fetterson, Mittie's first cousin; Alvenia Morrison and Vivian and Rachel Houston, Mittie's granddaughters; Rachel Houston and Lamont "Smoky" Houston, Mittie's great-grandchildren; Heidi Williamson, Mittie's great-great-granddaughter; Richard and Joe Hudson, R. A. Hudson's grandsons; Emma Hinson, Adam Morgan's granddaughter; Gladys Cox, Bud Huey's granddaughter; the Burleyson family; Sam Ardrey, Dr. J. J. Rone's grandson, who welcomed me into the old Ross house; Betty Thomas and Robert Thomas, E. T. Cansler's granddaughter and great-grandson; Penelope Niven, J. M. Niven's granddaughter.

Ruth Ezzell, a Heritage Room volunteer and Marvin historian whose husband was related to a witness to the will, made sure the story could move to nonfiction with her faithful correspondence and encouragement.

Some just took an interest in the story. Joe Moore, whose family has kept weather records at Rock Rest since the 1890s, provided weather data. My colleagues at Trinity School at Greenlawn gave advice and encouragement, as did my former colleagues at the *Charlotte Observer,* Frye Gaillard, Steve Lyttle, and Davie Hinshaw. Ralph Novotney, a real estate lawyer from Los Angeles, interpreted the will and the deeds.

The Union County Public Library, the Union Heritage Room, the Union County Historical Society, the Carolinas Genealogical Society, the North Carolina State Archives, the Union County Register of Deeds office, the Union County Clerk of Court office, Kathy Galvin at the St. Joseph County (Indiana) Public Library's interlibrary loan department, the Franklin County (North Carolina) Public Library (and Franklin County historian Joe Pearce), Banks Presbyterian Church, Marvin United Methodist Church, Bonds Grove United Methodist Church, the Western North Carolina Conference of the United Methodist Church, First Presbyterian Church in Monroe, Livingstone College, and Barium Springs Home for Children provided important resources. The North Caroliniana Society awarded a grant for research.

My mother, Beverly Stowe, provided lodging and meals for my research trips and accompanied me on some excursions. My brother, Dr. William B. Stowe, gave important guidance on the writing. My whole family, including my wife, Donna, and my children, some of whom have no memory of life when Daddy was not working on The Book, kept me going all these years.

INHERIT THE LAND

PROLOGUE

Tom Houston . . . was called by the Marvin people
"Miss Mag's son-in-law"

—R. A. HUDSON, 1921

The sad-eyed Southern squire on the witness stand could have predicted that night's late-spring killing frost by the dry north wind whipping the high-arched windows in the second-story Courtroom. He could not have predicted the fallout from an offhand remark while he was explaining his ledger to a hostile lawyer: "I think Tom Houston's account is in that book. He was called by the Marvin people 'Miss Mag's son-in-law.'"

Here was the heart of the case on trial in Monroe, North Carolina, in April 1921. Was Maggie Ross crazy about the black people her family raised? Or was she just plain crazy?

Maggie, a cousin to the recent governor, was the richest woman in Union County when she died nearly a year earlier. Tom was a sharecropper who couldn't even write his name. Maggie's will bequeathed her homeplace to Tom's wife, Mittie Bell, and her father, Bob Ross. Bob had grown up like a baby brother to Maggie from the time he was two years old and she was thirty-five. Mittie, in turn, went to live with Maggie and her sister as soon as she was walking. The spinsters built a grand house for Mittie and Tom after they married in 1907 and wrote identical wills later that

Tom Houston

year, a few weeks after the Houstons had their first child. Eight hundred acres, hundreds of dollars in cash, and two of the white family's three gold watches went to the black family.

The lawyer grilling the witness, John J. Parker, savored the "son-in-law" suggestion. Tense lines eased for a moment in his large, high-domed head. Parker, looming above the stand at more than six feet tall, needed such a break. He was sure he had lost the race for governor six months earlier because he couldn't shake his Republican Party's ancient identification with the rights of negroes. Impossible, then, that he could lose this case, so black and white, when he was taking the side of the white family. After all, some of the jurors were sons of Confederate veterans. One grew up on his grandfather's plantation when scores of slaves were carding wool for gray uniforms.

They had heard that Miss Maggie had called Mittie's daughter her "darling granddaughter." They had heard that before Mittie was married, she gave birth to a baby in Miss Maggie's bed, the baby died, and the white women paid the doctor not to tell. Now they were hearing that Miss Maggie called Mittie's husband her son-in-law.

No jury in the South would give a black man and a black woman eight hundred acres in a white community, especially when one hundred nine of Maggie's cousins were claiming the land. This was the white man's world. Maggie supped with black people; slept in the same bed as a little black girl; shared shoes, dresses, even underwear; and shielded her from the shame due her sin. Southern women with sense didn't act that way. Such testimony proved that she wasn't simply sentimental or sometimes charitable with these people. She wasn't just doting; she was a dotard.

Tom Houston was called by the Marvin people "Miss Mag's son-in-law." That showed her state of mind. That's what this trial was all about.

PART I

Worlds Apart

1

THE MARVIN PEOPLE

From a line of ancestors who had fought for freedom
in the Revolutionary War and believed in the
Fatherhood of God and the brotherhood of man
came the community of Marvin.

—MARVIN HISTORIAN, 1960s

For two hundred years, the gentle red-earth hills and the dusty-brown draws and bottoms in the far western corner of Union County, where the border with South Carolina runs northwest on some surveyor's plot and the Mecklenburg County line angles northeast along Sixmile Creek, yielded some of the best cotton in the county. A few of the oldest families held kings' grants from colonial times, but most had come down the Great Wagon Road from the North, like the Polks, who had produced President James K. Polk nine miles to the north, and the Jacksons, who had produced President Andrew Jackson eight miles to the south. The soft pines fell for farmers clearing the fertile land, and plenty of thick oaks shaded homesites on stately knolls that commanded views of a rippling landscape inviting such names as Pleasant Valley and Forest Home, Bonds Grove and Sandy Ridge. The dry winds came from the northwest and the wet winds from the southwest, the sun set over South Carolina, and the forest floors lay thick with generations of leaves hardly rustled by human feet. An Indian trading path ran north of the land, out to the Catawba Nation on the big river to the west, and the settlement of the Waxhaws, a branch of the Catawbas, lay to the south starting at Twelvemile Creek, but the region remained largely overlooked even in antiquity. Day and night, summer and winter, snow and heat, dusty dry and creek-swelling wet, the soil produced acorns and hickories for the squirrels and lush banks of fragrant honeysuckle for the bees and the butterflies, thickets of blackberries for the rabbits, and tender grass and saplings for the deer—and gathered strength for the decades when it would be put to the plow, yielding thousands of bales of cotton to fuel a civilization.

The earliest homes went up in the decade before the Revolution, but only a few farmers—large landowners, small slaveholders—worked the ground before fifteen of their sons went off to fight for Southern Independence. Most of William and John King's family died of smallpox, and Sir Frederick Ezzell of Germany bought the three hundred acres King George III had given them. Acres apart along the winding paths settled Howeys and Howies, Stephensons and Squires, Rosses and Rones, Pierces, Brooms, Parkses, and McIlwaines. Of the men who followed General Lee, three gave their lives for the Cause. The others marched home to build a new world after the collapse of the Confederacy. Their slaves were freed, but the people still needed work and the fields still needed people to work them. The land was still rich, though its owners were poor. Its yield could keep them all alive.

Buckhill Baptist Church was already built on one of the hills near the South Carolina line, but the Baptist style, complete with an immersion pool at the spring nearby, proved a poor fit for the kind of community the farmers were planting. Loyd Rone was the only Methodist in the neighborhood until John Squires moved nearby in 1865. Methodist preaching services started at the log Stephenson School House, already host to an old Sunday school, in 1872. In hot weather, the worshipers built a brush arbor for services—there Rone's daughter and Squires' daughter were baptized—and in winter they built roaring fires in the schoolhouse fireplace. Every first and third Sunday afternoon, Dr. W. D. Lee would draw crowds for preaching. In 1874, Rone and Squires agreed to build a permanent church: Rone, who donated the land, provided the

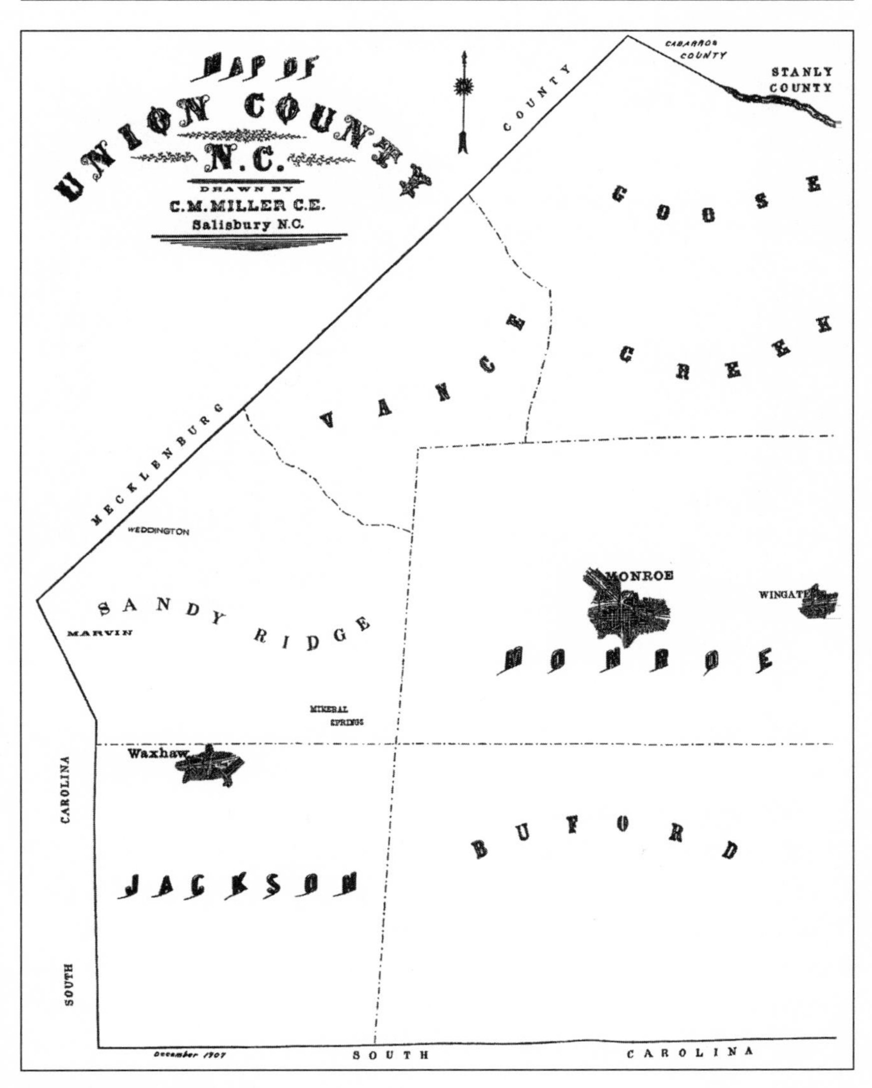

Union County Map, 1907

brick and paid the masons; Squires provided the wood and paid the carpenters. Thomas Jefferson Ezzell, their neighbor, agreed to pay for the paint and the painters even though he was not a member of the church. Work started in December. A cold snap that winter froze the mortar and

Marvin Methodist Church (courtesy of the Union County Historical Society)

plaster, but the red-brick building, briefly called Rone's Chapel, opened in the summer.

At the formal dedication in October 1875, the church was christened for Most Rev. Enoch Mather Marvin, a Confederate chaplain from Missouri who became a bishop of the Methodist Episcopal Church South in 1866. Bishop Marvin, who had worked the Oklahoma Indian Mission, was as revered for his humility as for his oratory. After delivering the commencement address at Washington College in Lexington, Virginia, he turned down a dinner invitation from General Lee in order to sup with the village blacksmith. The community, as well as the church, adopted his name.

The old Sunday school moved from the whitewashed schoolhouse next door, but it remained open to all denominations. Presbyterians Billy McIlwaine, son of the community doctor, and a Scotsman named Donaldson helped Mr. Squires lead the free-flowing Bible class discussions. Starting in the summer of 1875, the Methodists invited a

Presbyterian minister, G. Springs Robinson, to hold services twice a month in their building. The sharing continued until the Presbyterians opened Banks Chapel in 1878.

By tradition, temperament, and blood, many of the families in the community were Presbyterians. For years, most of them traveled, when the roads were passable, to Providence Presbyterian Church across Six-mile Creek and well into Mecklenburg County. Providence's pastor, Rev. William Banks of South Carolina, started Presbyterian preaching services once a month at Wolfsville Academy, a school at Providence and New Town roads, before he died in 1875, and Rev. Robinson continued meetings there until the Methodists invited him to use their building. Rev. Billy McIlwaine, the onetime Bible teacher, was preaching at Hopewell Presbyterian in northwestern Mecklenburg County when he felt moved to hire a buggy, drive thirty miles to his old stomping grounds, and canvass his neighbors for construction of a new Presbyterian chapel. By the end of the day, he collected six hundred fifty dollars, and his father donated land for the building, separated from the Methodists only by a broad field. John Squires built the sturdy gable-roofed structure with double entrance doors framed with panels and windows.

In 1886, Dr. James John Rone, Loyd Rone's son, built the most magnificent house in Marvin on the strip of land he had inherited between the two church buildings. Dr. Rone was the husband of Mary Lavinia McIlwaine, Dr. W. A. McIlwaine's daughter and sister to Rev. Billy McIlwaine and Rev. Bobby McIlwaine. The union of Marvin's greatest benefactor clans, Methodist and Presbyterian, and the raising of their grand home, the soul of the community between its two spiritual centers, confirmed a standard of harmony and beauty—aesthetic, religious, and familial—to which the settlers had long aspired.

The house was two rooms over two rooms in the front: bedroom to the right, sitting room to the left on the first floor, with a wide foyer between in front and a narrow hall running past the banistered staircase to the back. The arrangement presented passersby on New Town Road the view of a wide, tall face flanked by chimneys, and Dr. Rone ornamented that face with a massive Victorian two-story porch for nearly its whole width. The porch was built freestanding under a roof supported by four square-tapered two-story columns, and its elaborate millwork included turned columns, turned balusters, a turned spindle-frieze, and scroll-sawn brackets. The afternoon sun filled the porch, and the front yard faced the sunset so as to catch the last rays of evening light. A one-story, two-room wing—a dining room and kitchen sharing a central chimney—ran behind the sitting room. Back porches ran the length of the kitchen and the width of the downstairs bedroom. Inside, dark-finished pine boards fit snugly for smooth walls and ceilings and floors, and triangular molding strips softened the corners of the rooms. The house sat near the front of the property, with room for one carriage to drive easily between the road and the row of oaks outside a white, double-gated picket fence. The driveway entered from the Methodist side and arched around to the back, where the picket fence cornered to divide the drive from the yard.

The Rones understood their role in Marvin. Mary Lavinia was brought up in sight of her new home, in the doctor's house that in its time commanded the community at a fork in the main road. She had fallen in love with J. J. while they were both studying at Erskine College in Due West, South Carolina, before he went to the Medical College of Vanderbilt University in Nashville. She knew how to keep up with the latest fashions, and she made the home a hub of hospitality for the community. The Rones were bringing up two daughters of their own, Blanche, who was eight when they moved into the house, and Anabel, who was seven. Neighbors' children feigned illness just to stay overnight at the house for the doctor's observation and his wife's cooking. The yield of the rich garden, the fruit trees, the fields, the barnyard, and the beehives flowed into Mary Lavinia's kitchen. Her art filled the house with the fragrance of fried chicken and fried ham, fluffy buttermilk biscuits and crisp cracklin' cornbread, blackberry cobbler and pound cake, green beans shimmering in bacon-laced pot likker and dill pickles steeping in pottery crocks of vinegar. Folks who came to spend the day pitched in to help with peeling potatoes and plucking hens, shucking corn and shelling peas, and they shared in the celebratory supper at the long table in the dining room.

Strangers driving on the road that connected Monroe and Fort Mill inquired at the nearby store about the impressive scene at the core of the community—church, mansion, church, with ceaseless activity in the middle all week and solemn gatherings at the sides on Sunday mornings. Marvin folks proudly replied that the second generation of the churches' leading families lived there, a sign of the faith, hope, and charity that marked their little village, and established the course it would take as it grew. The neighbors felt secure that the radiance of that history and that striking tableau between the curves in the road cast all of them in a favorable light and brightened a straight path to a prosperous future.

But after only five years, Dr. Rone abruptly abandoned the community, moved his family to Pineville, and began to practice medicine there. The move was a matter of conscience, the neighbors whispered—moral, and probably something medical, too. A leading citizen in the community had gotten his stepdaughter pregnant. The woman had delivered—the stories weren't clear whether Dr. Rone was present—and they had thrown the baby down a well to hide their shame. Dr. Rone would no more practice medicine in Marvin. They said that before he left, he met the guilty neighbor late one afternoon on a lonely road and, in the deepening shadows, horsewhipped him for his crime. Within a few years, the doctor left the state to take over an ill classmate's practice in Missouri, where he died in 1899. By then, incest, murder, and vigilante justice had turned out to be tired topics in Marvin.

Most people, especially the elders, knew something about the Rosses. They lived on old family land only two miles away from the center of the community, although their orientation seemed in the other direction down New Town Road, toward Union Methodist Episcopal Church South, where they had buried their mother in 1886. Everyone knew that Miss Susan and her children—Mr. Dennis and Miss Sallie and Miss Maggie—had taken in a black child, Bob Ross, years ago and raised him to manhood. Everyone knew that he had married and sired a

Banks Presbyterian Church (courtesy of the Union County Historical Society)

daughter the year after Miss Susan died and that the child was living with the white sisters and their brother. Everyone also knew that Miss Susan's children were as industrious and ambitious as their mother had been, that they had added field after field to their inheritance from Grandfather Jonathan Burleyson and had risen among the biggest cotton producers in Sandy Ridge Township. But no one could have predicted that such a family, if it could be called a family, would be moving into the house that Dr. Rone and Miss Mary Lavinia had made the very heart of Marvin. The light between the two churches had faded when the couple moved out of their home. For some neighbors, it turned to darkness when the strange set of siblings and servants moved in.

"Them Ross women is odd," whispered folks who only recently had been spreading the word about the baby in the well. But in the tenant cabins and the sturdy clapboard farmhouses, another whisper soon followed: "Them Ross women is good." Their well-known wealth, amassed from their grandfather's estate and their own thrifty skill, flowed freely to neighbors, black and white, when they fell on hard times and to churches, black and white, that the women had helped take root. They deeded two acres to help start Marvin African Methodist Episcopal Zion Church in 1901 so that black people west of Providence Road wouldn't have to walk all the way to Redding Springs for church. Miss Maggie subscribed five hundred dollars to Banks Presbyterian Church when the time came to build a new sanctuary. Workers dismantled an old Indian mound to fashion the rock foundation for the church. Maggie gave a three hundred dollar piano, a pulpit Bible, and a leather-bound hymnal in memory of her sister. When Miss Sallie died in 1909, her obituary recorded the kind of goodness she lived and revealed the public approval of that life:

> Originally endowed with a strong constitution, she early formed such habits as to secure for herself an unusually long life. She rose early each day; she addressed herself with energy to her daily tasks; she was temperate in all things—in dress, in food and drink, in rest and labor. And she had her reward in a quiet life of many years. . . . And be it said to her honor, that her success in business was not attained by failure to pay honest debts, by exacting exorbitant interest, or by withholding the hire of the laborer. No advantage was ever taken of the poor, the needy or the distressed, whether white or colored. So far from this every honest, faithful tenant had an unfailing friend and wise counselor in Miss Sallie Ross.
>
> But whilst she gave her attention to the business of this world, she was not unmindful of the claims of the world to come. She publicly avowed her faith in Jesus Christ as her personal Savior, and united with Banks Presbyterian Church and lived and died a member of this church. Her religion was not of the demonstrative kind which proclaims itself publicly and on special occasions where it can be "seen of men." Hers was of the kind that prefers to reveal itself quietly all the year round in the payment of honest debts, in dealing kindly and mercifully with those dependent upon her, and in keeping her promises to the letter whether made to rich or poor, white or black.

The respect that the Rosses by nature showed to all, black or white, their neighbors by custom came to reflect. When Miss Sallie and Miss Maggie told the road commissioners to check with Bob Ross about laying a road through their land, they went and talked to him. When he showed up at the white tenants' doors to collect rent for the women, they paid him. Miss Jennie Helms at Crane's Store usually wrote only the first names of tenants and black customers in the store ledger, but when Bob came to buy fifteen pounds of nails or forty cents' worth of molasses or fifteen cents' worth of candles, the flowery script recorded "RB Ross."

Marvin was still an out-of-the-way place, a world unto itself. The fields provided work for nearly everyone. The Rosses' and the Cranes' and the Stephensons' gins turned the crop into seedless bales. Frank Crane ran a grist mill and a sawmill and a postal station before Rural Free Delivery and a telephone exchange after the mail routes arrived. Mr. McKinney ran the blacksmith's shop. Crane's Store and Ezzell's Store stocked the coffee and tobacco, kerosene and cattle powder, sugar, quinine, and bluing that the farmers and their wives wanted. The tenants, black and white, needed the work, and the landowners, all white, needed the workers. To live, they must let live. Many might whisper about the Rosses' odd ways—some might even sneer—but they were neighbors, and Marvin folk were neighborly.

2

THE WHITE MAN'S WORLD OF VIOLENCE

If it is necessary, every negro in the State will be lynched. It will be done to maintain white supremacy.

—MISSISSIPPI GOV. JAMES K. VARDAMAN (1904–1908)

In much of the world beyond Marvin—the neighboring towns, the next state, across the South, and even up North—not brotherhood but lynching was the rule. Hatred begot violence, and violence seemed to beget more hatred. Union County, created in 1842 from the union of eastern Mecklenburg and western Anson counties, straddled a sort of seam in upland North Carolina's economy, and hence its racial strains. To the east, as the land grew flatter and more sandy, it supported plantations with thousands of acres of cotton and tobacco, and the descendants of slaves who worked those fields accounted for 40 percent of the population as close as Anson County. To the west, as curving creeks crisscrossed the rumpled clay soil, most farmers counted a few hundred acres and took on a few tenant farmers, black and white, to help their families tend the cotton. Black people made up less than 20 percent of the population, but the county's history counted its share of terror against them.

Among the most mysterious were the whispers about the name of Niggerhead Creek that flowed in the northeastern side of the county.

More mundane versions said the water was named for the round, black stones in the creek bed, but more lurid tales invoked history rather than science. Most involved a slave, maybe named Henry, who killed his white master's wife while the master was away visiting their sons at war. He was executed—in some versions, by a crowd on the spot, in some by the one-armed Confederate sheriff in Monroe after a quick trial—and his skull stuck on a pole in the creek to warn other would-be revolutionaries in those waning days of slavery.

Race violence ran deep in Union County. The oldest brick building in the county seat was the two-story Monroe City Hall, originally a jail built with the blood money of a slaveholder from Weddington, Marvin's older neighbor to the east. In 1847, John Medlin and another man dragged one of his slaves behind a wagon from their farm some twelve miles northeast to Monroe. He was dead when they arrived, and Mr. Medlin was convicted of murder. He pled "benefit of clergy" under an old English law that required only that he could read and write to buy his way out of prison. The county used his three-thousand-dollar fine to replace its log jail and invite more elegant construction in its three-year-old county seat. One of Maggie and Sallie's cousins, Lessie Ross, married Mr. Medlin's grandson, Williford Crook.

Mob violence was more common. One Sunday evening in the late spring of 1898, two thousand people surrounded the jail in Cabarrus County (just north of the Rocky River from Union), broke into the cells, and dragged two black men nearly two miles down dirt roads to a dogwood tree where they hanged the men and filled their bodies with buckshot. They accused Tom Johnson and Joe Kiser, who had run away from his wife and children in Union County to live with another woman, of raping twelve-year-old Amy Hartsell and slashing her throat, nearly decapitating her, while her parents were at church earlier that day.

"While the people were at the jail, a number of people tried to persuade them to allow the law to settle the matter," the *Concord Times* reported. "But there was no thought in the minds of those people of letting the perpetrators of such a shocking crime live a single day longer. A crime so foul, so horrible, so damnable, they argued, demanded swift and summary punishment."

Such an eye-for-eye approach even swayed a preacher who tried to stop the lynching and prayed for the men while the crowd fell silent. He wrote to the *Charlotte Observer*: "This was my purpose—to prevent the lynching; but when I failed, it is a satisfaction to feel that these men were guilty of this double crime unparalleled in the history of the country. It was not the wild, mad mob your correspondent represented it to be, and they quietly persisted in doing what they thought was right. I do not hesitate to say that my sympathy was with them, although my judgment was against lynching and I did all that I could to prevent it."

Another mob formed swiftly to the south on a November day in 1903. Will Porter, who worked in Monroe, was on a business trip when he caught Joe Nelson loading a boxcar in Jefferson, South Carolina. Joe was accused of raping Will's little sister on the family's farm in Chesterfield County, along the southern border of Union County. Will tossed Joe into his buggy and headed for the sheriff. A crowd gathered, grabbed Joe out of the buggy, and hanged him on the spot by the side of the road.

Much less than rape or murder was required for a lynch mob to form. In 1916, a mob in Abbeville, South Carolina, about fifty miles from Marvin, hanged Anthony P. Crawford from a pine tree because the black landowning cotton farmer's wealth angered the white farmers gathered at the gin one October afternoon. Such lynchings often resulted in white annexation of black land, either because neighboring farmers simply took over title or because bereft black families could no longer pay their mortgages and taxes, and their property was sold at auction.

Lynchings anywhere—Illinois, Kentucky, Pennsylvania, Oklahoma—made front-page news in Union County newspapers that provided fodder for talk in Crane's Store. Sometimes the bloodlust spilled across the color line, as in a dispatch from Cairo, Illinois, published on November 16, 1909:

> Will James, the negro who murdered Miss Annie Pelley, was killed here tonight by a mob. James was strung up to the public arch, the rope broke and at least five hundred shots were poured into his body. . . . Women present were the first to pull the rope. When it broke, the frenzy of the mob was uncontrollable and they fired volley after volley into James' body, shooting him to pieces. The mob then dragged

the body over the streets for more than a mile to Twenty-sixth and Elm streets, in an alley, and burned it where the murder was committed.

Henry Salzner, white, a photographer who killed his wife last July with an axe, was taken from jail at 11:10 o'clock tonight by a mob and hanged to a telegraph pole and his body riddled with bullets. This lynching followed closely on the lynching of Will James.

Near-lynchings also made news. An unidentified black man, charged with making an indecent proposition and winking at a white girl in Hickory, about seventy miles northwest of Marvin, was spirited in a buggy to nearby Newton while Judge W. B. Council distracted the mob that showed up at the jail. In Shelby, it took a congressman to stop the crowd that came to avenge the shooting of the police chief.

North Carolina newspapers condemned the lynchings. After the Shelby incident, *Monroe Journal* editor R. F. Beasley unleashed a sarcastic column:

A negro shot and killed the chief of police of Shelby Saturday, and a mob got up early yesterday morning to try, sentence and execute him. It seems that Congressman Webb persuaded the crowd not to do it, and his personal influence gave the law an opportunity to be tried. Oh, we are coming along all right. First we lynched 'em for crimes against women and children, and everybody approved; then we burned 'em. Then lynching and burning were thought to be the proper thing for cold blooded murderers and not long ago, in South Carolina, they "fixed" one for plain "sass." By and by we will express our disapproval of verdicts of justices of the peace by lynching the prisoners, just to show magistrates what small potatoes they are. And we expect to see the good day come when it will be just the thing for temperate and judicial mobs, exercising of course proper care, to lynch fellows who disagree with them on political or other questions. We are a progressive people.

In January 1904, the *Journal* printed a Sunday dispatch from Dodsville, Mississippi: "Luther Holbert and his wife, negroes, were burned at the stake here by a mob of over 1,000 persons, for the killing of James Eastland, a prominent white planter and John Carr, a negro, on Wednesday morning at the Eastland plantation two miles from this city. The burning of Holbert and his wife closes a tragedy which has cost eight lives, has engaged 200 men and two packs of bloodhounds in a four days' chase across four counties and has stirred this section of Mississippi to such a state of excitement as it has never before experienced in its history."

Later, Beasley published Booker T. Washington's response to the violence. Washington pointed out that the three burnings in two weeks—all in broad daylight and two "on Sunday afternoon in sight of a Christian church"—had nothing to do with the sexually charged accusation of rape, more heinous to many white men than murder.

"In the midst of the nation's prosperous life, few, I fear, take time to consider whither these brutal and inhuman practices are leading us," Washington wrote. "The custom of burning human beings has become so common as scarcely to attract interest or unusual attention. . . . I maintain that the only protection of our civilization is a fair and calm trial of all people charged with crime, and in their legal punishment if proved guilty. There is no excuse to depart from legal methods. The laws are as a rule made by the white people and their execution is by the hands of the white people, so that there is little probability of any guilty colored man escaping."

Beasley agreed, calling Washington's view "so true, so temperate and set for conditions so serious." After a race battle in Atlanta in the fall of 1906, the editor became more incensed: "Even Russia is pointing the finger of scorn at us. And as the atmosphere clears, the horror of the mob's work in Atlanta—like the work of all mobs—gets worse. It is said that no man really knows the number of negroes who were killed."

When Congressman Heflin of Alabama shot a black man on a crowded streetcar on Pennsylvania Avenue in 1908, Beasley excoriated him: "The idea of a member of the highest legislative body in the country on his way to deliver a temperance lecture in a church, with a pistol in his pocket is a sight for gods and men. The reception of no amount of threatening letters can excuse such conduct."

The news columns shared the editor's contempt: "A negro named Austin, on April 30th was pursued in a swamp in Hampton county, S.C. and shot and killed three of the men who were attempting to capture him. Nearly a month later, last week, he was captured and died from the wounds while being taken to Hampton. Here one of the most disgraceful scenes ever known in America took place, equaling in brutality an Indian outrage such as the savages practiced in digging up and mutilating a body. The body was taken from the officers who brought it, and the head and fingers and toes were cut off. Members of the mob took the bits of flesh for mementoes. After this the body was singed and then hanged from a tree in front of the courthouse."

On August 4, 1906, Beasley featured on his front page, with a rare black border, an editorial from the *Charlotte Observer* titled "The Remedy, the Only One," calling for drastic measures to end the violence:

> Lynch law is on the increase in North Carolina. There is no negro vote, no negro legislation now, but there is a growing disrespect, not to say contempt, on the part of the white for the laws which they themselves make. The mob hoots and jeers Senators, judges and other officers, whom it helped to elect, when they get up before it to expostulate with it and pray of it to observe the laws which it helped to frame. There must be an end to this, or worse days will come. . . .We are saying now, in the hope that the message will carry to the Governor, the judges, all sheriffs and all others charged with enforcement of the laws, that there is no hope of curing this disease, which is spreading rapidly, except by the shedding of blood. When a North Carolina mob is fired into by deputies or the military, and a dozen or fifteen of the law breakers are killed, there will be an instant end to mob law in the State. The longer the application of the remedy is delayed, the faster the disease will spread. It should be applied to the next mob that thunders at the gates of a jail. But the execution should not be entrusted to the local militia; the chances are that it would fail. The militia of another county should be ordered, where it is practicable, as it generally is, for there are nearly always premonitory murmurings which indicate the coming of the mob and give time for preparations for it. And power should be given the Governor to remove the sheriff who fails to give the command to shoot when to shoot is necessary . . .
>
> Lynchings will not end in North Carolina until the killing of lynchers begins. Then it will end.

But Beasley and his fellow editors were not only opposed to violence. They took a paternal-style pride in the fact that North Carolina invested about five dollars in "uplift of the negro"—health, education, and welfare—for every dollar the state collected in taxes from them, and the papers took pains to promote positive news about black people. The

Journal wrote about a Marvin neighbor in 1906: "William Ivey of Sandy Ridge Township is a young colored man whose good character and success as a farmer should be an example to others of his race. He has taken advantage of the good times to get a start. Four years ago he says he had nothing but two loads of hay and was in debt nineteen dollars. Now he has two good mules, wagon, buggy, barns, and corn and other feed enough to run him this year. In addition to having paid for all these things he now has $150 ahead in cash."

One story praised a former slave who showed up at an eighty-two-year-old woman's house in 1906 to pay for a coat she made him in 1865: "Mrs. Cox said she did not want any payment, but the old darky insisted on it, saying that his failure to pay had worried him so much lately that he could not stand it any more. It is supposed that old George had been attending a protracted meeting and got religion. What ever the cause, he has certainly brought forth fruits meet for repentance."

Another made a moral model of a black man named Wesley Bossard, who snatched the pistol from the man who killed his son but then refused to take revenge on the killer: "What would you have done in a like circumstance, Mr. Good Citizen? Would you have turned the weapon on the man you had seen kill your son the instant before, or would you have done as did old Wesley, the negro hackman?"

Beasley joined the chorus when black Dr. J. S. Massey, who opened the first hospital in Monroe, black or white, was falsely accused (and exonerated) of sending obscene material through the mail: "There was fully a score of the leading business and professional white men of the town, and most of them without having been subpoenaed. They all gave the defendant a good character in no uncertain terms, and some of them had known him since boyhood, and several of them were physicians. A man, black or white, who so lives that he can establish a reputation like this has something to fall back on that cannot be estimated in money. Because Dr. Massey's influence has been good and his conduct always becoming, these gentlemen were glad to give him the benefit of their testimony, and this paper is glad to give publicity to their action." Dr. Massey's family in 1886 had gone on an expedition with the families of other former slaves from Waxhaw to Liberia, where his father died. The hardships in Africa drove his mother to bring the family back to Union County.

In 1907, Confederate veterans asked the state to provide pensions for their "faithful servants." As the years advanced, the papers marked the passing of former slaves with a lingering wistfulness. On February 12, 1907, the *Journal* reprinted a *Charlotte Observer* obituary under the headline "The Passing Away of Another Old-time Darkey":

> Prince Broom, a negro of the old-time stock, died at his home in Providence township last Tuesday night of pneumonia. He was about 70 years old. Prince was owned by Mr. G. D. Broom of Union County in slavery time. For 30 years he worked for the late Mr. Hugh M. Parks of this county. During his long life he was never charged with a crime and but once was he a witness in a law suit. As Mr. Parks' stable man, he carried the keys to the barn, the crib, the grainery and the smoke-house and in his care everything was safe for any length of time. Prince Broom was a country hog butcher. He could kill, clean, cut up and salt away the fattened hogs better than any man in the neighborhood. He must have helped to kill 2,000 hogs in his day. Every good house wife in the neighborhood called on him when the hogs were to be killed. . . . A number of white people will attend the funeral.

The white editors seemed reluctant to part with those last links to what they saw as the well-ordered civilization of slavery days, reluctant to face a future without those living evidences of proper roles among the races, as the obituary concluded: "There are but few old time darkies in Providence now. They are Ben Dunn, Byer Howie and Anderson Smith. Recently Jarvis Stitt, Jake Robinson, a slave of the late Captain James B. Robinson, and Prince Broom has passed away."

The *Journal* printed an unnerving picture of those roles reversed, an African Methodist Episcopal bishop's claim that humans were created black but some unfortunates bleached out. "And in their unnatural pallor many of these bleached men, all of whom were made black at the beginning, now look with contempt and indifference—often with prejudice and hate—upon their brother, because the negro has retained the color that God gave them," Rev. Henry M. Turner told a conference crowd. "We should write books of our own, poems of our own, scientific treatises of our own, in harmony with our color and our race. And don't learn songs like 'Wash Me and I Shall Be Whiter Than Snow'—a song that I would not tolerate sung in my presence."

But Beasley also ran on the front page, without comment, a prophecy from a local Baptist deacon named John Henry that came closer to reflecting the editor's own hopes:

> Between 1 and 2 o'clock there came a message to me sent from God by the Holy Ghost, telling me to tell all the folks, tell all the children of God, to come together and let the light of the Holy Ghost shine. Every one that intends to hold out till the end, pray that the Holy Ghost might conduct the prayer meeting services through the holy days of Christmas. Don't one fight the other, but come together, let the unconverted part of the world know that there is power and virtue and reality in the religion of our lord and savior Jesus Christ. The devil has had his time—that's how come the chain gang here and so many trouble in our mind. Let the Holy Ghost have a chance. There is power enough in the word of God to save us all. Amen.

3

THE WHITE MAN'S WORLD OF POWER

We have fixed the negro's bounds and determined his habitation in perfect accord with his nature and necessities, and in the place assigned him he is, as a race, content to dwell.

—T. WALTER BICKETT, 1903

North Carolina's establishment could eschew violence against black people because it had accomplished a far more peaceful, pragmatic, and permanent way to ensure white supremacy. In the Old North State, the experiment with equality that started with Emancipation and crested in Fusion collapsed on August 2, 1900. The passage of the Suffrage Amendment established as law what the election of 1898 had accomplished by Redshirt terror—the removal of black people from the political process. The amendment to the state constitution imposed a literacy test for voting—registrants must be able to read and write some section of the constitution—but its "grandfather clause" allowed illiterate people to vote if their ancestors had voted before January 1, 1867—that is, if their ancestors were white. The amendment passed 187, 217 to 128, 285.

The Democratic Party championed the change to establish forever the restored control that it had lost in 1894, when the Republican and Populist parties agreed to Fusion, supported a ticket that included some from each party, and took control of the General Assembly. That legislature passed a resolution honoring Frederick Douglass when he died and passed laws that made it easier for black citizens to vote and to win elections. In 1896, the Fusionists, with strong support from blacks, elected Republican Daniel Russell governor, and he appointed some black people to state boards and agencies. Several hundred blacks became justices of the peace, school committeemen, aldermen, and police. Republican federal officials in the McKinley administration appointed some to be postmasters. Then, days before the 1898 election, Democratic Redshirts appeared on horseback to intimidate black voters, and Furnifold Simmons, chairman of the state Democratic Executive Committee, published an appeal to galvanize white voters. Simmons's vivid picture of life under Fusion played especially on the sex-charged fears of white men whose women might be subject to the will of black men.

> The most memorable campaign ever waged in North Carolina is approaching its end. It has been a campaign of startling and momentous developments. The issues which have overshadowed all others have been the questions of honest and economical State Government and WHITE SUPREMACY. . . . A proud race, which has never known a master, which has never bent to the yoke of any other race, by the irresistible power of fusion laws and fusion legislation has been placed under the control or dominion of that race which ranks lowest, save one, in the human family. . . . WHITE WOMEN, of pure Anglo-Saxon blood, have been arrested upon groundless charges, by negro constables, and arraigned, tried and sentenced by negro magistrates . . .
>
> NEGRO CONGRESSMEN, NEGRO SOLICITORS, NEGRO REVENUE OFFICERS, NEGRO COLLECTORS OF CUSTOMS, NEGROES in charge of white institutions, NEGROES in charge of white schools, NEGROES holding inquests over white dead, NEGROES controlling the finances of great cities, NEGROES in control of the sanitation and police of great cities, NEGRO CONSTABLES arresting white women and white men, NEGRO MAGISTRATES trying white women and white men, white convicts chained to NEGRO CONVICTS, and forced to social equality with them . . .
>
> The Battle has been fought, the victory is within our reach. North Carolina is a WHITE MAN'S STATE, and WHITE MEN will rule it, and they will crush the party of negro domination beneath a majority so overwhelming that no other party will ever again dare to establish negro rule here.

On November 8, lily-white Democrats elected 134 of the 170 members of the General Assembly. Two days later in Wilmington, six hundred armed whites destroyed the newspaper office of black editor Alexander Manly, black city officials resigned, hundreds of black people fled north, and a new city government organized. "Negro rule is at an end forever," the *News and Observer* proclaimed in the state capital three days later. "The events . . . at Wilmington and elsewhere place that fact beyond all question."

After the coup of ballots and blood, when violence was no longer necessary, the establishment scorned lynching. The white men in charge of North Carolina after the turn of the twentieth century wanted a peaceful, prosperous, paternalistic existence, with black people a settled, subservient element of their society, like the plow mules and the hunting dogs.

"The negro is fast discovering that the South is the only place for him," sneered the *Greensboro Record*, reporting a boycott of black chauffeurs by the New York elite in 1913. "The sensible negro knows that the people of the South are not going to tolerate anything like social equality, but they know the race is given fair treatment and an almost equal chance."

Charles Petty of Spartanburg, South Carolina, wrote in the *Progressive Farmer* in 1905 about the importance of black workers: "In this State, negroes make and gather three-fourths of the cotton crop. The first duty of the landlords is to make this labor more effective. It can be done. Build better houses for them. Employ them for long terms so that they may plant gardens and set out fruit trees and have a milk cow. Give them a square deal."

Editor Beasley, who had reprinted Booker T. Washington's appeal against burning blacks alive and endorsed Washington's push for industrial education rather than the right to vote, shared the opinion of the scandalized South when President Theodore Roosevelt hosted the black leader for a meal. Part of the horror involved the chance that a black man's knee might brush a white woman's thigh under the table. When Washington ate at a whites-only hotel restaurant in Hamlet, North Carolina, the ensuing uproar so engulfed the state that a Trinity College professor who praised the black leader lost his job. When a white chambermaid in Indianapolis refused to make up the bed where Washington had slept, the hotel fired her, but she received telegrams of congratulation from around the country and twenty-five dollars from a village in Georgia.

Beasley took a stand equally opposed to equality and violence. "This paper believes that Mr. Roosevelt is a real enemy to the South because he holds views different from the South's on the race question, and by giving prominence to those views has opened old wounds that might have been healed had he not antagonized the views of this section," he wrote.

> Further, there is little doubt that he would, if he could, injure the South by seeking in some legal way to exploit his view. But all this does not warrant the Southern leaders and papers in inflaming the public mind in these really vicious attacks. The truth is, that the one who is injured most is the one we forbid to strike back—the black man. The continued cry of social equality where there is none, and can be none, but inflames the public mind and creates the belief among the ignorant and the prejudiced that any kind of mistreatment of the inferior race is justifiable. This is not right. We cannot afford to let the negro rule us, as he has in times past; but the great constitutional amendment has done away with that. We cannot afford social equality, but really the negro doesn't want that. And we cannot afford to be unjust and unnecessarily harsh with the black man.

On Christmas Day 1906, the editor endorsed President Roosevelt's dismissal of three companies of black soldiers after some from the companies attacked the town of Brownsville, Texas.

"There are some things that negroes are not fit for," Beasley wrote.

> This paper is not a negro hater, in fact it has a contempt for the thoughtless vaporings of white men who make wholesale charges against the colored race. We know that there are thousands of that race who are idle, vicious, insolent and worthless. But on the other hand there are more thousands of them who work hard, try to live honest lives by their labor, and are good citizens. To say such a thing is rank heresy, of course, but it has the commendable feature of being the truth. When the critics sought to damn the Master because he conversed with the bad woman, He asked the one who was without sin to cast the first stone. 'Tis true that there are many worthless negroes, but before we can condemn the race as a whole we must get rid of a good many worthless white people, or else fall a victim to our own logic. There are just two difficulties to be experienced in discussing the negro question. One is that many of us want to measure him by the white man's standard. The other is that we look at the question entirely from our own selfish

standpoint: we want the negro to work for us, at our price, to suit our convenience and to thankfully receive whatever treatment we see fit to accord him.

The race question rose on every subject from the federal census to the telephone book. In the summer of 1909, distraught Democratic congressmen appealed to President Taft to order that no black people would be hired below the Mason-Dixon line as enumerators for the 1910 census because they wanted no black strangers having cause to go into white homes. In Asheville, the "time-honored tradition" of marking a star by black people's listings in the telephone directory got a publisher in trouble: A prominent white citizen sued because a star had been inadvertently printed next to his name, and a prominent black hotel owner suffered ridicule from his buddies because no star showed up next to his.

Editor Beasley, quick to defend "good colored people" against the broad hatred of the lynchers, felt no qualms about writing "A Bad Nigger Captured" for a headline or including, in his column of church notes and human-interest happenings, a withering critique of many he met on the street:

A town negro of the genuine loafing variety, and there's plenty of them, may do a good many other things, but he is not going to work at anything more onerous than carrying a message or a package—and the package has to be mighty light, too. Notice a gathering of them on the corner and ask one if he wants a job, and he'll put you through a category of minute questions designed to see just how hard the proposed exertion is to be. If he finds it anything but the lightest or finds that you don't want to pay a double price for it, he will claim a previous engagement and is just then waiting for his man to come along. One may approach a dozen ragged darkies without finding one who will agree to cut a cord of wood. And if one agrees to do it, the chances are that he'll throw up the job incomplete.

Charity and Children magazine picked up Beasley's assessment of black leaders' responsibility for the sex offenses that spawned so many lynchings.

The Monroe *Journal* writes temperately and sensibly in the issue of last week on the nameless crime, putting the blame for the prevalence of the evil upon the educated and influential negroes who, instead of using their power to suppress the evil among the brutal and vile, spend all their strength and influence demonizing mob law. They, as the *Journal* well says, have the matter in their own hands. The newspapers can not reach the rapists, for they do not read newspapers, but the leaders among the negroes are in close touch with all classes and are perfectly able to make public sentiment so strong that the evil will be greatly lessened, if not entirely suppressed. But these leaders rarely say a word against the crime for which so many negroes are lynched; on the other hand, they intensify race hatred by assailing the mob, which will continue to kill every negro who lays his brutal hand upon an innocent woman, and they are entirely silent about the crime which causes the dethronement of law, which we all deplore.

In the world, and the newspapers, of the Jim Crow South, blacks were a race apart, separate and unequal, even speaking a language barely recognizable as human. The *Journal* ran an occasional column of Uncle Commodore's philosophy, from "Monroe's most famous nigger": "The fust time ah yeerd erbout that ole nigger, Charlie Blair, a-askin' dat young nigger gal ter mahy 'im, ah des nachully bus' out laffin'—mm-m ah! At de same time, ah was dat mad ah could-a bus' his old haid an' laid 'im out fer his funerl stid er weddin'. De goins on of some dese old niggers'd turn the milk o human kineness ter clabber."

Commodore was sitting on the steps of his cabin cleaning chicken heads. "Yer 'member dat old Sockertees yer wus tellin' me erbout—de ole, what-do-yer-call 'im, phisolopher—dat saw er lot of gol' an' silver, an' sed he wuz glad dere wuz so many things he could git erlong widout? Yassir, dats de man, ol Sockertees; an' ah'm des lak dat. Ef ah kaint get er whole chicken, ah kin get erlong right smart wid de brains ah get outen day haids."

"De nigger dat says he done got 'ligion, an' keeps a-loafin' eroun' an' tellin' me 'bout it, better go ter wuk. Dere's some shoats in my hawgpen, an' ah allus keeps de mos' keerful gyard on dem wen he comes eroun': yassir."

No black person ever spoke in the newspaper without such phonetics. When someone asked Uncle Solomon Richardson why leaders had suspended Clarksville Camp Meeting in southern Union County after attacks from South Carolina blacks with sticks, razors, rocks, and pistols that broke up Sunday services, he explained: "Laik o faith. Our folks is fearder of them niggers doun Souf den they's got faith in de Lawd; dey's afeared He won't protect 'em." The exaggerated dialect even showed up in the Heath-Morrow Company's advertising in July 1919: "As our colored friends might say:/'Am ye gwyne to de Fo'th uf July Celebrasion in Monroe?'/'Co'se I is, nigger! ' "

On the prevailing white view, the good blacks, like the old slaves, embraced their lower place. When the pastor at the black Presbyterian church in Waxhaw announced that he was moving to Sumter, South Carolina, the *Waxhaw Enterprise* praised him for matching the model:

> We believe that the good white people of this community will endorse the statement that Rev. J. Gregg, during his residence of several years here, has fully proved himself, in almost every respect, a model and worthy colored man and leader of his race. He is well educated, exceedingly modest and retiring in disposition, and altogether inoffensive to anyone. He has at heart the best interests of his race and labors earnestly and faithfully at all times for its betterment. Above all, he is a worthy example to every colored man in the community. This much is said here because the *Enterprise* believes that proper recognition and encouragement should be extended to all deserving colored men.

Above all, on this view the Suffrage Amendment established a permanent order in society that made lynchings and burnings unnecessary.

"In North Carolina the negro has been eliminated from politics, and every good citizen is glad of it," T. J. Pence wrote in the *Raleigh News and Observer* in 1910, an opinion that Beasley reprinted with its attack on the Republican Party.

> I had entertained the thought that the color question would not be again injected into politics, but I was mistaken. It has been raised by the Republican Congressional Campaign Committee. There is a chapter in the Republican campaign text book, published by the Congressional Campaign Committee, entitled "Our Colored Citizens," which can only be described as disgusting in its appeal for the negro vote. . . . Here is one gem culled from the chapter:
>
> The platform adopted by the Republican party at Chicago in 1908 contains a plank which stands squarely and unequivocally for all the civil and political rights of the Afro-American people. There can be no question in the mind of any honorable, thinking, sane Afro-American as to which party he should support in this campaign. No truer sentiment has ever been uttered than that of the great Douglass when he said: "the Republican party is the ship: all else the sea."

> One of the proud boasts of the Republican campaign book is that there are 14,397 negroes in the employ of the Federal government, and that they receive in salaries each year the grand sum of $8,255,761.

The amendment was the touchstone of all political thought, even on the subject of prohibition. "For it is coming to be known that, great as the good that has resulted from the retirement of the negroes from politics in the South (and that blessing to both races cannot be overestimated), the retirement of the saloon has been, if possible, a greater blessing," Editor Beasley wrote. "The saloons are a damnation to any people, but in the South they are a peculiar damnation to the colored race, and consequently to the white. The effects of the school house and the pulpit for the uplift of the black man were almost wholly set at naught by the saloon, and if there was ever a godsend equal in direct beneficence to an interposition for heaven, it was the abolition of the whiskey traffic for these people."

Walter Bickett, son of the Misses Ross's first cousin, Thomas Bickett, had moved to Louisburg to practice law when his analysis of the amendment attracted the attention that made him the "Little Giant" of North Carolina politics—he was elected attorney general in 1908 and 1912, governor in 1916. In a 1903 letter to the editor of the *Raleigh News and Observer*, reprinted in the *Monroe Journal*, he called on editors to deny a political "negro problem" in the state:

> At the risk of being boiled in oil for heresy, I beg to submit that no writer on the negro question whose article has come to my notice has touched the real, vital and pressing negro problem which we of this good day have to face. That problem, as every man or woman who is put upon his *voir dire* will swear, is threefold:
>
> How to get a competent negro woman in the kitchen.
>
> How to get and keep a kind and trustworthy negro woman in the nursery.
>
> How to get and keep plenty of negroes in the cotton patch.
>
> Now, as I am a lawyer and have never been a candidate, I have had no means of acquiring sufficient knowledge of agriculture to entitle me to be heard up on the cotton patch proposition, but on the kitchen and nursery question I can speak "as one having authority."
>
> It is well enough for our statesmen, who dip into the future far as human eyes can see and for our shrewd politicians, who dip only as far as the next election, to indulge in learned theories about the negroes as a social and political factor in our midst. But, sir, the real negro question is not political, is not social, it is domestic.

The fear of the negro which is ever before the eyes of the women of today is that said negro will not turn up in time to "edit the gravy department" in the morning. The negro who is on the nerves of the men of this hour and who is causing their heads to gray, "but not with years," is the one whom we seek eagerly but do not find at her post in the nursery, and consequently the pious men of this country, contrary to their religious scruples, are forced in the uncanny hours of the night to do skirt dance stunts to the bellicose lamentations of their latest born.

These, sir, are living, wide awake questions, questions which vitally affect the health, wealth, morals and religion of the land, and unless they are solved and that right quickly, our agricultural industries will wane, our churches will be filled with men who have lost of the last vestige of their religion, those evil-minded lawyers who run the divorce mills will feed and fatten on excess of toil, and the august and honorable institution of marriage will fall into disrepute and disfavor among the people.

So why did Dinah go away
When we all wanted her to stay?

is a song as full of pathos as the mournful "Song of the Shirt."

Mr. Editor, we need the negro in our business. He suits the South, and the South suits him, and the man who says a word to engender strife and prejudice between us is an enemy of both races. The only fangs the negro ever had consisted of ballots, and those were artistically and scientifically extracted by the constitutional amendment, and today they are, as a people, harmless as blind puppies. A hundred white men in this county can easily and without strife and without friction keep them exactly where they belong.

There are three of these people on my place, and my four-year-old son can and does rule every one of them as absolutely as a Czar. Any one of them would fight to the last ditch for him, and I would not swap them off for any other labor on earth. Mr. John Temple Graves is a brilliant orator, but I submit, when he talks about exporting my cook and your nurse, he is undermining the very foundations of society, and an injunction should be sued out against him requiring him to shut up. In a recent issue of your paper you said, speaking of the negro question, that "nobody's opinion is worth much." You were absolutely correct, and why? For the very same and very sufficient reason that nobody's opinion would be worth much as to what sort of timber the North Pole is made of. The fruitful writers on this subject violate every principle of logic by assuming the existence of a condition in the South which is absolutely nonexistent. I repeat, there is no political or social negro problem. These questions are *res adjudicata*. We have fixed the negro's bounds and determined his habitation in perfect accord with his nature and necessities, and in the place assigned him he is, as a race, content to dwell. The constitutional amendment put him out of commission politically, and there is no sort of trouble about his social status. It is as hard for a white man to get into a social pew for which he is not scheduled as it is for a camel to do the needle act, and there need be no fear about the negro's doing so.

I insist that North Carolina, and most of the Southern States, have settled these questions wisely and well, that we are in no sort of trouble about them, and that if the penny-a-liners in the North persist in getting excited and turning red in the face and saying bad things about a negro problem down here, then they will simply occupy the ridiculous position of the man who went into convulsions because he dreamed that his neighbor had the colic.

The only way the negro can become a problem is for newspaper and magazine writers to keep on calling him one. If there is not a let-up along this line, the negro will after a while deny that he is a negro and insist that he is a problem. All men know that the press is all powerful, and I submit that, if the Southern press will at once begin to deny vehemently that we have a negro problem in the South, if it will daily call sharp attention to the peaceful and harmonious relations which actually exist between the races; if it will publish in big headlines that the South are the best friends the negroes have in the world, and that ninety and nine of the negroes fully understand that and appreciate it—if the press will adopt this course I will go bond that in a year the negro problem, so called, will be no more heard of.

Every one at all familiar with the construction of political platforms knows that it is just as easy to "point with pride" as it is to "view with alarm." It requires no greater strain upon the conscience to "congratulate" than it does to "deplore." And I suggest the following plank to be incorporated in the next platform adopted by the next Democratic State convention: "We point with pride to the peaceful and friendly relations which exist between the whites and blacks in North Carolina. We congratulate the people that the Democratic party has in its wisdom and virtue removed all cause for prejudice and bad feeling between the races by eliminating the negro from politics, and we congratulate the negro for recognizing that this was done for his ultimate good and for quietly submitting to the new order of things. We view with alarm the growing troubles which an unjust Republican policy is engendering between labor and capital in the North. We deplore the existence of so many strikes and so much strife and bloodshed in States suffering under Republican misrule, and we cite these, our unfortunate sister States, to the peace and order and contentment which prevail throughout the South as an example of what Democracy, triumphant, can and will do for a people."

In all sincerity, Mr. Editor, I say, let the doctrine of good will be preached, and verily every word that is written will come to pass.

This article is not controversial. It is a plea for peace and for the diffusion among all classes and conditions in our beloved State of that perfect love which "casteth out fear." Let a policy of this sort be adopted and the "sounding of joy" of Dinah beating the biscuits in the kitchen will again make the men of this country thank God for the room that is inside of them. The voice of Aunt 'Cindy in the nursery crooning, soft and low,

Doan' you cry, ma honey,
Doan you weep no mo',

will again sweetly lead the little ones to the "Land by the Lollipop Sea." The fields will again be full of happy coons, working joyfully and singing of the "coal black gal and the watermillion hangin' on de vine," and those sentinels whose beat is the sky-line will report that there is perfect peace and all is well in Dixie.

Even after the U.S. Supreme Court declared the grandfather clause unconstitutional in 1915, Union County lived in the world of its favorite son. The day the Ross will verdict came down in 1921, Monroe was holding a municipal election. Rumor had it that scores of blacks had voted in the election—thirty in one ward alone—but poll holder J. G. Rogers vehemently denied the charge.

"Eleven, not over fourteen, votes were cast by the negroes," he told the *Journal.* "Many negroes endeavored to vote, it is true, but they were denied the privilege when they admitted they were of republican politics."

4

THE COURT

Experience has demonstrated that the participation of the negro in the political life of the South is harmful to him and to the community, and is a fruitful source of that racial prejudice which works to his injury.

—JOHN J. PARKER, 1920

The black-and-white world of the Rosses of Marvin and the black and white world outside collided in the Union County Courthouse in Monroe on March 31, 1921. The impact attracted the top lawyers in the state—"an imposing array of counsel," the *Journal* noticed. The mayor of Monroe was on one side, the son of the Chief Justice of the state Supreme Court on the other. Christian denomination and political party, alma mater and past professional partnerships—the gap between the lawyers' walnut-stained tables in the courtroom sliced across all ordinary allegiances. Attorneys John Sikes, A. M. Stack, Frank Armfield, and J. C. M. Vann had been at the Democratic state convention together in 1914 with R. B. Redwine and R. A. Hudson, executors of the will over which they were now divided. Redwine and John J. Parker were both trustees of the University of North Carolina. The cousins' suit had thrown together the family of the previous term's Democratic governor with the upstart young Republican who tried to succeed him, both of them Monroe boys with long pedigrees. Lawyers, witnesses, jurors, court officials had attended state bar association meetings together, belonged to the Shrine Club together, taken the first airplane ride in the county together. Now they stood separated by the sharp line of race in a case, further fraught with the lure of land and gold and the whispers of illicit sex and moral degeneracy, to decide the will of the dead.

Attorneys for the Caveators

John Johnston Parker was born in 1885 in Monroe to Dan Parker, a Baptist meat market owner, and Frances Iredell Johnston, descendant of two governors and a U.S. Supreme Court justice appointed by George Washington. His grandfather died for the Confederacy at Chancellorsville and was buried in an unmarked Virginia grave. His mother helped found the Episcopal church in town. As a teenager, "Johnny Bull" worked in the original Belk Brothers retail store in Monroe. He earned his Phi Beta Kappa key at the University of North Carolina, where he graduated in 1907 and took a law degree in 1908. Raising eyebrows among his Chapel Hill colleagues and his deeply Democratic family, he devoted himself to Republican politics. He joined the party in 1908 and campaigned for its congressional candidate in Greensboro, where he had gone to practice law. With his support, John Motley Morehead won the Fifth District seat.

Because his mother was dying, Parker returned to Monroe and opened a law practice, with Amos M. Stack and Gilliam Craig as partners, in 1909. The next year, at the age of twenty-five, he ran for Congress in the Seventh District. President Taft was counting on him. The incumbent, Robert Page, charged that he would turn the state over to "Radicals and Negroes"—the Democrats' attack on the Republicans since Fusion. Parker lost by two thousand two hundred votes out of twenty-five thousand cast, as Democrats swept the state once more. In 1916, when he ran for attorney general, he received only four hundred votes out of twenty-four hundred cast in his home county. Walter Bickett, who had been attorney general, was elected governor that year.

A few months before he received the Republican nomination for governor in 1920, Parker tried, in a speech at Chapel Hill, to match the Democrats' "lily-white" stand. When he accepted the nomination, a hopeless race given his party's place in the state, the thirty-five-year-old lawyer was determined to try. In his acceptance speech in Greensboro, he again said: "The negro as a class does not desire to enter politics. The Republican Party of North Carolina does not desire him to do so. We recognize the fact that he has not yet reached the state in his development where he can share the burden and responsibility of government. This being true, and every intelligent man in North Carolina knows that it is true, the attempt of certain petty Democratic politicians to inject the race issue into every campaign is most reprehensible. I say it deliberately, there is no more dangerous or contemptible enemy of the state than the men who for personal or political advantage will attempt to kindle the flame of racial prejudice and hatred."

After his nomination, black Republicans in Union County held their own convention and declared that, because of Parker, they would vote for some candidates outside the party. "The regular Republican party of the state has eliminated us from the party," they wrote to the *Journal*. "The constitution of North Carolina guarantees us the right of suffrage. We feel, like our white brothers, that the ballot is our most defensive weapon, and a proper use of it is necessary for the good and safety of the state and nation. We concede the ruling of this country to the dominant race, but since we are forced to share in its bitters, we think we ought not to be maligned because we want to taste some of the sweets." Editor Beasley remarked when he ran their letter: "One thing is for certain—they are not going to vote for Mr. Parker."

Weeks before the election, Parker wrote to his hometown newspaper: "The Republican Party of North Carolina is as much a white man's party as the Democratic Party. I have been to every convention since 1908 and I can truthfully say that I never sat in a convention with a negro delegate, which is more than my opponent can say."

He spent the day before the election crisscrossing his home county—Marshville in the morning, Waxhaw in the afternoon, Monroe at night.

He carried twenty-seven of the state's one hundred counties and got two hundred thirty thousand votes, eighty thousand fewer than Cameron Morrison. In Union County, he got one thousand five hundred five votes—one hundred one more than his party's presidential candidate—and carried three precincts but lost to Morrison by two thousand five hundred thirty. He lost his own precinct by nearly six hundred votes. In Marvin, the count was eighty for Morrison, nine for Parker.

As the campaign wore on, Parker prepared for the Ross will case. Five months later, he was the lead attorney for the Union County cousins of Miss Maggie, trying to set aside her will, written while he was in law school, that left her land to a black man and a black woman.

His partner in the firm, Amos M. Stack, was on the team. Stack, fifty-eight years old, was the seventh son of a southeastern Union County farmer who had died six weeks before Amos was born in 1863. He graduated from Trinity College in 1884, got a law license in 1885 and moved to Winston-Salem to help found the *Sentinel* newspaper. In 1886, after reading law with D. A. Covington in Monroe, he moved to Stokes County to practice law. Stack, a Democrat, won election to the state senate from that Republican district in 1893. He returned to Union County and became a partner with R. B. Redwine in 1900, partly because his house in Danbury had burned, partly because he preferred Monroe's schools and partly because the death of Covington left a vacancy in the city's bar. He moved to Parker's practice in 1909. Governor Kitchin appointed him solicitor, and he won election to the office in the next campaign, but in April 1914, he resigned. The growth of recorder's courts in neighboring counties had so reduced the pay that the job wasn't worth his effort. In his spare time, he gave lectures on an extensive trip he had taken to Egypt, the Holy Land, and Europe.

The Mecklenburg County cousins hired Walter Clark, son of Chief Justice Walter Clark, the youngest major in the Confederate army and the author of a five-volume *History of North Carolina Troops, 1861–1865.* The younger lawyer, a leading Methodist layman, was a captain in the 113th Field Artillery that included the Bickett Battery, named for the wartime governor.

Attorneys for the Propounders

Leading the defense of the will was E. T. Cansler, whose grandfather, Philip Kanzler, had been the largest landowner in Lincoln County and among the largest slaveholders in western North Carolina. E. T.'s father, John Poindexter Cansler, went to Marion, North Carolina, to manage the family's mountain property when he married Catherine Murphy, daughter of the Irishman Judge William Murphy and the English woman Martha Brown, who buried the family silver when the Yankees invaded. Confederate Lt. John Poindexter was badly wounded in the battle of Sharpsburg, and he left most of the raising of their four children to Catherine when he came home from the war. John and Catherine both died in 1870. E. T. went to Charlotte to read law at the office that Zebulon Vance, North Carolina's Civil War governor, started in 1866 with Charlotte mayor Clement Dowd and Robert Johnston, the youngest general in the Army of the Confederacy. He earned his license quickly and developed a reputation for fierce litigation—and for championing the underdog. When he visited the chalet he built in 1911 at his beloved Little Switzerland, the resort he and a partner built partly on old family mountain land, he took his photographic memory and encyclopedic knowledge of the law to court for mountaineers otherwise ill-equipped to deal with their crafty adversaries.

The sentiments of Miss Sallie and Miss Maggie seemed not strange to Cansler, who gave a house to his black field hand, Bish, and a hundred acres of prime Mecklenburg County farmland to his black chauffeur, Dolph. He believed in justice, rights, a fair shake for anyone, especially in court, and he despised the autocratic manner of his best friend and oft-times adversary Heriot Clarkson. The two sometimes grew so heated at trial that they would resort to kicks and fisticuffs, and news that they were on opposing sides drew crowds hoping to catch a show at the courtroom circus.

Cansler's colleague, John Cuthbertson Sikes, Jr., was elected mayor of Monroe in May 1919 with no opposition. He tried to resign the office in August 1920, but the aldermen refused his resignation. He was appointed alderman-at-large in 1916 and beat two opponents for the seat in the 1917 election. His father had been a road commissioner. Democratic Party leaders were trying to recruit him to run for district attorney, an honor he declined, and he felt he should to devote more time to his law practice. The city was growing too fast for the part-time job he had accepted. Water mains had been enlarged, sewer lines had been extended, and the responsibilities of the swelling budget demanded more than Sikes thought he could provide, but he accepted the leaders' decision. Ten years earlier, when he was in partnership with R. B. Redwine, he had represented Will Blount, a black bricklayer who was charged with murdering W. R. Outen, an accountant.

With them worked Frank Armfield, fifty years old, another Trinity College graduate with a law license from Chapel Hill who wrote poetry in his spare time. He had practiced in Monroe and served one term as mayor, until he moved to Concord. His partner, the boyish-faced John Coleman McRae Vann, thirty-three years old, son of a Monroe lawyer, also graduated from the University of North Carolina. Vann had already served as mayor and state representative, and he had run unsuccessfully for Congress. Their new partner, Jesse Fearrington Milliken of Chatham County, newly moved to Monroe after a stint in the army where he rose to second lieutenant with the 117th Field Artillery, had graduated from the University of North Carolina and earned his law license in 1910.

Two and a half years earlier, Cansler and Armfield had won acquittal for Gaston Means in a sensational trial in Concord that brought both witnesses and lawyers from New York. Means was accused of killing Maude King, the widow of a Chicago millionaire, when the two were alone and she was practicing with a small pistol he gave her. He had been managing her accounts, and the million dollars she inherited had disappeared. He was also accused of working as a German spy. The jury, agreeing with Cansler and Armfield's defense, ruled that King died accidentally. "These two barristers exhibit a marked deference for each other and are a good team," the *Monroe Journal* reported as the Ross will trial began. "Mr. Armfield is a specialist on authority, while Mr. Cansler is hardly equaled in this state as a trial lawyer."

The propounders' team included Monroe lawyers Walter Bennett Love and William Oscar Lemmond. Love, like Parker a Republican who had studied law in Chapel Hill and been president of his class, was the men's Bible teacher at Central Methodist Church. He taught school in Union County to earn money for law school and held a patronage postmaster job before he went into full-time law practice. Bow-tie-wearing "Bunk" Lemmond, a Wake Forest College graduate with an office in the courthouse, had been a judge of recorder's court since 1916. He played the fiddle in his spare time. Lemmond had inherited the law practice of W. J. Pratt, who had inherited the practice of Henry B. Adams, and thus the safe that contained the Rosses' wills.

The Judge

Forty-four-year-old John Bispham Ray, who wielded the gavel over this assembly, was a near-rookie mountain judge who had gone to school a total of twelve months in his life. He was elected to the General Assembly at age twenty-six and, in the same year he was admitted to the North Carolina bar, authored a law that bore his name, making the manufacture and sale of liquor a felony in Yancey County. Since then, he had written two law books and helped start the Black Mountain Railway while practicing law in Burnsville and raising seven children with his wife Pansy. He and his father, Garrett D. Ray, owned a collection of more than a thousand Indian hatchets, bushels of arrowheads, coins and curios from around the world, and every North Carolina mineral, including more Cantinite crystal than the Smithsonian Institute and a rare smoky quartz within a beryl. The collection had won prizes from the Chicago World's Fair and the Paris Exposition.

Ray was appointed a judge of the 18th Judicial District of North Carolina a few months before the Ross case. On January 31, he read one of the longest charges to a grand jury ever heard in the Union County Courthouse. The speech included a plea for the protection of birds, based partly on the number of insects they consume. "I firmly believe that the human race would perish within five years should all the birds of the world be exterminated," he said. "Out in Mississippi, a large landowner employed men to kill the birds because he believed they were puncturing his cotton bolls. Investigation, however, showed him that the birds were destroying weevils instead of bolls, and he hereafter devised means for their protection instead of having them exterminated."

In the February term in Monroe, Judge Ray took the odd step of assigning fifteen dollars a month from three defendants' fines for the support of another defendant's wife and five small children. John Knight, a white man, was convicted of making liquor and sentenced to two years on the chain gang. The three black men who had been implicated with him paid a total fine of two hundred fifty dollars. When Knight's attorney objected to the sentence because Knight's family was destitute, Judge Ray threatened to give the money to the county schools. Knight quickly agreed to the subsidy, and the judge reduced the sentence to eighteen months. Knight's defense attorney was John J. Parker. "Judge Ray showed excellent good judgment," Beasley's *Journal* observed, "and earned the commendation of the scores of lawyers and court attendants who were present."

The Jurors

The lawyers came from the at-odds worlds of the Ross sisters and their caveator cousins on questions of race and right. They would argue, and Judge Ray would preside, but they would not decide the case. That was for twelve white men in two rows of swivel seats, many of them chafing at their misfortune to have been snagged on the street. The jury search, including more than one hundred interviews on the stand, had gathered men from five different townships in the county—J. I. Fuller, P. M. Abernethy, G. J. Griffin, S. S. Presson, and F. P. Deese from Monroe; H. W. Pigg and H. Marshal Baucom from Goose Creek to the northwest; T. C. Eubanks from Buford to the south; A. E. Morgan from New Salem to the northeast; and J. O. B. Huey from Jackson to the southwest. None from Sandy Ridge, much less from the strange little world of Marvin.

James Orr Bennett Huey, known as Bud, was the son of the clerk of court James Calvin Huey, one of Lee's soldiers paroled by Grant at Appomattox. Bud was in his forties, farming on his father's land, going to the Unity Associate Reformed Presbyterian Church his father helped organize. Just the previous summer, he saw lightning strike his ten-year-old daughter on her way in from a neighbor's house and raced from his front porch to help—but she was dead when he reached her. Pascal M. Abernethy, a veterinarian, was a son of the former pastor at Central United Methodist Church. Holmes Morris, an auto mechanic, was in his twenties. Frank Deese, no known relation to the Deese caveators, was a clerk at W. C. Deese Store, and G. W. Davis was superintendent at G. M. Tucker Manufacturing. J. I. Fuller had moved from Wadesboro to become a policeman in Monroe, on the five-man force with Chief J. Wright Spoon, Frank Irby, J. F. King, and Jesse A. Helms, who had just found out that his wife was pregnant.

Their avowal of no opinion in the case of white women's leaving their land to black people surprised some. Henry Pigg's father, Andrew Jackson Pigg, had been a Confederate prisoner of war. When Henry was three, the invading Yankees raided their farm, taking all their livestock and shooting off the beak of the one rooster that reached a hiding place under the house.

Adam Efird Morgan was born when his grandfather's plantation was carding wool for Confederate uniforms and making saddles and harnesses for Confederate horses in round-the-clock shifts. Drury Morgan reigned over an estate, straddling the Rocky River on the county's north border, whose center was a three-story, three-millstone grist mill powered by four wheels in a three-quarter-mile millrace dug by his dozens of slaves. He had a trading post that sold salt, coffee, syrup, scissors, knives, forks, and needles, and he had seven four-horse wagons to haul his goods. He had a post office, a sawmill, a tannery, a cotton gin, a patented wheat smutter, a blacksmith, a barber, a shoemaker, a tailor, and many boys apprenticed to him to learn the trades on his barony. "Add" could remember riding around the plantation with his dark-eyed Grandfather Dru on a thoroughbred horse. His father, Henery, had tried to go into the Lutheran seminary, but trouble with his eyes sent him back to the land. He brought up his family near the mill, and Adam, who became a miller, helped build the Morgan Academy on the land in 1897. He was within three weeks of his fifty-eighth birthday when he took his seat on the Ross will jury. Adam brought an air of appropriate seriousness to the juror's chair. He was a thin man, small-featured except for his broad hands, with dark eyebrows and wire-rimmed glasses and a drooping mustache that made him seem to be frowning—a generally sober, scholarly air. He would be coming from the northern edge of the county to Monroe every day now for who knows how long, and he would have to decide whether to award eight hundred acres of cotton land along the southwestern edge to an old lady's black apprentice or to the governor's family.

PART II

The Rosses

5

SUSAN

My will and desire is that my daughter Susannah have liberty to use and occupy as much of said described tract including the house in which she now resides as she can work.

—WILL OF JONATHAN BURLEYSON, 1852

Susannah Burleyson Ross was sixty-five years old when she started her third family. She figured she deserved another chance. Things had not worked out so well with the first two. The family she grew up with was all dead or dispersed, and the family she formed when she married Nathaniel Ross in 1827 was well on its way to the same end.

Her father, Jonathan Burleyson, was a son of Isaac Burleyson, Sr., from Montgomery County, a member of Captain Polk's Company of North Carolina Militia in the Revolution, where he helped fight Tories around Fayetteville in eastern North Carolina. Jonathan migrated southwest to Mecklenburg County about 1800 and settled east of Sixmile Creek with his wife, Sarah. Susan was the third of their six children, the first four coming at two-year intervals—Dennis Clay, Mary, Susannah, John B. Little sister Margaret Ann was born in 1819, and little brother Jasper Jonathan in 1826, the year before Susan married.

Nathan, as he was known, was one of the ten children of Martin and Peggy Brown Ross, who came from Martin County about the time

Jonathan Burleyson arrived. Nathan was thirty-six years old at the wedding—nearly twice Susannah's age and only nine years younger than her father. Their children came every two or three years—Jackson J., Sarah A., John N., Dennis Clay, Margaret A.—but Nathan was a poor provider, and Jonathan worried about his daughter's future.

Meanwhile, in 1834, Jonathan's sister Jane and her husband, William Castle, moved to Mississippi after Andrew Jackson's removal of the Indians to Oklahoma opened the Deep South cotton land to cheap settlement. Brother David moved two years later to Chickasaw County, Mississippi, and Susan's brothers followed their relatives—John B. and Jasper Jonathan to Panola County, Mississippi, in 1841, Dennis Clay in 1847. That was a year of grief for Susan. Little sister Margaret, who had married a Gribble, died in January at just twenty-six years old; Susan's second son, John N., died in March at age twelve. Two trips to the cold Union Methodist Church South cemetery exactly two months apart. Two years later, Nathan's nephews Amon and William went to the gold fields of California and were lost at sea; nephew Ellison went to Mississippi, and nephew Martin went to Texas.

But those were Rosses, and Susan was hardly a Ross. Nathan's failures drove Jonathan to a drastic move when he wrote his will on December 3, 1852, insuring his daughter's future but ending her marriage: "My will and desire is that my daughter Susannah have liberty to use and occupy as much of said tract including the house in which she now resides as she can work. But in no event shall her husband Nathan Ross have a right of entry upon my plantation nor the use of any of my property willed to my daughter Susannah." Jonathan did not trust Nathan or forgive the poverty imposed on his daughter and her household. He wrote: "To Nathan Ross I will and bequeath one hundred and thirty dollars which he owes me for money I paid out for him and nothing more of my estate."

By the time Jonathan died in October 1857, Susan's oldest son Jackson was already living with his grandparents. Jonathan's will gave Sarah the family's female slave, Mary, and the choice of their two male slaves, Ben and Will. When she chose Will, Ben went to Mississippi to work for John and his wife Ellen. He married out there, to a woman named Charity, and had two sons of his own, Jonathan and Joseph. On May 16, 1859, Sarah entered into a covenant with her son John, who had acquired the shares of the four other siblings, and her twenty-two-year-old grandson Dennis, as trustee for Susan and her other children, so that she could live on the land for the rest of her life and they would inherit. The Burleysons by then owned 535 acres, known as the Howie or Lawson land, on the Tar Kiln Branch east of Sixmile Creek between Sir Frederick Ezzell's estate and the lands of Robert G. Howard, a friend who attended Union Methodist Church with the Burleysons. Nathan, as Jonathan's will required, was banned—Susan sent him away. Jackson struck out for the West, like his aunts and uncles, and wasn't heard from again, although some news came back that he died in 1860. The second of Susan's sons gone.

Susan's mother, Sarah, died on July 21, 1861. Her executor, Samuel Hoey Walkup, sold Will at auction on September 3 for seven hundred ninety-two Confederate dollars to Joseph Adams. Adams paid three hundred dollars in 1862 and four hundred ninety-two in May 1863. Walkup, a lawyer in Monroe and a general in the state militia, was Jonathan Burleyson's "trusty friend." Just a year earlier, he had been a guest of President James Buchanan in the White House, where his bride, Minnie, played "The Battle of Waterloo" on the piano. He was already famous for gathering eyewitness evidence that Andrew Jackson had been born in North Carolina, despite South Carolina's claims. Now he was on his way to join the 48th North Carolina Regiment and fight for the Confederacy.

So was Susan's son, Dennis, who joined Mallett's Battalion and was wounded at the Battle of Kinston on December 14, 1862. The next year came news that Uncle Dennis Clay Burleyson and his wife Sarah Bonds Burleyson had sold all their possessions in Lafayette County, Mississippi, and mysteriously disappeared. After the war, on February 28, 1868, Susan and Dennis bought out John B.'s four-fifths interest in Jonathan's land for four hundred twenty-eight dollars—one dollar an acre. Now this was their land, as the mid-nineteenth-century legal language described it, marked by the northeast corner of an old field adjoining James

N. Houston below Robert Newton's old sawmill, running a straight line from there to John McCorkle's barn, angled at hickory, persimmon, black gum, ironwood, post oak, water oak, and black oak trees, stumps and stones and an elbow in the wagon road—"to have and to hold to the sole and separate use and benefit of the said Susan Ross for and during the time of her natural life and at her death to whomsoever she may direct by her last will & testament or in case she does not devise it by her last will and testament nor otherwise dispose of it during her lifetime the remainder to descend equally to her children, viz, to Sarah A. Ross, Margaret M. Ross and Dennis Clay Ross, to them and their heirs in fee simple forever."

In August, Nathan Ross died and the family buried him with Margaret Burleyson Gribble and John N. Ross in the Union Methodist Church South cemetery, marked only:

Sacred
to the memory of
Nathan Ross
DIED
Aug. 4 A.D. 1868
aged 77 Yrs. 10 Mos.
14 days.

They had not been a family for more than a decade by then.

It took more time than that to close Susan's father's estate. Adams sued over Will, preventing Colonel Walkup from settling for years. He had invested eight hundred dollars of the estate's income, including money from the sale of Will, in Confederate bonds, now worthless. After the executor's claims, Susan's share of the cash from her father's estate came to twenty-one dollars and three cents. The decree settling her parents' estate came down on March 10, 1874. The land was hers, five hundred thirty-five acres, and at last she could have the family she wanted. That family needed a child. Sallie was forty. Dennis was thirty-seven. Maggie was thirty-five. The chance that any of them would yet yield offspring had dropped to nil. Her other two sons were gone. But North Carolina had provided a way.

The General Assembly that ratified the Thirteenth Amendment emancipating the slaves also passed an apprenticeship law designed to preserve a social order in the state. Thomas Jefferson had compared owning slaves to holding a wolf by the ears—you didn't like it, but you didn't want to let go. Now that the slaves were free, the legislature was groping for a new stability. Chapter 5 of the public statutes, published in 1873, provided the binding of apprentices by indenture to a "master or mistress," including infants with absentee fathers. The apprentice was promised food, clothing, and shelter, and education in reading and writing.

In the fall of 1874, Susan applied for Robert B. Ross, the two-year-old son of Rosa Ross, onetime slave of her husband's family, unmarried. He needed her, she thought. And she needed him. The probate judge apprenticed him to her, and Rosa appealed without success to the Supreme Court. Sheriff John Wilson Griffin, with the order in the case of *State and Susan Ross vs. Rosa Ross and Robert Ross* in hand, took Bob from Rosa's arms, both of them screaming, and delivered him to Susan at the Burleyson homeplace on October 30. There he lived with Dennis and Sallie and Maggie as they set about enlarging the territory that Susan had received from her family. Susan bought seventy-two acres from Fulton and Amanda Howard for five hundred dollars in 1879 and forty-five more from the Howards for nine hundred thirteen dollars in January 1886. When she died on November 20, 1886, her new family was established on the land, Dennis and Sallie were positioned to expand its territory, and Bob was close to carrying it forward for another generation.

6

BOB AND DENNIS

The master shall provide for the apprentice . . . such other education, sum of money, or articles of furniture or implements of trade, as may be agreed on between the court and the master, and inserted in the indenture.

—BATTLE'S REVISAL OF THE PUBLIC STATUTES OF NORTH CAROLINA, 1873

The probate judge apprenticed Bob Ross to Susan, but he learned his trade from Dennis Clay. Dennis had been the man of the house since his mother left his father when she took possession of her father's land in 1859. He was, like his mother, more Burleyson than Ross, named for his Burleyson uncle, sharing Susan's ambition, managing with her to add field after field to the Burleyson homeplace.

Dennis was, like all Confederate veterans and especially wounded ones, officially revered in his community, although some whispered about the black boy who died at his hands years ago and about his free-spending bachelor ways. He had been a private in Mallett's Battalion, nineteen officers and four hundred sixty men under Col. Peter Mallett, the 19th Battalion of the 68th North Carolina Infantry. They, along with Radcliffe's Regiment and Bunting's and Starr's light batteries from North Carolina, fought with Gen. Nathan G. Evans' brigade from South

Carolina—two thousand Confederates in all—against more than ten thousand Yankees under Maj. Gen. John G. Foster at the Battle of Kinston on December 14, 1862. More than four hundred Confederates were captured that bitter-cold day when they were trapped between the enemy and a blazing bridge across the Neuse River, which their own general had ordered fired to save the main body of his troops, which were escaping through the town. Private Ross got away with only a wound.

Nearly twenty men from the community fought for the Confederacy. Three died. Job Squier Crane, the "Little Yankee" who was born in New Jersey in 1822 and moved to Union County in his twenties, was held under house arrest for questionable allegiance through more than a year of the war. When a rich neighbor asked to hire him as a replacement for the man's youngest son, cabinetmaker Crane chose instead, in the summer of 1863, to volunteer for the duration with Company F of the 49th North Carolina Regiment. He lost an index finger when he was shot during a skirmish in June 1864. The Little Yankee returned home to his wife and nine children and had his tenth child ten months later.

Dennis sired no sons, but when Susan brought Bob into the house he soon found himself teaching the youngster what he knew best—cotton farming. Bob plowed in the fields with him, planted, chopped, picked, and ginned the cotton from their increasing acres, at first under the eye and then by the side of the man who was old enough to be his father. They were together on the land, in the barn, in the stable, at the gin, in the living room, at the kitchen table; they even shared the same bedroom. Dennis knew the poverty of the old days, the days of Nathan and then of the war, when his sisters had to plow instead of going to school, and he was determined never to have the household in such shape again. For the farmer, there was one sure hope: cotton. The South shared the sentiments of Henry Grady, editor of the *Atlanta Constitution*, when it came to the crop:

> What a royal plant it is! The sun that shines on it is tempered by the prayers of all people. The shower that falls whispering on its leaves is heard around the world. The frost that chills it and the dew that descends from the stars is noted, and the trespass of a little worm on its green leaf is more to England than the advance of

> the Russian army on her Asian posts. It is gold from the time it puts forth its tiny shoot. Its fiber is current in every bank, and when loosing its fleeces to the sun it floats a sunny banner that glorifies the field of the humble farmer, that man is marshaled under a flag that will compel the allegiance of the world and wring a subsidy from every nation on earth. It is the heritage that God gave to this people forever as their own when he arched our skies, established our mountains, tempered the sunshine and measured the rain. Ours and our children's forever. As princely a talent as ever came from His hand to mortal stewardship.

When the *Monroe Journal* reprinted Grady's paean, the editor added: "The royal plant is now in flower and every day throughout the Southland millions of busy fingers are gathering the whitened locks. No wonder the Southern people love it—it is the never-failing storehouse whence come the necessities as well as the luxuries of life. If it prospers, they prosper. With anxious eyes, they watch its growth, and when harvest time comes round, if the yield is not as great as expected there is bitter disappointment. How often has the hardworking father figured on being able to buy another needed implement or animal, or to build another barn if the crop was good!"

The Rosses prospered. Bob's mother, Rosa, now married to Samuel Howie, moved to a tenant house on their land. Even after Susan died, Dennis and Sallie and Maggie increased their holdings—sixty-one acres from W. A. Howard, one hundred seventeen acres from an estate that Dr. Rone administered, eight acres along Sixmile Creek and nine acres in Marvin from Frank and Arkanta Crane, two hundred twenty-six acres along the creek from L. A. Helms and his wife, ninety-nine acres on Providence Road from W. C. Traywick and his wife, five tracts from R. L. White. The Marvin lands totaled about five hundred acres, the homeplace lands about eight hundred.

Soon after Susan died, Bob, tall, deeply dark, and handsome, married Alice Fetterson and brought her to the plantation, but he continued to work the land with Dennis. On September 23, 1887, Alice gave birth to a daughter, Mittie Bell, and Dennis's sisters started calculating when they could bring the girl to live with them as Bob had. She had already gone to stay in their house in 1891 when Alice gave birth to a son, Waydie. The boy lived only eight months and ten days, from March 8 to November 18. The Rosses raised a monument over his little grave off New Town Road:

Sleep on sweet babe
And take thy rest
God called thee home
He thought it best

Bob and Alice had no more children. She left him about 1908 and moved in with Jackson Massey, sorrowing Bob and scandalizing the sisters. Alice and Jackson married in 1910, months after Sallie died.

When Dennis and his sisters bought Dr. Rone's house between the churches, two miles from the homeplace, they moved Mittie with them. Bob, at twenty, took more responsibility for the stables and the gin and the fields on the old land. He took on even more after Dennis died, just four years after the family had settled into its new home. Dennis had been working at the gin when he was caught in the machinery and ripped so severely that he had to be carried to his room upstairs. His mangled body clung to life for less than a week. Harriet Taylor and Lafayette A. Gallant and Mrs. McIlwaine, who had been sitting up with him, were there when Dennis died. Tirzah Coan, their second cousin who lived a quarter-mile away, came in time to close his eyes. Sallie and Maggie erected a tall monument over his grave at Union Methodist Church cemetery, near their father, their mother, their little brother, and their Aunt Margaret Gribble. They had the marker inscribed:

With loving hands we ministered to him.
With crushed hearts we buried him.
But we hope to meet him again
In that land beyond the river.
Erected by his only two surviving sisters.

The sisters hired Richard A. Hudson, one of the section's leading farmers, who lived on Providence Road, to help manage their business after Dennis died, but Bob's work went on. He ran the gin for the tenants and the neighbors. He bought supplies at the store. He collected rent from the tenants, black and white. He looked after the stables and the fields. Sallie bought him a subscription to the *Monroe Enquirer*. In 1898, the year of the Redshirt riders and the Wilmington Massacre, Maggie and Sallie gave two acres for Marvin African Methodist Episcopal Zion, a new church for Bob and Mittie and their friends west of Providence Road so they would no longer have to walk all the way to Redding Springs near Wolfsville for services. Aunt Rosa Howie was on the roll of the sainted founders, with Uncle Ned Houston, Granny Ann Robinson, Uncle Craig Kirkpatrick, Uncle Bob Duncan, Uncle Green Ardrey, and Uncle Anthony Miller. The sisters got around to writing the deed, legally selling the congregation the land for one dollar, in 1901.

Frank Crane, one of five men charged by the county with laying out a big road through the old Burleyson land, knew not long after Dennis died that the sisters planned to give their homeplace to Bob. When he visited them to talk about the project, they told him: "That is our land up there and you can come and lay out this road wherever you like, but we would like for you to lay it off to suit Bob Ross, for that is his land as soon as we are done with it." When the neighbors appealed the county commissioners' decision to establish the road, Sallie hired lawyer Robert Redwine, the son of an old friend from Union Methodist, to defend it. He won. The road curved close around the knoll where Bob was living in Jonathan Burleyson's home, a paintless gray two-story with a one-story extension, two chimneys, and a dark root cellar. Bob had installed lightning rods to protect the old structure.

When Bob came to their house in a hurry one summer afternoon because the mowing machine was broken, Sallie gave him twenty dollars to get it fixed. "We give him all he makes," she explained to an astonished neighbor, meaning they collected no rent from his crops, "and then we help him." After Sallie died, Bob's barn burned and Maggie replaced it. J. M. Niven, the county commissioner who ran a store at Waxhaw, asked Maggie whether she wanted to maintain Sallie's account arrangement—to give Bob whatever goods and groceries he wanted, and she would pay the bill. "Let Bobbie have such supplies as he needs," Maggie told him. "He's a good boy, and I want him to have what he needs."

Bob and Maggie were both lonely—he bereft of wife, she of sister—and they shared that loneliness best with each other. She would sometimes go up the road to spend the day with him at his house, her grandfather's old house, on the homeplace. He was like a little brother and a grown son all in one, and she had no delight except in his family's prosperity. Only he of all their family had been fruitful, and in his line, thin but strong as Mittie Bell, lay all their future.

7

MITTIE BELL

This Ross family made it clear that Grandma Mittie was part of them no matter what.

—ALVENIA HOUSTON MORRISON, 2002

Mittie Bell had rubbed a blister on her heel and needed a comfortable pair of shoes to wear to Redding Springs Camp Meeting, so she went into the front room and asked Miss Maggie if she could borrow hers. After all, Mittie at age eighteen and Maggie at sixty wore the same size—dresses, jackets, even underwear. Mittie once wore Maggie's silk dress to a camp meeting, and she often wore Maggie's everyday dresses around the house. Almost every month they would go shopping together at the Belk store in Waxhaw. When a dress caught her eye, Mittie would insist that Maggie buy it, and she almost always won. The store manager knew that if he could interest Mittie in an item, Maggie would buy it. They both took a size 4½ or 5 in shoes. Maggie had good taste in shoes, too, always buying something between a pump and a lady's casual. Today, she hesitated to let Mittie wear them out.

"Maggie, you give her your shoes," urged Sallie, who, taller and thinner than Mittie and Maggie, wore a size 7 or 8. Margaret Garrison, who had grown up across the street and was visiting from Charlotte, frowned when Maggie yielded, but Mittie slipped on the shoes and skipped off to the camp meeting. Sure, she could take the horse and buggy, too. Steve would bring it around.

Mittie was, the women explained to the neighbors, their little girl. She had lived with them since she could walk—they had needed no court order for Bob and Alice to let her join their household. They bought a trundle bed to slide from under their bed at night so she could sleep in the room with them. When she was older, they gave her a single bed in Maggie's room. Sometimes when she was nine or ten she would wake up, afraid of the dark or a bad dream, and crawl into bed with Maggie. When she wanted a treat from Mr. Frank's store, they would give her a dime, sometimes even a dime and a nickel. Margaret made clothes for her. So did Jennie Helms at the store. When preachers and such people showed up at the house, Mittie tied a cloth on her head and waited on the white folks' table as the guests expected. But when familiar neighbors dropped by—the Rosses called Margaret and her mother Harriet Taylor "cousin" though they were no blood kin—they dropped the formalities.

"Come on, Mittie, you can stand here by me at the table," Maggie told the girl when Harriet Taylor was over for lunch. "Cousin Hettie doesn't care. You can stand by me at the table."

Mittie grew into a generous, outgoing woman, known for her cooking skills—the women taught her to make scratch cakes and sweet potato custards by letting her throw away unsuccessful attempts—and for her engaging personality. She had an oval face and a light skin tone that, with her high cheekbones and sharp nose, suggested a trace of Indian in her ancestry. She carried her five-six or five-seven frame, neither skinny nor heavy, with grace and confidence.

When she finished what schooling was available to her at their knee and at the Colored School in Marvin, the sisters wanted Mittie to continue her education at Livingstone College. The school, which was started in 1879 by the African Methodist Episcopal Zion Church and named in 1887 for David Livingstone, the British explorer of Africa, admitted her. When the day came for Mittie to go in 1903, Sallie was sick. Margaret went with Maggie on the Southern Railway train from Charlotte to Salisbury to drop her off. But after two or three months, Bob and Maggie had to go back and pick her up. She didn't want to finish the term. They spent the night on campus, eating dinner on a tray in Mittie's room, and brought her home the next day.

The women sent Mittie to Livingstone again the next year, and again she was too homesick to stay. The next year, when she came home again, she was really sick, and they sent Steve Walkup to Lancaster County to fetch Dr. Potts. He arrived in his buggy, examined her in an upstairs room in the house, and came down to tell the sisters sad news: Mittie was pregnant. She did not leave the house again for the term of her pregnancy, and when her labor began, in the harvest season, they sent again for Dr. Potts. He delivered the child in the downstairs bedroom where Maggie slept, where Mittie as a child had crawled into bed with her. The baby died. They buried its body in the garden behind the house and told no one.

On April 14, 1907, Mittie married Tom Houston, son of Ned Houston, who worked on Dr. McIlwaine's land. He was a slender man, not quite six feet tall, darker than Mittie and elegantly handsome, with dreamy wide eyes in his narrow face and a mustache that matched his striking-dark eyebrows and framed his firm lips with an effect of dash and charm. He was a little older than Mittie, born on Independence Day 1886. He was not as educated as she—his life had been in the fields—but he wooed her in ways that won the approval of both her parents and the old women who looked after her. Sallie and Maggie gave them a cow for a wedding present. This time, when Mittie had a baby, she was married. The birth of Florence Tucker Houston, on October 19, 1907, put to rest the nightmare of the buried baby and opened the family to the future. The next year, Sallie and Maggie hired S. H. Fincher to build a house for her family.

The clapboard one-story house, its main section forty feet square with a towering roof, rose on brick piers in a piney grove, in sight of the knoll at the road's bend where Bob and Alice lived in the old Burleyson house. Across the wrap-around porch with its tongue-in-groove floor and ceiling, one passed through an ornate door flanked by deeply layered panels and narrow windowpanes to a grand center hall nearly ten feet wide. Vertical beaded board ran the length of the hall on both sides to a thick chair rail's height, with horizontal beaded board above. The hall opened onto four rooms—two on the left, two on the right—each about fifteen by twenty feet, each trimmed elaborately with millwork around the doors and windows, each pair sharing a brick chimney. Fireplaces opened in the center of each room's interior wall, and a door between fireplace and outer wall connected the neighboring rooms. The kitchen, even bigger than the front rooms, stretched off the north side of the back with its own small chimney. Few white people, and no tenants black or white that anyone knew, had such a home. Tom planted oak saplings and chinaberry trees in the front yard, dug a garden patch in a sunlit spot to one side, and started an orchard of plums, apples, and pears in the back yard.

Mittie, like her father, was happy for her child to spend most of her time at the Ross women's house as she grew up. When she had her first son in 1909, she named him Dennis Clyde, the third generation of Dennis C.'s in the Ross family. Mittie and Tom had a second son, Charlie, in 1912; Robert in 1913; Collins in 1916; Ervin in 1917. Florence was still spending much of her time at the big house, and Maggie was still helping the growing family. One day Mittie showed up and asked Maggie to give her a cow because she needed milk for the children. Maggie chided her for selling her wedding-present cow and told her she wouldn't give her another—but she would give one to Florence, and Mittie better not sell it. Maggie happened to have two cows giving milk at the time and, although she jealously guarded the income from butter at eighteen cents a pound, she gave Mittie one and bought a replacement from Clyde Ezzell. Later, Mittie came back for another cow and Maggie sent her to Mr. Ezzell, who had one for sale. He wanted seventy-five dollars. Maggie wouldn't spend it. Mittie came back and said that her mother, Alice, had a cow she'd sell for sixty dollars. Maggie bought it for her.

When Mittie came to visit, she took home eggs, butter, meat, sugar, flour—whatever she wanted. Sometimes she would get money. Sometimes she baked custards. The sisters vied to take care of Florence, bathing and dressing and fussing over her like doting grandparents. They called her "my darling granddaughter," and when she was older she slept in Maggie's bed during her extended visits, just as Mittie had done.

After Sallie died and Harriet Grier moved in to cook for Maggie, Mittie sometimes came to stay a week or two. She slept with Harriet on a pallet on the floor in Maggie's bedroom. She visited less as more of her boys were born and the children took more of her time. Mittie and Harriet did not get along. Once when Maggie was depressed and Mittie was trying to cheer her up by pulling on her nose and ears, Harriet intervened.

"That's the way I do Miss Mag when she has the blues," Mittie explained, but Harriet drew back a fist to force her away.

"Thank God, I have got somebody to take up for me," Maggie said, but Mittie kept playing with Maggie's face and laughing as if the lady's protest—"Oh, quit, Mittie"—were part of the jest.

Once, she and Tom stopped by after a trip to Charlotte and Mittie complained to Maggie that she couldn't find a dress she wanted for ten dollars.

"I ain't got no money," Maggie answered.

"I can't get a dress for ten dollars—the devil!" Mittie retorted "I have been to Charlotte two times, and I can't get a dress for ten dollars." She stormed out of the room. Maggie followed her to the front porch and called Tom.

"Tom, Mittie is mad," she said through a deep, almost fearful, frown. "She wants a dress. You come soon in the morning and you can go up on that early train and be back by one or two o'clock."

The next night, Tom stopped by to report that he had made the trip. He had bought Mittie a dress, but not the one she wanted. It was already sold.

Mittie never doubted her place in the family, and she broached no challenge from outsiders. About two months after Florence was born, Mittie noticed Sallie showing some jewelry, two rings and a pin, to Margaret Garrison and heard her say "Cousin Mag, here are some things I value more than anything on earth, and I want you to take care of them."

"Miss Sallie, you told me you were going to give that ring to me," Mittie objected, but Sallie waved her off: "I will make Mag give you hers."

Some years later, Mittie saw Maggie giving two candlesticks to Margaret and reminded her: "Miss Maggie, you promised me these candlesticks."

Maggie, embarrassed, took one back from Margaret as a compromise: "You won't care if I give Mittie one, will you?"

8

SALLIE AND MAGGIE

In their youth, the Misses Ross took much interest in community affairs, but as they grew older, they became very reticent, and mingled less and less with the outside world.

—MONROE JOURNAL, 1920

It took two daughters to carry forward the shrewd and soft sides of Susan Burleyson Ross. Sallie, "the business end of the firm," as one neighbor put it, inherited her ambition, her aggressive dealing, her eye for a bargain. Maggie mirrored her mother's compassion, her charitable giving, her concern for the downtrodden. Each, of course, shared some of the other's gifts, whether by nature, nurture, or a lifetime of living together. Maggie could hold her own in a horse trade, and Sallie could give away an armload of bedding to a neighbor whose house burned down. But they possessed clear specialties, like the head and heart of a human body, and together they were "the Misses Ross," one identifiable organism. As Nathan's children, they were poor, forced to plow the fields while others went to school, and only the generosity of a friend at Union Methodist gave them any chance at an education. Andrew Jackson Clark, who was about ten years older than the sisters, farmed in the summer and taught in the winter. From his free lessons, both women learned to read and write and do some arithmetic, but Maggie's heart was not nearly as engaged as Sallie's head. The elder learned to compute interest; the younger could make change only with an effort she would rather not exert. Sallie was the sister working along-side Dennis to keep investing the cotton money in more land, making more cotton, buying more land. Maggie was the one more likely to be bathing and dressing Mittie Bell.

Dr. W. H. Crowell from Steele Creek, who took over Dr. Rone's practice in Marvin, boarded with the Rosses for more than a year while he was courting Ida Ardrey. They married on January 1, 1896, and lived in his upstairs room until they moved into their own home on February 5. The old women amused the young doctor with their antique airs and superstitions. Maggie told him she believed in ghosts, and she could hold him for hours with detailed stories of the distant past, although she couldn't remember Sunday's dinner by Wednesday. He also noticed that she had gloomy spells, but she wasn't his patient and he didn't prescribe for her.

When Dennis died later that year, Sallie knew she needed help. Bob could look after the crops, but someone needed to work with her on the trading. Dr. S. H. Ezzell, son of their neighbor Thomas Jefferson Ezzell and his first wife Amanda, had recently started practicing medicine, and he stayed in the house for several days after the funeral. A little later, he stayed with them for a week to work on Dennis's books and add up the tenants' accounts. He soon learned to ask Sallie when he had questions—Maggie knew next to nothing of the business. She spent most of her time sitting quietly in her rocking chair, sometimes not even responding when he spoke to her. She missed Dennis, and as the more sensitive of his two surviving sisters, she brooded on the ravages death wrought in her family—mother, father, brothers, and this one ripped so suddenly and so violently.

A few weeks later, Sallie sent for Dick Hudson to help them with the work. He and Barber Sullivan sold some mules and crops from the tenants and took the tenants' mortgages. A few months later, the sisters asked him to market two hundred bales of cotton that had come off the land. The buyers offered five thousand dollars, a price Mr. Hudson considered too low, but the sisters told him to sell. Sallie gave him a list of debts—Dennis's debts—and sent him to Charlotte to pay them.

That took almost all the money, in a year when the average national income was four hundred thirty dollars. Eggs sold for nineteen cents a dozen, milk for twenty-seven cents a gallon, bread for five cents a pound, unsliced. The gossips were right about Dennis's profligate spending, but except for the confidential agent, no one need know.

The next spring, Sallie sent for Hudson to sell another two hundred bales, and he was able to get a better price, almost seven thousand dollars. When he brought her the money this time, wrapped in a newspaper, she asked what bank they should use. He suggested the Commercial in Charlotte and took her to meet the cashier, Addison G. Brenizer. Later that year, the sisters asked him to manage their affairs permanently and offered him fifty dollars a year. For more than ten years, he sold their cotton, raised their money, and ran their errands, dropping by at least once a week to discuss the business. He wrote checks for the tenants' supply bills, advised them on rents, looked after the buildings, and made contracts for new barns and tenant houses. They bought no more land after Dennis died, but they sold only one tract, just over the line in Lancaster County, South Carolina, to their second cousin, George Washington Ross.

The women were not well. Dr. W. O. Nisbet, who grew up in Union County, treated Sallie at home for a spell of sickness in 1898, when he was practicing in Waxhaw. She was so ill that he spent the night in the house to watch her progress. Two years later, after the doctor had moved to Charlotte, Maggie took her to his home for two days more of treatment. In 1905, Sallie had to go to the Presbyterian Hospital in Charlotte for eleven days to get treatment for her bladder and kidney trouble. Dr. Nisbet, who helped start the hospital in 1903 in the Arlington Hotel on West Trade Street, took care of her there. Sallie spent much of 1907 in bed with bladder trouble. By April 12, Dr. H. Q. Alexander had been to their house eighteen times to treat her.

Maggie had never been as strong as Sallie. She was thin and frail, and wrinkles had early crisscrossed her face, making her appear even more delicate than she was. Her nervousness and her melancholy, her hand-wringing and frequent long face, accented the air of weakness. She had suffered digestive trouble for years. When Dr. Nisbet came to the house to treat Sallie in 1898, he gave Maggie a prescription for a laxative and something for her stomach. In 1904, when he saw her at his office in Charlotte, he diagnosed her with catarrh of the stomach and floating kidney and gave her a band to wear around her waist to support her internal organs. As she aged, she suffered crying spells at least weekly, trouble sleeping at night, and Bright's disease, a chronic kidney inflammation for which she took tiny pills. She complained about her stomach and her rheumatism. She was distracted, body and soul, by her aches and pains and her fear of wretched loneliness should death strike her home once more.

In 1905, the sisters settled their religious affiliation: They joined Banks Presbyterian Church next door. They had attended Waxhaw Baptist Church, Union Methodist Episcopal Church South, Bonds Grove Methodist Episcopal Church South, Marvin Methodist Episcopal Church South, and, in August, Pleasant Grove Camp Meeting. At one point, one sister was a Baptist and the other a Methodist. They had always been drawn to Banks. Dr. William A. McIlwaine, their neighbor and physician when they first moved into the Rone house, had given the land for Banks Chapel and was its Sunday school superintendent for years. The story of his death was a set piece of Marvin's history. On Sunday, February 18, 1894, he led the prayer, announced the hymn "We Are Marching on to Zion," sat on the front seat, and died. "His soul flew off to Glory," the obituary said, and awe-struck worshipers took off their coats to cover his body. The day of his funeral, buggies clogged roads to the cemetery from every direction, and black and white people joined in mourning: "We've lost the best friend we've had." His tall gray and white monument in the small cemetery, next to the two sons he had buried early, read simply: "For fifty years he healed the sick."

The year 1905 also brought deep grief to the sisters—Mittie came home from college again, this time pregnant. They knew the old story whispered around the community about the stepdaughter's baby, the outrage that had driven Dr. Rone from Marvin. They were sorry, Sallie told Dr. Potts, an understatement of their anguish. They had tried to raise her right—and they would stand by her. As the doctor was leaving, Sallie pressed a two-dollar gold piece into his hand and asked him not to mention the birth. Burying that baby was the hardest thing they had done since they buried Dennis nine years earlier, and they could erect no monument on the grave.

Two years later, when Mittie, happily matched with Tom Houston, delivered a daughter, the sisters rejoiced that they had lived to see the family reach another generation. They also summoned their lawyers to come and put on paper what they wanted to happen to their empire when their bodies rested in the little Presbyterian cemetery across the road.

9

THE NEIGHBORS

O poortith cauld, and restless love,
Ye wrack my peace between ye;
Yet poortith a' I could forgive,
An 'twere na for my Jeanie.

O why should Fate sic pleasure have,
Life's dearest bands untwining?
Or why sae sweet a flower as love
Depend on Fortune's shining?

The warld's wealth, when I think on,
It's pride and a' the lave o't;
O fie on silly coward man,
That he should be the slave o't!

—ROBERT BURNS, 1793

Five years after the neighbors adopted Marvin Methodist Church's name, the United States Post Office rejected the word for its official address. The community could have its own Star Route post office for weekly mail pickup, but "Marvin" was too much like "Morven" in Anson County. Find something less confusing, the postal officials ordered. So folks got together at Frank Crane's new store to talk it over. During the meeting, somebody pulled a practical joke, setting up a needle in a seat so that a tug on a thread would lift the point just as the victim was sitting down. A robust yell, a hearty laugh all around, and down to business. By the end of the meeting, they had decided: The place would be called Poortith—Scottish for Poverty, made appealing by Robert Burns' poem that contends sorrow comes not from cold poverty but from restless love. J. B. Squires came up with the idea. Mr. Frank became postmaster on June 21, 1880.

They were a people who took themselves not too seriously, who shared their Poverty with a mutual respect deep enough for personal humor. A couple of teenagers once climbed on the roof of Amos McIlwaine's house and called down the chimney, "Amos! Amos!" He was so rattled by the eerie voice that he replied "Yes, Lord! What can I do, Lord?" One evening after an ice storm, the men in Mr. Frank's store offered Amos and a friend a dollar for each magnolia leaf they would bring back from the tree uphill in the Marvin Methodist Cemetery. The men's sheet-draped co-conspirator was already lying by a gravestone to rise just as the adventurers topped the hill. Terrified by the ghostly vision, one slipped on the ice as they dashed back toward the store, pleading with the other: "Don't leave me! Please, don't leave me!" Newcomers, even schoolteachers, were sometimes taken on snipe hunts to the blackjacks and sometimes left to wait all night at the head of a ditch. If the pranks went too far, Aunt Nannie Rone chided the pranksters. Much of the county shared in an April Fool's gag on Mr. Frank's nephew, James Crane. During the night, someone took his horse from his stable, and when he awoke he alerted the neighbors that a horse thief was abroad. He notified the police in Waxhaw and Monroe to be on the lookout. Search parties went out and tracked the horse for some distance before losing the trail. At last, they called the joke: The horse had been in Mr. Frank's barn all along!

Mr. Frank, postmaster of Poortith, was more or less mayor of Marvin, and his store was tantamount to town hall in the farming village. He was a large man, with a thick, drooping mustache that could strain soup and a hairline that receded past the crest of his head. He almost always wore a white shirt and dark trousers and vest; he would add a coat on cooler days. He kept thirty-seven cents in his vest pocket in case some sport, seeking to impress his girlfriend over the weekend and unworthy of more money, asked for a loan. For his own finances, he relied on the Rosses, who kept thousands in their house and acted as a bank for many of the neighbors. Mr. Frank borrowed five hundred dollars from them once, then two hundred dollars and smaller amounts over the years. He could send someone up the hill to bring back five dollars or two-fifty or whatever he needed in the store whenever he needed it.

He was born in 1859, son of Job Crane, the "Little Yankee" who became a wounded Confederate, and he married the Widow Helms in 1882. They met when he was chopping wood for the Parkses, next door to where Arkanta had moved with her three daughters after her husband, Amon Helms, died. It was a warm, humid day, so Frank took off his jacket and hung it over a nearby fence while he worked. When he went to get the jacket, it was gone. Arkanta took it to her house to make the broad-shouldered, blue-eyed neighbor come and meet her. The ploy worked: They fell in love. His mother, Lydia, told Job to break up the romance or get out of the house, so Job went to live with his sister for a while. "Miss Lydie" let her husband come home after the wedding, but she refused to acknowledge the marriage even after "Miss Kantie" gave birth to James Thomas. Not until the fall of 1885, when she heard that their second son, Frank Ernest, was born with a crippled foot did Miss Lydie relent and visit the family. The board at Marvin Methodist summoned the women and ordered them to settle their differences. Miss Kantie was willing to forgive, if not forget, and the relations thawed. They took Ernest to Atlanta for surgery, and he came back wearing an iron brace that the blacksmith John McKinney had to extend from time to time. The boy learned to use the brace as a weapon when he was angry at his playmates. Mittie Bell Ross, who made friends when her family moved nearby in 1892, knew the weight of its kick.

Mr. Frank went into retailing after a stint in his late teens at W. M. Parks's sawmill, when he saved enough money to rent a building and buy a stock of groceries. He was boarding at Dr. Rone's house at the time. He was soon able to build his own building, and the site, near a bend in New Town Road and a side-road intersection that led into South

Carolina, became the core of the community. Ezzell's Store sat snugly in the far side of the intersection. Mr. Frank ran a grist mill, a sawmill, a lumber yard, and a molasses mill for the community across New Town Road from his store. He and the Ross sisters shared a vineyard where their lots met in the back.

In 1906, Mr. Frank built a new house between his store and the Methodist Church, an elegant Queen Anne befitting his station in the community—white-painted with green shutters and a slate roof using material he had brought down from Charlotte on mule-drawn wagons. Arkanta died in 1910 and was buried in the Methodist cemetery. Miss Jennie, whose sisters had married off, presided over the house until Ernest married Bessie Perry in 1916 and they moved into the mansion. Jennie spent more of her time at the store, where she kept the books in a flowing script, except for the days when migraines kept her at home. Then Mr. Frank, in his heavy scrawl, penciled the five cents for Calumet baking powder, three-fifty for ten pounds of Top tobacco, or twenty-two cents for rice and ale.

The store had windows with shuttered hinges on each side of its double front door. The building was one open room inside, lined on each side with long counters set out from shelf-filled walls and heated with a wood stove toward the rear. On the dry goods side, cardboard boxes of men's hats and work shoes filled the top shelf, and the lower shelves held bolts of cloth—brown sheeting, hickory shirting, cottonade for pants (a dime a yard for everyday, fifty cents for finer material), carefully-covered fine linens and lawns, drill cloth for men's underwear; a case of spool cotton; a few boxes of ball thread for coarse sewing and patching. A glass showcase at the end of the counter displayed silk handkerchiefs, Hoyt's German Cologne at a dime a bottle, pins, needles, buttons, cufflinks, hat-pins. One lower shelf held slates, pencils, foolscap paper for copy books, Blue Back Spellers, and a few other books for school. A box of horseshoe nails sat on the floor next to stacks of horseshoes and mule shoes.

At the back of the store, spikes driven into the wall held coils of rope, trace chains, hame strings, collar pads, horse collars, bridles, and reins. On the floor were boxes of ax heads, a crate of ax handles, pitchforks, shovels, spades, and weeding hoes. Behind the door was a tank of kerosene. A platform in the back held a barrel of vinegar and barrels of molasses of different grades—fifty cents or seventy-five cents a gallon. One back corner of the room was walled off to hold cracked cotton—bolls not fully open—so the lint could be pulled free and sold without ginning. Near the back west corner, Miss Jennie operated the Marvin Telephone Co. that Mr. Frank owned with Jonas Plyler and C. E. Parks. One line ran west up New Town Road, the other east down the road. When a caller reached the switchboard, a flag dropped, showing a red sign. Miss Jennie would plug in, hear whom the caller was trying to reach, plug in her end of the line, and crank a bell at board level with the receiver's signal—one short, two long; three short; whatever code the company had assigned.

Along the other long wall, the grocery counter held a keg of gunpowder and a small scale with one-ounce weights—gunpowder cost five cents an ounce—and a larger scale that could weigh up to thirty pounds. The hoop cheese on the counter cost fifteen cents a pound. Customers brought their own white cotton bags to buy sugar by the pound. One shelf behind the grocery counter held snuff and tobacco—Brown's Mule was the most popular—and Mr. Frank had a cutter handy so you could buy part of a plug. Cans of sardines and salmon and pound boxes of soda were stacked on the grocery shelves. Saltine crackers and ginger snaps came in thirty-pound packages. Pickles and salt fish came by the barrel.

In the crop season, workers came to the store for cheese and brown sugar that they mixed for lunch and washed down with a swig from the common dipper in the pail drawn from the well pump outside. In cold weather, they raked hot coals into an apron around the Franklin stove to bake potatoes and onions that filled the room with a warm pungence. One Christmas Eve, Jim Crane showed up in the crowded store wearing the gas mask his brother Ernest had used in France during the World War. The alien appearance so frightened his eleven-year-old son Frank that the boy fell backwards off the counter where he was sitting, dashed outside, and hid under a fig tree behind the store. Some others in the store fled across the road to a tenant house. The fast ones locked the door, and the slower ones had to hide under the house.

Crane bought farm-fresh produce from neighbors who came with baskets filled with their butter and eggs and left with the baskets filled with his vanilla, soap, thread, tobacco, and candy. They could get credit to their account or cash for their crops. Onions and beans brought a dollar a bushel, corn and peas thirty-five cents a bushel, young chickens fifteen cents each, fat hens a quarter, cotton, market price—which could swing wildly from three cents to seventeen cents a pound. Children would bring bags of peanuts to trade for what they wanted when they came to the store on Saturdays or—on order from their parents—after the school across the road closed for the day. Steve Walkup or Craig Kirkpatrick or Jim Lymus left early in the morning to take two-mule or four-mule wagons loaded with the produce to the R. H. Field Commission House in Charlotte, and Mr. Frank followed in his buggy to make the trade. The driver stayed overnight in a campground with the empty wagon, then loaded it in the morning with goods for the store and drove home. By the end of the day, when the wagon arrived, plenty of neighbors gathered to get a look at the new merchandise and help unload.

A couple times a year, a pair of traveling salesmen came around with patent medicine and other goods advertised on brightly colored advertising cards they passed out to the children. Covered wagons came down from the Appalachian Mountains bringing tobacco, apples, cabbages, and chestnuts. The drivers camped near Mr. Frank's store, filling the air with the smell of frying country ham and boiling coffee, and the men and boys from the neighborhood joined them in the evenings around the campfire to get news of the outside world.

Regular news came from the postmen and the newspapers that passed through the store—the *Waxhaw Enterprise*, the *Monroe Journal* and its rival *Enquirer*, the *Charlotte News* and its rival *Observer*. The men worried, in turn, about Pancho Villa and the Russo-Japanese War, the Kaiser and the drowning of Ney McNeely of Waxhaw when his plane was shot down over the Mediterranean on his way to become consul in Aden, Arabia. They worried constantly about weather—droughts that parched the red upland, hailstorms that beat down stalks, floods that soaked the unpicked bolls—and cotton prices, ever suspicious of manipulation by the federal government and the cotton spinners. C. C. McIlwaine, who lived just beyond the Rosses from the store, often held the floor. When Capt. Will Heath of Monroe, president of the National Cotton Manufacturers' Association, proposed importing Italian workers for the fields, McIlwaine ridiculed the idea: "Why, the rascals would strike before breakfast!" When Southern farmers organized to hold their bales for higher prices, Dick Hudson represented the township at a state meeting.

In election years, the talk around the Franklin intensified, and candidates sometimes showed up to join in. The Democrats found almost as much disappointment in national elections, with the exception of Wilson's, as satisfaction in county races. In 1905, Dick Hudson was appointed county commissioner when A. J. Brooks died. McIlwaine and J. S. Howie were the townships' delegates to the party's congressional convention in 1908, when Mr. Frank, C. O. Howard, George Sutton, J. S. DeLaney, J. D. Hemby, and Dick Hudson went to the state convention. In 1913, Crane, Howie, and Sutton were on a special school committee for the township.

The idlers often found less weighty things to talk about as they sat on nail kegs and played checkers, went out in the yard to pitch horseshoes, or organized Saturday shooting matches. The *Journal* routinely reported oddities of interest to farmers—the first cotton bloom each year, an ear of corn with a tiny shuck grown around every kernel, a woman who rescued fourteen eggs from the belly of a black snake she killed, returned them to the nest, and got them to hatch. "Mr. C. W. Medlin of Goose Creek reports that from a big double-yolk egg on his farm two chickens, one entirely white and one entirely black, were produced," the paper passed along one spring. "One was duck legged and one was long legged, he says, and so were not much of twins after all."

The regulars were always ready to leave their chat to help a neighbor in need. When word came that somebody was sick and unable to tend his crops, the men in the store would arrange to show up the next day with plows and hoes to get the friend's fields in shape again. Life in Poortith, so far from "cold poverty," was generous, warm, and shared.

10

THE TENANTS

They lived largely to themselves on their farm . . .
surrounded by numerous colored tenants. In a way,
they had an empire of their own.

—*MONROE JOURNAL*, 1920

Will Body had but one hope. The wagons from the A. W. Heath Company were in his yard to take his goods, and W. H. Collins from the store in Waxhaw had the papers to prove that he had not paid his account. Talk to Miss Maggie, the black tenant told the white merchant. When Mr. Collins went to her house and told her what was happening, she hurried down to Crane's store and telephoned Dick Hudson. He came over, and she told him to pay Mr. Collins a fair price for the merchandise. Will was spared.

Such was the safety of residence in Rosstown. Whether across the old road from the family's mansion or along the new road that Crane's crew laid out through the homeplace after Dennis died, to farm for the Rosses was to feel like family. The landlords made sure you enjoyed decent housing, fair rents, and cash to tide you over when you needed it.

Some of the tenants were blood kin. Tirzah Coan, who moved onto New Town Road land with her husband, Joseph Doctor Coan in 1894, was a second cousin—their grandmothers were sisters—and close as a sister to Sallie and Maggie. The Coans rented the land until 1911, when Maggie sold them their house on twenty-four and a half acres for thirty dollars an acre, telling them, "I want you to have a home of your own in Marvin." Doc continued to rent some of her farmland. Their houses were just about a quarter-mile apart, and the cousins visited back and forth regularly. Tirzah, childless and more than twenty years younger than the sisters, helped with their cooking and sewing as they aged. She helped prepare both Dennis and Sallie for burial. Not long after Dennis died, she had a three-month spell of sickness that left her weak. Her health so deteriorated across the years that soon after the land sale her rheumatism kept her confined to the house. Maggie visited her more often.

Some of the tenants were close as family. Harriet Taylor, who met the Rosses in 1871, called Susan "aunt" and the sisters "cousin," though they were no blood kin. So did her daughter, Margaret, who was thirteen when the family moved to the Rosses' land from Lancaster County in 1888. They moved to the Ardrey land, then the McIlwaine land before Mr. Taylor died, but they kept visiting the Rosses regularly. Sometime after Dennis died, the Widow Taylor quit keeping house and divided her time between Salisbury and her son Robert White's house in Lancaster County. She stayed with the sisters two, three, four, sometimes six weeks at a time. She helped in 1905 when Maggie had the grippe. Every now and then, the women would give her a few dollars for her service. After Sallie died, she stayed three months, and Maggie gave her thirty dollars.

Margaret came back to stay with the sisters for a week or ten days at a time after she married William Garrison and moved to Charlotte in 1901. She went with Maggie to take Mittie to Livingstone College in 1903, and she was staying with them when Mittie came home in 1905 and Dr. Potts diagnosed her pregnancy. The sisters visited Margaret in Charlotte, where she had started a boarding house, two or three times a year. Maggie continued to go see her, sometimes with Mittie, after Sallie died and Margaret had expanded her business. She stayed for three or four days at a time, always adding a visit to her Gribble kin, and once, when Margaret took her to Dr. W. H. Hoffman in Charlotte to have her teeth fixed, she stayed three weeks.

None of the tenants lacked anything the Rosses could give them. Ed Yarbrough moved across New Town Road from the Ross house in 1901 with his mother-in-law, Fannie Forbis, and his sons, Collie and Ross. The sisters gave him some honeybees for his yard, and for fifteen years he tended their bees and made gums for their combs with lumber and nails the landlord provided. Maggie loaned him two hundred fifty dollars after Sallie died, but she wouldn't consider selling the Watson tract to him. She hired him and his brother Ambrose to build a house for Jim Crane in 1913 so Frank Crane's nephew would return to her farm. Most of her lumber came from Charlie Parks, the neighbor whose family had first taken young Frank as an apprentice.

Jim grew up in an old house on the land his father Silas rented for years. He went to the McIlwaine farm for a year, but Maggie agreed to build a nice five-room house for him about three hundred yards from her house, and he came back at Christmas. A year or two later, when late rains soaked the cotton crop, Jim talked her into knocking a bale off everyone's rent—cutting it from five bales to four. Later, when he was going to Fort Mill to trade his wagon for a new one, she asked him to order one for her. She went upstairs and gave him a hundred twenty-five dollars for the wagon.

In 1911, Maggie bought the old Banks Chapel for two hundred dollars and had it moved across New Town Road, just east of the cemetery. She paid Noah Helms sixty-five dollars to add a second story, converting the old church into a tenant house. In 1915, Ambrose Yarborough offered to rent for five years if Maggie would build him a new house. She refused the longer contract but built the house anyway. They moved an old building away from its homesite, and S. H. Fincher built a new one. Maggie made sure he placed the house so that a big tree on the lot shaded the front porch.

Steve Walkup, who lived across the road from the women when they bought the house, went to work for them about 1900. He had worked for Frank Crane, driving the wagons to Charlotte for the store's trading, and he still rented some farmland in addition to the odd jobs he did around the house for the women. He and his wife Emma had two daughters, Annie and Bird, and three sons, Ed, Walter, and Stephen. They shared the house with Emma's mother, the revered Granny Ann Robinson, who was a founder of Marvin AME Zion, and Emma's brothers Dock, Ned, and Ed. Amos McIlwaine, who had lived in a cabin around the New Town Road bend, moved onto Maggie's place after Sallie died. He stayed around the yard and built their fires. Amos was mentally slow—the neighbors called him a half-wit—and he was quick to point out that he was not a "'sponsible person" when he was about to get in trouble.

On the homeplace, Maggie paid five hundred dollars to build a new tenant house for Banks Stephens, who had rented from her since 1901 and married Mary Kimbrell in 1906. When he complained that the house was not ceiled, she went down to see—and ordered the work finished. "No one should live like that," Maggie said. Banks's rent was two thousand seven hundred fifty pounds of cotton. Cotton sold by the bale, so Banks, like the other tenants, took his receipts from Crane's gin to the landlord to settle up at the end of the season. One year, Maggie owed him thirteen dollars fifty-six cents. Never one for figures, she confused the numbers in her head as she went upstairs for the money and came back with thirty-six dollars fifty cents. He took what she owed and handed the rest back: "That belongs to you." Maggie, embarrassed, took it and laughed: "Oh, I ain't got no sense nohow." Later, Banks came to borrow twelve hundred dollars. She sent Dick Hudson with him to the bank in Waxhaw to draw up the note and get the money.

Banks and other tenants at the homeplace, including his brother, Oscar Stephens, who farmed ten years for the women, typically paid their rent to Bob Ross. Oscar and his wife Ella had three sons and shared the house with three in-laws. Bob and Mittie and Tom Houston paid no rent—whatever they raised belonged to them, and anything they needed the Rosses provided, including a five hundred dollar barn when Bob's old one burned and the house that S. H. Fincher built for Mittie and Tom after their marriage. He also built a house for Billy Ardrey that year.

Much of the management of the Ross plantation fell to Dick Hudson after Dennis died. He sold that year's cotton, part in the fall, part in the following spring, and Sallie arranged to pay him fifty dollars a year to take over some of the business her brother had handled. After Sallie died, he took over much more work, and Maggie tripled his pay.

Mr. Hudson let contracts for tenant houses and barns, drew bank notes for the large loans the women granted, reported their taxes, kept the tenants' accounts, and signed checks for their supplies at the store: "Maggie Ross, by R. A. Hudson." He kept track of the two dollars here and three dollars there that she loaned the tenants, and he settled up with them when the crops came in every year. In January and July, he went to two banks in Charlotte, the Commercial and the National, to collect her 4 percent interest. Every month, he went to Waxhaw to pay the tenants' accounts at the store. Every two or three weeks, she sent for him—sometimes to go seventeen miles to Charlotte, sometimes to Monroe, sometimes to Waxhaw, sometimes to a tenant's house to check whether it needed repair.

Hudson was one of the leading farmers of Sandy Ridge Township, prominent in both the cotton association and Democratic politics, eventually appointed a county commissioner. He lived on Providence Road, three and a half miles from the Rosses, next to his in-laws, the Howards, from whose family Susan had bought land to expand her farm. Hudson had a store at the road in front of his house that some of the homeplace tenants found handy.

Sallie Hudson remembered going with Amanda Howard to the Burleyson homeplace and meeting the Rosses when she was twelve years old. The sisters were more than fifteen years older than their friends, and they doted like grandmothers on the Hudsons' son Richard and Harry Hood, the son of their older daughter Pearl, who was more like a brother than a nephew to Richard. The boys were in college at the same time—Richard at Clemson Agricultural College of South Carolina, Harry at North Carolina Agricultural & Mechanical in Raleigh. Sallie took it on herself to look after the old ladies, and she was regularly in their house to help them when they were sick. She had grown into a stout farmer's wife, barrel-shaped and double-chinned, with close-cropped white hair, square-set lips, and piercing eyes—large enough, in both heart and body, to care for not only her own family but any neighbor in need. Maggie and Sallie loved her. When they were well, they made the trip to Sallie's house to spend the day, usually lounging under the giant oak in the front yard along Providence Road, within sight of the new road and not far from the old Wolfsville School.

One evening in 1907, Dick Hudson found the sisters sitting on their back porch just when, in a speak-of-the-devil way, they had been wishing he would appear. They were planning their will, and they were thinking of giving fifteen hundred dollars to his teenage son Richard. But they were debating whether to give his grandson Harry Hood, who was about Richard's age, part of the money.

11

THE WILL

I devise, bequeath and give all my property, real and personal, of whatever nature, kind or description, to my sister, Maggie A. Ross, during her life, with the request that she keep the property as it is.

—SALLIE ROSS, 1907

At 10:30 on a fall morning in 1907, Robert B. Redwine and Henry B. Adams, traveling together in a buggy from their law offices in Monroe, reached the Ross house. The message that Steve Walkup brought gave no hint what Miss Maggie and Miss Sallie wanted with them. Adams, a large, affable man with thick, snow-white hair just long enough to sweep back, had been practicing in Monroe since 1872, after graduating from Trinity College and studying law for two years. He was elected to the state house in 1884 and the state senate in 1886 and recently moved his office into the Law Building. He was Dick Hudson's attorney.

Redwine, son of an old friend from Union Methodist, opened his practice in Monroe in 1891 after he graduated from the University of North Carolina. He was the women's lawyer. He came late to law after farming and retailing, and he had won election to the recent term of the General Assembly. His dark hair was thinning, retreating high above slightly crossed eyes that, with his mouth-covering bushy mustache and deeply cleft round chin, gave him an air of perpetual bemusement. He

R. B. Redwine

was appointed a county commissioner in 1895 but resigned the next year. The partnership of Redwine and David Covington was appointed general counsel to county commissioners when Populists took over the board in 1896, and the next year they won a bid to rent two offices in the courthouse for one hundred dollars a year. Redwine established a partnership with Amos M. Stack in 1900, when he built the red-brick Law Building in Monroe. The men dissolved that partnership in 1905, and Redwine became partners with John C. Sikes in 1906. In 1902, Stack and *Monroe Journal* editor R. F. Beasley wrote in a book about Monroe: "Mr. Redwine has always enjoyed a large practice, both civil and criminal. He has the absolute confidence of his clients and makes their interests his own. He is, both in and out of the court house, the personification of honor and integrity. He stands unflinchingly by principle and truth as he sees them."

At the Ross house, a black woman opened the door for the lawyers. Maggie and Sallie were waiting in a room to the left off the hall. They chatted briefly about old times at Union Methodist—Sallie remembered that Jack Clark, their teacher, was Redwine's uncle—but the talk soon turned to the future. Sallie had celebrated her seventy-sixth birthday a few weeks earlier. She was approaching seventy-seven, the number on their father's tombstone, the age at which their mother had died. Maggie, at sixty-eight, was at least as frail as her older sister. They had decided to write their wills—identical wills save for the bequests of their watches and chains. Adams would take notes so he could write up the items. The women were distributing more than ten thousand dollars in the bank and three thousand six hundred dollars in gold coin stitched into two shot pokes and stuffed into a drawer upstairs. Their fourteen hundred acres, some of the finest cotton-growing soil in Union County, was worth about thirty thousand dollars.

After Maggie mentioned that she wanted Dick Hudson to be her executor, Sallie did most of the talking. She asked Redwine to be her executor. He agreed. The four of them sat together around a table in the formal room lined with dark-stained heart-pine flushboards floor, ceiling, and walls. A fire crackled at the brick hearth under the built-in pine mantel. The women had a long list of beneficiaries, beginning with their watches and chains—Sallie's to Dick Hudson's wife, Sallie, Maggie's to Mittie Bell. Dennis, they said, wanted Bob to get his.

They ordered the bodies of Susan and Dennis and John moved from Union Methodist Cemetery to Banks Presbyterian Cemetery across the street from their home, with a new monument that would cost up to two thousand dollars to mark the family plot. They gave the church a thousand dollars to maintain the graveyard. They told the executors to use three hundred to build an iron fence around the old cemetery where their father and aunt and grandparents were buried and to keep the grounds respectable. They gave the trustees of Marvin Methodist Episcopal Church South four hundred dollars to do as they wished and five hundred dollars to establish a library, and Bonds Grove Methodist Episcopal Church South three hundred dollars. They gave Banks Presbyterian Church the Rone mansion, five hundred dollars for a library, three hundred dollars for any use, and another hundred dollars to help buy an organ. They gave a thousand dollars to Presbyterian Hospital in Charlotte to furnish rooms in their memory and Dennis's, fifteen hundred dollars to the Piedmont Industrial School in Charlotte that Rev. J. A. Baldwin started, one thousand dollars to the Board of Missions of the Western North Carolina Conference of the Methodist Episcopal Church South, two thousand dollars to the Synod of the Presbyterian Church of North Carolina for home missions, and two thousand dollars to the Barium Spring Presbyterian Orphanage north of Charlotte.

The orphanage, a favorite project of Rev. Billy McIlwaine, started when a black woman in Charlotte took in some white kids after their mother died and their father left them. Some Presbyterian ladies riding through the neighborhood in 1883 noticed the children, took them in, and started a home and hospital for such children. When they asked the

Presbyterian Synod to take over the work, Reverend McIlwaine was the denomination's agent for education and became chairman of a special committee to find a site. The orphanage was serving nearly one hundred seventy-five children at an average cost of less than ten dollars a month. Maggie and Sallie, seeing their own story mirrored in the home's history, wanted to help.

The women and the lawyers recessed to the kitchen for dinner at noon, then returned to the sitting room to finish the task, which took most of the day. They put in five hundred dollars for Sallie Hudson and one thousand dollars for Dick Hudson in trust for his son Richard and five hundred for his grandson Harris Hood. They marked five hundred dollars each for Will Garrison and his wife, Maggie; one thousand dollars for Dr. W. O. Nisbet; five hundred dollars for Harriet Taylor; five hundred dollars for Elias Crane's daughter Margaret Jackson Crane; two hundred dollars for Fannie Forbis and one hundred dollars each in trust for her grandsons Collie Yarborough and Ross Yarborough; two hundred dollars to Stephen Walkup; one hundred dollars each to Billy Ardrey, Henry Featherstone, Winnie Featherstone, Calvin Featherstone, all black tenants on the land; one hundred dollars each to Bob's wife, Alice, and Mittie's husband, Tom; five hundred dollars in trust for Bob, five hundred for his mother, Rosa Howie, five hundred for Mittie, five hundred for the infant Florence. They expected to sell part of the land to pay those legacies, which totaled more than twenty thousand dollars. But not the Burleyson homeplace.

That would go to Bob and Mittie Bell. All eight hundred acres, counting some of the land Susan added to her inheritance. Maggie and Sallie gave Bob the half of the land with the gin house, the barn, the stables at the house where he was living. He and Mittie would divide the kitchen furniture and any money that was left after the legacies were paid. They gave Bob the stock, the farming utensils, the farm machinery on the homeplace. They gave Mittie the dark mahogany pump organ, the bed, the bedstead, the bureau, the washstand, the chairs, the carpet, all the furnishings in the front parlor. All for Bob and Mittie Bell.

Adams jotted the items down without comment. He took his notes back to Monroe and typed the wills, in required legal form, on his own typewriter:

I, Maggie A. Ross, of Union County, North Carolina, being of sound mind and desiring to declare what disposition shall be made of my property after my death, do make, publish and declare my last will and testament as follows:

Item 1. I desire that my body shall receive a respectable Christian burial, in a nice metallic coffin, which shall be placed in a substantial box and covered with a lid, and I commend my spirit to God, who gave it, with the hope that I may be numbered among his redeemed. . . . Item 3: I bequeath to Mittie Belle Houston, wife of Thomas Houston, colored, after the death of my sister, Sallie A. Ross, my watch and chain. . . . Item 41. My sister Sallie A. Ross and I have by mutual agreement made our respective wills and testaments disposing of our property to the same person, in the same sums or amounts and alike in every particular, except as to our watches and chains, and I devise and bequeath my property to her for love with the distinct understanding and direction that she shall dispose of our joint property as I have herein disposed of the same, if I survive her.

On November 15, 1907, Adams wrote to Sallie and Maggie, giving them a chance to make sure they had bequeathed their property as they intended and guaranteeing that the execution would be in order:

It has required a little longer time to write your wills than I anticipated, however, I enclose them to you this evening by registered mail, so as to insure their safe delivery. In executing them, it is necessary that each of you sign your name to your respective wills on the line just above the word Testatrix in the presence of the witnesses, whom you will request to attest the fact that you are making your will and request them to sign their names in your presence and in the presence of each other; in other words you must request them to bear witness to the fact that you are making your will and that they are requested to witness the fact and sign their names. You and the witnesses must all see each other sign your names.

If you have any property in South Carolina, it will be necessary for you to have THREE witnesses. When you have signed them, you can return a copy of each to me, if you desire me to keep it. Read the wills carefully and see that they dispose of your property as you desire it done and if they do not do so, return them to me for correction in any particular and I will make the correction.

Sometime before the war, some ancestor of Steve Walkup must have belonged to someone in Jonathan Burleyson's executor's family.

He was born the year after the war ended, and he had once worked for the Cranes. He moved his family—wife, two daughters, three sons, three brothers-in-law, and his mother-in-law—across the street from the Rosses in 1900. He farmed part of their cotton land as a tenant and did their chores—caring for their stock, cultivating their garden, tending their flowers, starting their fires in winter. On November 20, 1907, he went on yet another errand—summoning George W. Sutton and Charles C. McIlwaine and Earle Jeter Ezzell to the big house. It was a cloudy day, and there had been a halo around the moon for the last three nights—a portent of rain—but the fog of the day before had lifted, and the warm air felt clean.

Esquire Sutton had met the Ross women when he moved to Marvin in 1884. Mr. Ezzell had known them all his life (he was born in 1881) but had been in their home only five or six times before. McIlwaine was an old family friend, the brother of the preachers Billy and Bobby McIlwaine and of Mary Lavinia Rone. He had first seen the Ross women at Waxhaw Baptist Church before the war and now attended Banks with them. He had visited their home frequently since 1867, both the Burleyson homeplace and their new house, and the women had been in his home every two or three months. McIlwaine reached the sisters' house last. The men, unsure why they had been summoned, were escorted into a room alone, but Sallie and Maggie soon joined them.

"We have sent for you men to come and see us sign our wills," Sallie explained. "You are the three that we wanted to sign these as witnesses." Then she left the room and came back with a stack of blue-backed paper, folded over. "These are our wills and you are the three that we have selected to sign them."

Sutton asked whether they should read the wills. Sallie said "No." She kept the papers folded so that only the lines for the names showed.

It was the twenty-first anniversary of the death of their mother. The women were weeping, and Maggie had nothing to say while they took turns sitting at the little table to sign their names to the papers. The room, about fourteen feet square, was a sitting room, but Maggie's bed crowded most of the space. Sallie signed her will first, two copies, then McIlwaine, then Sutton and Ezzell, then Maggie, then the men again. The women never stopped sobbing and sniffling. As soon as they were finished, only ten or fifteen minutes after they arrived, with no offer of refreshment or rest, the men excused themselves and headed out of the room.

"We are much obliged to you," Miss Maggie whispered as they passed. "We are much obliged."

12

THE COUSINS

Maggie Ross died without ever having married,
and without leaving any lineal descendants, or any
brothers or sisters, or the descendants of such, any
uncles or aunts or first cousins, and your caveators,
who are second cousins, some of them third cousins,
and some of them fourth cousins, are the nearest
of kin of the said Maggie Ross.

—JOHN WESLEY DEES AND OTHERS, 1920

No one had seen John Wesley Dees visit the Ross house since Sallie died. Frank Crane remembered seeing him stop by once, when he was township constable, before he moved to Mecklenburg County about 1910. George Washington Ross was around more often. He lived just a half mile from the sisters when he moved from the McIlwaine place to the Billy Ardrey place in 1898, and he was back and forth on business several times when he was buying land in Lancaster County from them in 1901. Both men showed up for Maggie's funeral at Banks Presbyterian on May 24, a warm, clear Monday afternoon, not as hot as Sunday, with a brilliant sun filling the churchyard and the graveyard. The neighbors prepared Maggie in a twenty-dollar burial dress and put her in a two-hundred-dollar coffin, both bought from Waxhaw Furniture Company. They buried her next to the family monument she erected when Sallie died. The Widow Gribble and her daughter Sue and Sue's husband, C. P. Edwards, and a couple other cousins came, along with Harriet Taylor and Margaret Moore and the Hudsons and Bobby McIlwaine and the near neighbors.

Most people thought "Cousin Hettie" Taylor and "Cousin Maggie" Moore were among the handful of relatives at the service. They weren't. A turnout of actual cousins would have crowded the graveyard, but almost no one knew how far-flung the family was—especially on the Ross side, where it included people within two miles of Marvin who were strangers to the old woman. They were Manus, Dees, Parker, Bickett, Killough, Lee, Broom, Morris, Hinson, Thompson, Crook, Horn, Pemberton, Kiker, Stikeleather, Lawrence, Reader, Irby, Phifer, Hargett, Morrison, Nelsons, Carelock, Suthers, Griffin, Davis, Templeton, Fincher, Kiker, Owens, Marsh, Rogers, Harper, Moore, Haire, Presson, Jones, and Smith.

Martin Ross's oldest son, William, had no children, and Rebecca and Annie moved to Alabama, but Samuel and Hugh had four each, Arden seven, Marina six by Matthew Parker, Ellen seven by Wylie Parker, and Elizabeth six by James Bickett, Jr., Samuel's son Hilliard married Lucy Richardson and added ten children to the extended family. Samuel's daughter Louisa Jane married Bryant Dees and added seven, including John Wesley Dees. Maggie once told Margaret Garrison that John was the spitting image of her brother Dennis. John Wesley's brother John Robert married Martha Secrest and added eleven. Ezekiel's granddaughter Lizzie Morris married Manford Newton Manus and added six. Cousins married each other and made more cousins.

Elizabeth's husband, Jim, a Methodist preacher, owned Bickett's Tavern, one of the first buildings in Monroe. He was also the county's first jailer and saw the construction of the two-story brick building that replaced the original log jail. Jim and Elizabeth Bickett's son Thomas was a Confederate surgeon during the war. Their grandson Walter was by far the most famous of the clan—attorney general in 1908, governor in 1916. Born in 1869 to Thomas Winchester and Mary Covington Bickett, he graduated from Wake Forest College in 1890, studied law at the University of North Carolina, and received his law license in 1893. He moved to Louisburg in 1895 and married Fannie Yarborough, daughter of Col. William H. Yarborough, in 1898.

From the start, Walter Bickett made race relations a centerpiece of his law practice and his eventual political career. In 1909, he managed to establish an interpretation of North Carolina's one-eighth rule—that a person was legally black if at least one great-grandparent was black—to mean that the great-grandparent did not have any white blood. He was defending, in Franklin County Superior Court, a woman whose husband wanted to have their marriage annulled so that he would bear no responsibility for their child. He claimed she was black because one of her great-grandfathers was part black. When the state Supreme Court upheld Bickett's view in 1910, Chief Justice Walter Clark wrote: "If indeed, the plaintiff had discovered any minute strain of colored origin after the youth of his wife has been worn away for his pleasure and in his service, justice and generosity dictated that he keep to himself that of which the public was unaware, or, if the knowledge had become public and was disagreeable, the plaintiff, if possessed of any sentiment of manhood, would have shielded his wife and children by removing to another locality or to a state where the facts, if known, would not be deemed a stigma."

During his term as governor, in spite of preoccupation with the Great War, Bickett managed to establish a reformatory for black boys and a sanatorium to treat blacks with tuberculosis. He increased state spending on teacher training for blacks 500 percent, commuted the sentences of four hundred imprisoned blacks, and championed "equal accommodations for negroes and whites on the trains": "When a negro pays the same money, he is entitled to ride in a car as safe, as clean, and as comfortable as the white man rides in. It is best for both races that they ride in separate cars, but the accommodations should be the same." He fought lynching by sending troops to protect prisoners, bringing mob leaders to justice and once walking into a mob with its guns drawn and convincing it to disband. Only one person in legal custody was lynched during his four years in office.

"In North Carolina we have definitely decided that the happiness of both races requires that white government shall be supreme and unchallenged in our borders," he said in his address to a special session of the General Assembly in August 1920, when he called for a special commission to study his extensive legislative proposals for blacks. "Power is inseparably linked with responsibility; and when we deny to the negro any participation in the making of laws, we saddle upon ourselves a peculiar obligation to protect the negro in his life and property, and to help and encourage him in the pursuit of happiness."

In a newspaper interview after he visited Tuskegee Institute in January 1920, he invoked Booker T. Washington in calling for peace among the races and explained each side's role in southern society:

> I frankly concede that in the search for right relations, and in the climb of both races to higher levels, the burden rests upon the white man to point the way. We are the dominant race, but our very supremacy is a challenge to do justice. We cannot do the negro a great wrong without doing ourselves a greater injury. The white man owes it to his own traditions, to his own self-respect, and to his own self-preservation to guarantee to the negro the fullest protection of the law. The South in denying to the negro any participation in the making and in the administration of the law, makes him in a very sacred sense the ward of the law. The settled policy of the South to maintain a white government creates between that government and the negro the relation of guardian and ward, and every principle of American jurisprudence, every whisper of conscience and every instinct of decency require the guardian to foster and protect the welfare of his ward.

Walter gave Sallie and Maggie an enlarged photograph of his son William Yarborough Bickett riding his goat, Billy, and they hung it prominently in their sitting room among other family portraits. They had once displayed a large picture of Bob Gribble, but Maggie took it to his widow when Bob died. Margaret's descendants were their only Burleyson relatives left in North Carolina. After Sallie died, Mildred Kiker and one of the Jones cousins, who shopped regularly at Crane's Store, called on Maggie once or twice. George Ross made his payments on the South Carolina land until he cleared the loan in 1912. Nathan's line died out.

After Maggie's burial, the mourners crossed the road and went back into the house. Bobby McIlwaine and Dick Hudson went upstairs, to the east room, to look for the will. Aunt Harriet had given Sallie Hudson the key Maggie entrusted to her, and Sallie gave it to Dick. The key opened a small, old-fashioned trunk in the room, and the men searched through the papers. They found a roll of greenbacks. Bobby opened a large envelope, saw that it held blue sheets of paper, and put it down to look elsewhere. The cousins were waiting downstairs. The men looked around and found a shot poke, filled with gold coin and sewed up, in the little drawer of a chiffoneer. Bobby, still expecting white writing paper, went back to the envelope and inspected the blue-backed pages more closely. They were the wills of Maggie and Sallie Ross.

The light was failing, but Dick asked Bobby to read the wills aloud. He sat down while Bobby read, both unsure whether to show the papers to the relatives. At least they could answer questions if they had read the documents. Dick heard that Maggie had named him executor. Bobby, whose duties for the Presbyterian denomination covered Union and Anson counties, asked whether he could spend the summer in the house, since it was willed to Banks Church. When Bobby finished reading, they gathered up the gold and the greenbacks and put them into a hand satchel before they went downstairs. They did not read the will to the relatives. Dick took the satchel and the wills home with him. The next morning, he took them to Robert Redwine's law office in Monroe. The wills said he was the other executor. They clipped the stitches in the shot poke and counted the money—three thousand six hundred dollars in gold and eleven hundred dollars in greenbacks—and took the cash to the bank.

"Miss Ross is the last of her family, her nearest living relative being a second cousin," the *Journal* reported in a front-page obituary on Tuesday. "She was the wealthiest woman in the county. She was energetic and possessed an alert and capable mind." The next day, the executors probated Maggie's will and codicil before R. W. Lemmond, clerk of Superior Court of Union County. George Sutton, C. C. McIlwaine, and E. J. Ezzell, attested to their signatures on the paper.

For inheritance taxes, the homeplace was valued at eight hundred acres, seventy-five dollars per acre, total sixty thousand dollars. The Marvin land was valued at five hundred acres, seventy-five dollars per acre, total thirty-seven thousand dollars. The total value of lands was ninety-seven thousand five hundred dollars. On July 1, Dick Hudson and R. B. Redwine filed an account and inventory of the Maggie Ross estate. They had found four thousand five hundred thirty dollars and ten cents in the house, five thousand five hundred ninety-two dollars and thirty cents in a Bank of Waxhaw account, twenty thousand four hundred dollars in a Commercial National Bank account in Charlotte. Billy McIlwaine owed the estate two thousand sixty dollars and sixty-six cents, and Hudson owed one thousand twenty-nine dollars and eighty-three cents.

The executors divided the personal property on the estate between Bob and Mittie. Mittie got fifty-five pounds of ham, forty pounds of lard, thirty chickens, one cow, one pig, the parlor furnishings, the trunks, the sewing machine, the dining table, and the carpet. Bob got fifty-two pounds of ham, some middling meat, two hundred pounds of flour, two bushels of corn, one cow, one pig, one surrey and harness, fifteen hundred shingles, the bees, two beds, a bedstead, a bureau, a washstand, linoleum, carpet, a sideboard, the stove, the cupboard, and the refrigerator. They paid Richard Hudson, Jr., his thousand-dollar legacy, Steve Walkup his two hundred, and Billy Ardrey and Calvin Fetterson their hundred each. They started the scheduled payments to Bob and Mittie, fifty dollars each.

Even as the executors went about the distribution, John Dees and forty-five other cousins acted to halt it. On June 28, they filed a caveat, a warning against carrying out the will:

"That the paper writing . . . was not and is not the last will and testament of the said Maggie Ross, deceased, for the reason that the signature of the said Maggie Ross thereto was obtained by undue and improper influence upon the said Maggie Ross by Robert B. Ross and Mittie Bell Houston, and others whose names are not at this time known to caveators. . . . for the reason that at the time of the execution thereof and continuously thereafter, until her death, the said Maggie Ross did not have sufficient mental capacity to make and execute a will, for that she was not of sound and disposing memory at and during said time. . . . for the reason that the same was not executed in the manner required by law, and is not such a will as is authorized under the Statute of Wills. Wherefore, the cavators pray that the Clerk of this court shall transfer this cause to the Superior court for trial, at term, of the issues of *devisavit vel non*"—did she will it or not? C. P. Edwards and C. B. Ross signed as sureties and Egbert Gribble, Sue Gribble Edwards, Lillie Gribble Bradley, and Julia Alexander Morrison signed as principals to a two hundred dollar bond guaranteeing that the propounders would be paid if the suit failed.

The citation appeared in the *Monroe Journal* on July 2: "To Amos Ross, William Ross, Ellison Ross, Martha Ross, James Ross, Margaret Ross, Frances Ross, Kissler Ross, Bunyan Griffin, Margaret Jackson Crane, the non-resident heirs at law and next of kin of Rebecca Helms, of Ellen Parker, of Hugh Ross, of Ann Ross Bickett, of Jonathan Burleson, deceased, and to all other interested persons who may be interested in the estate of Maggie Ross, deceased, and to all persons interested in said estate, consisting of real and personal property." Dozens of interested parties appeared. On July 8, 1920, a Wake County sheriff's deputy read a citation to Governor Bickett notifying him of the caveat and inviting him to join at the August term of Union Superior Court. He did not sign on that day when sixty-three more cousins joined the original forty-six. Nine months later, the case went to trial.

PART III

The Trial

13

JURY

A propounder is an executor or other person in said propounded will or other testamentary paper, when he takes proceeding for obtaining probate in solemn form. A caveator is one who files a caveat to the probate of such will in common form. The word caveat means "let him beware," and is a formal notice or warning given by a party interested to a court, judge or administerial officer against the performance of certain acts within such designated person's jurisdiction.

—JUDGE J. BIS RAY, 1921

March 31, 1921

Sheriff Clifford Fowler, his black-banded white fedora in his hands and his basset-sad eyes cast down, eased into the courtroom. The tall, walnut-stained door swung silently behind him. It was past eleven o'clock at night. He did not want to tell Judge Ray the bad news. After ten hours of corralling, questioning, seating, and mostly rejecting jurors, they were one man short with the deadline looming. The state legislature agreed to allow this civil case, nearly a year old, to be heard in the March criminal term of Union County Superior Court because there was room on the docket. But the jury must be empanelled by midnight Thursday because the trial would surely extend beyond the weekend. Judge Ray agreed to postpone opening the case for three days because three principal attorneys were busy with another case in Mecklenburg County. Obeying an old law, High Sheriff Fowler had opened and closed court every day for three days, with Clerk of Court R. W. Lemmond sitting in the judge's swivel chair and recording that Judge Ray did not appear. This was the last day, the last hour, and there was no one else to drag into the courtroom. All afternoon, the sheriff had brought men from the movie theaters, from the churches, from the drugstores. He had stopped cars driving down the street and sent men up to the second-floor courtroom. Dozens were excused.

And why not? Half the county must be related to one or another of the one hundred nine cousins who had challenged the "paper writing purporting to be the will of Maggie A. Ross." Maybe not many people knew John Wesley Dees or George Washington Ross or the crowd from Mecklenburg County, but no one didn't know their cousin Governor Bickett, Union's most famous native son, who finished his term in January. The county's fighting men in the last war had named their unit for him. Sentiment was strong for naming the new high school for him. How to seat a Union County jury not kin to such a clan?

But the other requirement likely excluded even more: Jurors must not have expressed an opinion in favor of one side or the other. Much of the county, and even the state, had been abuzz with the case for nearly a year since the *Journal* published the full text of the will on May 28. "Both sides have been scouring the Marvin community for evidence, and the case promised to be one of the hardest fought ever heard in this county," the newspaper reported when the executors hired John C. Sikes, J. C. M. Vann, and E. T. Cansler to defend the will. In July, the *Greensboro News* published a long account of the controversy:

Alleging mental incompetency and undue influence on the part of the interested parties, forty odd relatives of the late old maid eccentric, Miss Maggie Ross, living in Union and Mecklenburg counties, have started action in the Union County Superior court in an attempt to break the will filed recently and which bequeaths the bulk of an estate estimated at around $200,000 to two negroes, Robert B. Ross and his daughter, Mittie Belle Houston. The law firm of Stack, Parker and Craig of Monroe is representing the Union county parties in the case, while Walter Clark, Jr., of Charlotte is employed by the Mecklenburg county people.

A hotly contested legal battle which, attorneys claim, may produce evidence of a sensational nature, promised to be the final of the remarkable history of the Ross family. . . . The history is a history of a rise from poverty to riches on the farm; but it is a story which also has its pathetic side, for as the Rosses grew rich, they grew reticent and lived almost to themselves. The enjoyment of social pleasures were unknown to them. They never married. Then the brother died and the two sisters were left to continue their lives alone. In 1909 Miss Sallie Ross died. The past May, Miss Maggie Ross followed her and with her death the will bequeathing the fruits of many years of toil to the two negroes was revealed. And now the contest case.

Surely, the sheriff figured, everybody in the county saw the *Monroe Journal* three weeks ago when the caveators announced their strategy on the front page:

That the late Maggie and Sallie Ross permitted Mittie Belle Houston, colored, one of the chief benefactors of their will, to give birth to an illegitimate child in the bed and room of the former, is one of the sensational allegations made in the bill of particulars filed with the clerk of court by the 100-odd caveators. . . . This particular allegation is set forth in full in the following section of the bill of particulars:

"That in the year 1905, the negroes had obtained such an influence and control over Maggie and Sallie Ross that Mittie Belle Houston when she was not married forced them to consent to her having a baby in the bedroom of Maggie Ross and in her bed although the mother of Mittie Belle was living elsewhere on the property of Maggie and Sallie Ross; That after the child was born, Mittie Belle had such control over Sallie and Maggie Ross that she forced them to conceal the birth of the bastard child and to have it secretly buried in their garden, which conduct was a felony under the laws of North Carolina, thereby obtaining over these aged and infirm women an absolutely dominating and controlling influence; that Mittie Belle forced Maggie and Sallie Ross to let her live in their home, not as a servant, but as a member of the household, upon terms of social equality, until her marriage in 1906 or 1907, when she forced them to build her a house, Bob Ross having previously forced them to allow him to take possession of and live in the home which they inherited from their mother, claiming it as his own and erecting lightning rods thereon, and to cultivate a large body of fertile land without paying any rent, taxes or other charges whatever."

Attempting to show further alleged influence exercised by Bob Ross and Mittie Bell Houston upon the Misses Ross, the caveators say:

"That after the negroes had obtained the dominating and controlling influence over the aged, infirm and helpless women, to-wit, sometime during the year 1907, knowing that the women who were then 76 and 68 years of age, respectively, would necessarily die within a short while and that their large estate which the negroes were enjoying and wished to continue to enjoy would pass into other hands, conceived the idea of having the estate willed to them; and knowing that such an unnatural, unjust, indecent will would so outrage the feelings of all those acquainted with the facts so as to invite a contest to set aside the will, cunningly schemed to bribe the community to assist them in upholding this unnatural and fraudulent will by having inserted therein small bequests of money and property to the Presbyterian and Methodist churches of Marvin (there being no Baptist church in the community), hoping thereby to enlist the aid of these great and powerful denominations in upholding the will; that thereupon they proceeded to use the dominating and controlling influence which they had obtained over the aged, infirm and helpless women, who were living alone without anyone to protect them, to force them to will them their property and to enter into a contract to make mutual wills so that when one should die the survivor would be powerless to prevent the negroes from receiving their joint property; and that by reason of that dominating and controlling influence the negroes, on or about November 20th, 1907, obtained from Maggie and Sallie Ross, paper writings alleged to be their wills, although caveators aver that they were not executed according to law, and that the women, and particularly Maggie Ross, did not have sufficient mind to make a will; and both, and particularly Maggie Ross, were weeping bitterly at the time of the alleged execution, thereby giving their pitiable protest against the wrong which they did not understand, but were powerless to protest.

"That the alleged wills bear in themselves overwhelming evidence of the dominating influence which the negroes had acquired and were exercising over the two aged, weak and defenseless women, for not only did Mittie Belle and Bob Ross obtain the bulk of the property for themselves, but had bequests inserted for the benefit of their relatives, viz: the father, mother, grandmother, husband and infant child of Mittie Belle; whereas the alleged wills ignored the relations of the women and the white people of the community who helped them in their sickness and trouble, ignoring even their cousin, Mrs. Tirzah Coan, who lived in the same community, who had helped them without charge in time of sickness and death, who had visited in their home, and worked for them without compensation, and whom they had professed to love as a sister, and had been led to believe that she would be remembered by them in their wills although their cousin was in ill health, old and poor and a tenant on their land; ignoring also other relatives for whom they cherished sincere affection, who were people of high character and responsibility and some of whom were in needy circumstances, and giving more than eight hundred acres of valuable land, in a white community, most of which they had inherited from their own kin people, and large money legacies and other personal property to two negroes to whom they were under no obligation whatever, and who had already obtained from them large sums of money and property.

"That thereafter the negroes continued to dominate the aged and infirm women, Mittie Belle compelling them to give her money and property and compelling them to lend money to her insolvent husband without security, and so completely dominated Maggie Ross that she would wear her clothes and her shoes and would take liberties with her person, twisting her nose, pulling her ears and taking other liberties which Maggie Ross would never have suffered at the hands of a negro if she had not been completely dominated and controlled by her."

How, the sheriff wondered, could anyone not form an opinion in this case?

Given the web of kinship and the glare of publicity, selection from the eighteen-man jury list started well at 2:30 P.M. W. E. Austin was excused for the term, but A. E. Morgan, T. C. Eubanks, G. W. Davis, Bud Howey, S. S. Presson, F. P. Deese, G. J. Griffin, H. W. Pigg, and H. Marshall Baucom were seated. Eight others were dismissed from the case. Sheriff Fowler started calling forward men out of the spectators' chairs, but none qualified. By the 5 P.M. recess, only the original nine were seated. When court reconvened at 7:30 P.M., Judge Ray sent Sheriff Fowler to the streets. Nearly four hours later, only two more men sat in the jury box—Holmes Morris and Dr. Pascal M. Abernethy, a veterinarian who begged to be excused because he had ten patients—mostly horses and cows—under his care. Judge Ray refused, although he agreed to consider the request in the morning. As the clock ticked, the issue appeared moot. Midnight was approaching, Sheriff Fowler had given up, and the whole exercise would have to start over in some other term.

Then the tall doors swung open, and Monroe police officer J. I. Fuller eased into the room. He had gotten off shift at eleven, he was on his way home, he had noticed the light in the courtroom and stopped to see what was going on.

Sheriff Fowler ordered him to the jury box.

No, he was not related to any of the parties.

No, he had not expressed an opinion about the case.

It was unusual to seat a police officer on a jury, but it was legal.

The jury is empanelled. Court convenes at 9:30 A.M. Friday.

As the crowd spilled out of the courtroom for a wee-hour trip for a short night's rest, Bud Huey walked across Lafayette Street to the Hotel Joffre. The court would pay the two dollars fifty cents for his room for the night, he told the clerk.

14

FIRST WITNESS

No civil case has ever attracted more attention in the Union County Superior court than the suit now in progress to break the will of the late Misses Maggie and Sallie Ross.

—MONROE JOURNAL, 1921

April 1, 1921

In the bright light of that Friday morning, the first day of April and suddenly much warmer than the cloudy night before, with the sun spilling through the tall windows and the crowd milling in the aisles and among the seats and along the walls, the exhilaration of the trial swept away the exhaustion of the jury selection. The thirty-five-year-old red-brick, slate-roofed courthouse, hosting the most celebrated assembly of lawyers ever gathered under its vaulted ceiling and lofty clock tower, pulsed with the fulfillment of its purpose. Its tall granite steps east and west welcomed the crowd that pressed across its thickly woodworked Victorian porches, through its towering, dark-stained doors, down its dim inner halls, and up the broad, heavy wooden staircase to the second-story courtroom. Fresh sawdust was spread on the floor to catch the common tobacco spit.

Not quite eleven years before, on Independence Day 1910, Attorney General Walter Bickett had orated at the dedication of the

Union County Courthouse (courtesy of the Union County Historical Society)

cannonball-topped obelisk to the Confederacy on the west side. Now his family came seeking justice inside. The events had in common an eager interest of dressed-up spectators—men in stiff white collars, ladies in long skirts—bright and abuzz as they awaited the show.

It was for such mornings as these that the courtroom's plaster frieze ran thick and green-gold along the stately cornice, that the thin gold-leaf trim traced the windows' wide arches, that the Declaration of Independence hung behind the judge's bench. For just such a crowd, the balcony hung over half the mezzanine seats; for just such a case, a quadrant was marked off for black spectators; for just such attorneys, the bar and the long tables and the heavy chairs glowed with deep-brown stain.

As soon as Judge Ray opened court, lawyer J. C. M. Vann told him that the propounders would not object to the release of Pascal Abernethy from the jury. The judge refused: "He ought to serve," he explained. "Jury service is one of three things required of a citizen," along with the paying of taxes and the working of roads. For the rest of the morning, as the lawyers argued a motion, jurors fanned and spectators dozed. Rev. George Atkinson and his new wife came from Salisbury to watch the trial. The day Maggie died, Reverend Atkinson was at First Presbyterian Church in Monroe to present a pulpit Bible in memory of his first wife, Frances, who died while he was pastor at the church.

The caveators wanted Judge Ray to strike the Further Answer of the Legatees and Devisees from the record. Barium Springs Presbyterian Orphanage, Presbyterian Hospital of Charlotte, North Carolina, the Home Mission Committee of the Synod of North Carolina, the Piedmont Industrial School, Bob and Mittie, the Hudsons, Jackie Crane, Harriet Taylor, and Dr. Nisbet, in addition to accepting the executors' reply to the caveators, maintained that Maggie and Sallie had a contract about their property that Maggie had recognized when she made the codicil, and neither she nor her "heirs at law" could violate that contract. They wanted the court to honor that contract.

During the arguments, E. T. Cansler rehearsed the rags-to-riches story of the sisters, a story fashioned from the same facts as the reporter's account and the caveators' bill of particulars, but with a far different flavor:

> It appears that early in life, these old women were neglected by their kin and looked down upon by their neighbors; that they were illiterate, being barely able to read and write; that they were close and saving in money matters and

unattractive in appearance; that they had no sweethearts or love affairs. Sometime during the seventies, their mother, who was then living with them, had bound to her a little negro by the name of Bob. This boy, Bob, was taken by the sheriff from his mother's arms and turned over to the Rosses. He was reared by them, sleeping in the house and in the room with their brother until he was grown. He was the servant and companion on all the trips of Dennis Ross, and after he was grown and married, a house was built for him near the "big house" of the old Ross homeplace where he has continued to reside since. Bob Ross' first child was named Mittie Bell, and when she became large enough to walk, was given by Bob and his wife to the Misses Ross to raise. They raised this girl in their home until she was sixteen or seventeen years old, when she married and moved into a home of her own upon the Ross place which was prepared for her by the Misses Ross.

After five hours of wrangling, Judge Ray ruled that the issue before the court was not whether Sallie and Maggie had made a contract but simply whether Maggie had devised the property to Bob and Mittie Bell. "Honors in the first scrimmage went to the caveators," the *Charlotte Observer* reported.

Bob Ross, who wore a corduroy suit to the trial, tried to sit through the reading of Miss Maggie's will in the afternoon. It was too much. Tears rolled down his cheeks as her words rolled across the courtroom. "I devise the old home place . . . so as to give to Robert B. Ross his half of the land to include the gin house, barn and the stables. Robert B. Ross shall have the half of said tract so devised to him during his life . . ." He wiped his eyes with a handkerchief, more tears came, and he slipped out of the room. The clerk was nearly finished with the forty-two items and the codicil when he returned. "Bob has been an interested spectator since the trial started," the *Journal* observed, "but to all appearances he is indifferent towards the outcome."

After the reading, the propounders called George Sutton, who had signed the will on November 20, 1907, and the codicil on September 9, 1909, to the stand for testimony. Because he was a witness of the law, both sides could cross-examine him. "At the time the will was signed by Miss Sallie Ross in my presence, I would say her mental condition was about normal, as it had been all her life as far as I have known her," he told Cansler. "I have never heard it discussed by any one else but what he had a normal mind at that time."

When Stack cross-examined him, Sutton went into more detail: "I do not remember anything that Miss Maggie Ross said while we were there, outside of her kind of boohoo that I positively recollect of. She never said anything about the papers or asked me to witness to them, to my recollection."

"Did you ask Miss Sallie if she wanted the will read?"

"Yes."

"What was her response?"

"She said no it wasn't necessary."

"Was the will read while you were there?"

"No."

"Did you see the pages of the will?"

"Yes. She brought them in folded up."

"What do you know about the content of that paper?"

"Nothing, except that it has my name on it."

"Do you know how much land Miss Maggie owned?"

"I think about fourteen hundred acres."

"What is your estimate of its worth in 1907 and 1909?"

"It is good land. I think that it would have been worth twenty-five dollars an acre."

"What about its worth in 1920?"

"I would say it had doubled in value, that is it would be worth in 1920 fifty dollars an acre. That around Marvin would sell for fifty or sixty dollars an acre."

"How would you describe Miss Maggie's mind when she signed the will?"

"It was about as it had been all her life, as I had known it, and there had been no sudden breakdown or relapse."

"You saw no changes in her mind?"

"No. She was not an idiot, but had a weak mind. At the time she signed her will her mind was just as it always had been."

"Did you ever hear her discuss schools or foreign missions or hospitals?"

"No. She used to give some money to the church but never a great deal. Their membership used to be in our church, that was the Methodist Church, and she gave us but very little."

The light was failing in the windows, and Judge Ray gaveled the first day of testimony to a close.

15

GEORGE SUTTON

For the benefit of the Country, I want this will broken.

—GEORGE WASHINGTON SUTTON, 1921

April 2, 1921

"At the time you signed this paper, Mr. Sutton, did you think Miss Sallie and Miss Maggie knew how to dispose of their property?" Cansler asked the witness, still on the stand as court resumed Saturday.

"Yes," Sutton answered. "I did not think anything else at the time but what she knew what she was doing. She was a weak woman, but I thought she knew how to dispose of their property."

"What if they had sold the property?"

"They could have sold it and I never would have thought anything but what they knew what they were doing, and the same way as to the will."

"You took her acknowledgement as Justice of the Peace when she made the deed to the school house lot. Did you think she had sense enough to make that deed?"

"Yes, or I would not have taken her acknowledgement."

"Did she know as she was signing that deed that she was being paid for it?"

"Yes."

Cansler handed him the proof of the will that Sutton had signed in front of Clerk Lemmond after Maggie died. He read it to the jury.

"Did you think you were swearing to the truth when you signed this and swore to it?" Cansler asked as he took back the paper.

"Yes."

"So you believe Miss Maggie signed the will, as you said here?"

The witness looked away and scowled. "If Miss Maggie Ross did not sign the will in my presence, she acknowledged it."

"Mr. Parker has made much of the fact that Miss Maggie was crying at the time they executed the wills. Wasn't Miss Sallie crying, too?"

"Yes, but I did not think either one of them was acting crazy, and never thought anything about Miss Maggie's crying."

"Did you wonder at the time whether she was capable of making a will?"

"No. I have never known anything else but what she had a sound mind; she was normal; I thought so at the time, or I would not have signed the will."

"Did she have a strong mind?"

"No, she was not a Solomon by any means."

"Do you think she would have confidence enough in herself to transact any business?"

"No."

"At the time you swore to the proof of the will before the Clerk, did you know the contents of the will?"

"No."

"Didn't you think it was a valid will?"

"Yes."

"When did you change your mind?"

"When I learned the contents of the will."

"When you learned the contents of the will?"

Sutton settled back in the seat. "I have stated that if they wanted to give those negroes something they could have deeded it to them and there would have been no contest about it. If they had done that, that would have been the last of it."

"Do you think you could write a will like this one, Mr. Sutton?"

"I myself have not got sense enough to make this will; an ordinary man could not make a will like that, but I could give the lawyer the information so he could have worded it; very few people could draw a will like this. Miss Maggie did not have capacity to make a will without the help of a lawyer."

"Speaking of giving information to lawyers, did you go to a lawyer's office last evening?"

Judge Ray stirred and stared sharply at Sutton, who looked into his lap and fidgeted.

"After court adjourned yesterday afternoon, I went to the office of Stack, Parker & Craig and went over the case with them. They had me summoned down here." His voice hardened, and he leaned forward before the lawyer or the judge could react. "For the benefit of the Country, I want this will broken. I do not want these negroes to have this property in our community. If the Ross women had the sense that I have got they would not make a will like that; if they had seen things like I do they would not have made a will like this, giving it to the negroes. If they had wanted to give the negroes two hundred or three hundred acres of land, that would have been all right and there would have been no litigation over it."

"Don't you think they had a right to do with their property what they pleased?"

"Of course, but if they had seen it like I do they would not have done it that way."

"If Mag Ross had made a deed for some land to Bob Ross in her lifetime, would you have thought her crazy?"

"No," Sutton said. "They could have sold all their land and made a deed to it. Miss Maggie could have made a deed to a hundred acres."

"So you think she had sense enough to make a deed?"

"I know that Miss Maggie after Miss Sallie's death sold some land to Doc Coan."

"What would have made you believe she had sense enough to make a will?"

"If she had made a will giving this property to white people or to a church I never would have thought anything else but that she had sense enough to make a will." He leaned forward to explain himself again. "I think this will ought to be broken for the good of the Country and community and not from a legal standpoint. According to my knowledge and my understanding they had a right to dispose of that property, they could have sold it, could have made a deed, could have deeded a part of it to the negroes and it would not have affected the whole community."

"Would you have thought the deed should be broken?

"No."

"Why do you want the will broken?"

"I think the will is worse because the property is somewhat entailed. I do not want them to have all of that property. I do not want them to own all the property around our churches and schools."

"But the lands around Marvin are to be sold at public auction, and the old Ross place is about a mile from Marvin."

"I know." His jaw set, his eyes flashed and his words spat like bullets. "If these women had willed their property to white people, I would have looked at the thing different, and I would not have thought anything else but what they had sense enough to make a will, and I would have never thought about coming in the Courthouse and answering anything else."

Cansler was finished. Amos Stack started his cross-examination by trying to clear up the embarrassing admission that Sutton had huddled with the lawyers.

"I was summoned by both sides here and have been in the office of counsel for the propounders several times, and have been in the office of the attorneys for the caveators several times and have tried to tell the same thing all the time," Sutton said.

Judge Ray broke in: "The Court says that the counsel for caveators did not have a right—when a witness is turned over for examination it is improper for attorneys to take him into their office during recess of Court and see what he will testify to."

"Object and except!" Stack was angry. "I want to be set straight before this jury. We did not do anything except what we had a right to do. He was our witness as much as the witness of the law, as the record will show we had subpoenaed first, so we had a right to take him to our office and see what he was going to testify so we would know how to cross-examine him, and because of this we were subjected to the criticism of the Court!"

Judge Ray refused to relent. Turning the witness over for redirect examination, like turning a witness over for cross-examination, means the attorney does not have the right to conference off the stand about his testimony, he explained: "For the counsel then to take the witness and examine him privately, after his evidence has been put on in chief, the Court is of the unalterable opinion that it was an improper act."

Sutton finished his answer to Stack: "The attorneys for the propounders have talked to me at home and here at Court; I can't tell everything we talked about, but I told them in my opinion if the Ross women had had sufficient mental capacity they would not have made a will as they did."

Stack changed the subject.

"Did Miss Mag Ross ever talk to you about the Barium Springs orphanage?"

"No."

"Did she ever mention the Presbyterian hospital or the Piedmont Industrial School in your presence?"

"No."

"Did she ever contribute anything to either?"

"Not that I know of."

"Did she ever talk to you about foreign missions?"

"No."

Cansler parroted the exchange when he took Sutton back for a third round of questioning.

"Did you ever know Mr. A. M. Stack to contribute to an orphanage?"

"No."

"Did you ever know him to contribute to a hospital?"

"No."

"Did you ever know him to contribute to foreign missions?"

"No."

Cansler pounced.

"This shows the court that Esquire Sutton's testimony cannot be construed as reflecting upon the mental capacity of Miss Mag Ross, as few of us know anything about the charitableness of even our closest friends," he declared to the jury, and he turned back to the witness. "If Maggie had known about those institutions, would they be natural bequests?"

"Yes. From a moral standpoint all of the bequests are natural. Except those to the negroes."

It was only midday, but Judge Ray recessed until Monday morning.

16

WITNESSES TO THE WILL

Propounders offer in evidence the original will of Miss Maggie Ross and the codicil thereto. Caveators object. Objection overruled, and caveators except. Propounders offer in evidence original will of Miss Sallie Ross. The caveators object; objection overruled, and the caveators except.

—CLERK OF UNION COUNTY SUPERIOR COURT, 1921

April 4, 1921

Early Monday morning, Vann was in the barbershop when he heard forty-one-year-old Bill Pierce talking about a deal he'd seen his father make with Ross women when he was a child. The lawyer got the traveling pharmaceutical salesman from Charlotte subpoenaed to testify.

When court reconvened, Cansler continued his examination, getting Sutton to catalog the relationship of the sisters to the people listed in the will.

"Bob Ross lived with the Ross family all his life," Sutton said. "He was the servant of their brother Dennis. His is probably fifty years old now and has never lived anywhere else that I know of. . . . Mittie Bell Houston is the daughter of Bob Ross and has lived with the Ross women ever since she was a little child. . . . Rosa Howie is Bob Ross' mother and has lived on the Ross place for a long time, thirty or forty years. . . . Dr. Nisbet is a physician of Charlotte, used to live in the Waxhaw community and was the physician of the Ross women."

But why, Stack wondered on re-re-cross-examination, did she leave money to Dr. Nisbet: "Wasn't Dr. Potts Mag Ross' physician for many years?"

"Yes."

"Would it not have been more natural, Esquire, for Mag Ross to have left that money to Dr. Potts instead of that Charlotte doctor?"

Judge Ray upheld Cansler's objection.

Stack persisted: "Why did the will not bequeath money to Tirzah Coan, a poor, paralyzed cousin, a natural object of Mag's bounty?"

Cansler objected more strenuously, charging that Stack was addressing the jury. Upheld. Sutton was dismissed.

Earle J. Ezzell, the county's dashing thirty-nine-year-old bachelor state representative, took the stand next to tell the same story of witnessing the Ross sisters' will. After the older farmer's testimony, which had taken parts of three days, the jaunty young lawmaker with the slicked-back black hair, half-squinting left eye, and square-set jaw clipped through the questions.

"We went in the room to the left of the hall as you go in from the front door, it was a bedroom," he said. "We were all in a small room, about fourteen by fourteen feet. Miss Maggie was present. I don't remember seeing her just at the time I signed the will, but she was in the room. Both of the ladies were crying."

Ezzell looked at the will and identified his signature.

"I signed that in the presence of Mr. McIlwaine, Mr. Sutton and Miss Maggie Ross."

"And what would you say Miss Maggie Ross' mental condition was at that time?"

"Good, so far as I know."

Cansler showed him the codicil, and he identified his signature.

"Mr. Sutton and myself signed the will there in the presence of Miss Maggie and Mr. Adams and I am not sure but I think Mr. Hudson was there."

"And how would you describe Miss Maggie at that time?"

"She seemed to be perfectly calm and her mental condition was good so far as I know."

"What about her health?" Stack asked on cross-examination.

"Miss Maggie was in very poor health," Ezzell replied. "I remember she was in bed for awhile, but I don't remember whether it was before or after the will was made. She was a nervous, frail woman given to despondency and melancholy. Miss Maggie was a woman to stay in the house a great deal and I never had an opportunity to discuss her property with her. The last years of her life she was not a strong-minded woman."

"Did you ever see Miss Sallie Ross and Mr. Hudson together?"

"Yes."

"Who did most of the talking when Miss Sallie Ross and Miss Maggie were together?"

"Miss Sallie."

Cansler took the witness back: "What exactly do you mean by 'the latter part of her life she was not a strong minded woman'"?

"I meant the last four or five years—not more than that. She died in 1920, and this will was made in 1907."

"You mentioned that Mr. Hudson transacted their business," Cansler said. "How would you describe Mr. Hudson's character?"

"Mr. Hudson has the reputation of being a good business man."

Cansler pressed for a stronger endorsement. Ezzell hesitated, then shocked the room by answering that Hudson did not have a reputation for strict integrity among the people of the community.

"It was quite a blow to the propounders," the *Journal* reported. "Mr. Ezzell tried to evade the question, but counsel for the propounders insisted, believing the Union County member of the legislature would endorse the general conception of Mr. Hudson's character, which, to say the least, has been good."

Charles C. McIlwaine, who gave the third account of the will-signing, was more sure than the others that he had seen the women sign their names, and he was the only one who remembered signing duplicate wills that day.

"Mr. Sutton and Mr. Ezzell and myself were standing to one side of the room and Miss Maggie was around the other way," he testified. "I saw her sign her name. Mr. Sutton and Mr. Ezzell were standing close behind her when she signed it. She was sitting down. After she got up, I sat down and signed my name." Cansler showed him the will, and he identified his own signature. "I saw Miss Maggie sign both papers and I signed four papers." He identified his own signature on the duplicate will.

"And what were these women doing while they signed their names?" Stack asked.

"Both of them were weeping, just sniffling."

With the three signatures attested, and over the caveators' objection, the propounders introduced the original wills and codicil in evidence.

All three witnesses to the signatures testified, but only one person was alive to tell about the day when Sallie and Maggie instructed Henry Adams what to write. R. B. Redwine, now fleshier and without his mustache, took the stand. Judge Ray allowed him to be removed from the record as an attorney for the propounders.

"Was Mittie Bell Houston present when the instructions were being given?" Mr. Cansler asked.

"There was a negro woman there who waited on the table, but there was nobody in the room except Mr. Adams, the two Ross women and myself."

"Did you have anything to do with the drawing of the will?"

"No, Mr. Adams did that. My impression is that Mr. Adams went back the next day, but I am not positive about that."

Cansler showed him the letter that Adams had written to the women on November 15, and he read it aloud. "When did you actually see this will for the first time?"

"Copies of the will of Miss Sallie and Miss Maggie Ross were turned over to me. They came out of a safe in W. O. Lemmond's office. The safe had originally belonged to Mr. Adams. Mr. Pratt bought the safe after Mr. Adams' death in 1915 and Mr. Pratt died in December 1918 and W. O. Lemmond, his administrator, moved his safe into his office. I found the wills in an envelope in the safe, along with similar papers. On the envelope on which these copies of the wills were found is written 'Wills of Miss Sallie A. Ross and Miss Maggie A. Ross' in Mr. Adams' handwriting." The copies were introduced in evidence as Exhibit C and Exhibit D.

Redwine described his visits to the Ross home, the work he did as their attorney, and the accounting he made as Maggie's executor.

"Mr. Hudson and I set a time to pay the legacies," he told Parker on cross-examination. "We saw there was plenty of time and we set the twenty-eighth day of June, is my recollection about it, and Mr. Hudson came here for the purpose, and before he came down, he paid part of some of the legacies. Some to Mittie Bell Houston, fifty dollars; R. B. Ross, fifty dollars; Yarborough, one hundred dollars; Calvin Featherstone, one hundred dollars; Stephen Walkup, two hundred dollars; and R. A. Hudson, Jr., one thousand dollars, making fifteen hundred dollars. We listed an account against Tom Houston for one thousand eight hundred forty-five dollars and sixty cents as worthless. I don't think it is in the form of a note. I am not certain. I guess it was an account but I do not say whether it was an account or not. I had Mr. Hudson's statement about it."

"What about Bob Ross?"

"My impression is we considered the account of R. B. Ross worthless."

"Were you consulted by Mr. Adams about the codicil that was made to Miss Maggie Ross's will, or told about it?" the propounders' lawyer asked. The caveators objected in vain.

"As I stated a few minutes ago, I was not in town when they were here when the codicil was drawn. The next morning Mr. Adams spoke to me about it and told me they had brought Miss Sallie's will down and he had advised that it was not necessary to probate that will unless they wanted to, advised Miss Maggie, and asked me what I thought about it, and I told him I thought that was correct."

"What, if anything, was said about the codicil?"

The caveators again objected in vain.

"Mr. Adams told me at the same time that Miss Maggie had made a codicil to her will. That was either the afternoon or next morning after they brought Miss Sallie's will down."

Preacher Billy McIlwaine had come from his home in Pensacola, Florida, to testify for Miss Maggie. He had grown up in sight of her house and had been her pastor from 1910 to 1917, when he came back from his missionary work in Alabama. Even when he was away, first to Indian Territory, then to Alabama, he had visited them at least every year. He still owned farmland in the neighborhood. He told about Maggie's contribution to the new Banks Church, her donation of a piano, her purchase of the old Banks Church.

"I am going to ask you a rather direct question," the lawyer said. "Did you ever make a horse trade with her?"

Reverend McIlwaine smiled. "Preachers don't generally make many horse trades, but I had a favorite animal I had caused to be shipped from Alabama, and when I knew I was going to leave this County and go to Florida, I proposed to sell this animal to her, especially so because I thought this animal would have a good home, and so I sold that animal to her. I asked one hundred fifty dollars for the animal, but I finally sold it to her for one hundred dollars. When I asked her a hundred and fifty dollars for the horse, she said it was too much. I want it distinctly understood that I regard her as a good trader. The animal was worth a hundred and fifty dollars. She had originally cost me three hundred dollars."

"Did you have other opportunities to talk to Maggie Ross about business?"

"She was a planter, a pretty large one, and I planted pretty largely too, and when I called at her home I talked business with her, and she had enough confidence in me to tell me her business, and she would tell me about her tenants that had fallen behind, etc., about her losses. She told me at one time or another the old barn at the old home place where Bob Ross lived, had burned, she told me of the reconstruction of that."

"Did you ever have occasion to talk with her about her will."

"Once when I was building that church, staying with her, I told her that I did not mean to meddle with her business, but there is one question that I believe that I would ask her, if she didn't object. I said I understand that you have made a will or wills and that you have given this home in which you live, adjoining the property of Banks Church, to this church after your death. I asked her if that was so. She told me it was correct. I asked no further questions."

Cross-examiner Walter Clark drew the preacher's scorn.

"I have been a preacher all my life," Reverend McIlwaine said. "I attended the A. R. P. College, but I took my training at Columbia, South Carolina, and at Princeton, New Jersey. I think that I am a fairly good preacher."

"Is it not also true, Reverend McIlwaine, that you are also a fairly good businessman—are you worth a million dollars?"

"I think that if I would see a million dollars that I would never get over it."

"Are you worth several hundred thousand dollars?"

"No."

"What happens whenever a preacher gets to have two gods, Reverend?"

"You know he is on the bad road."

"How many gods do you have? Six or seven?"

The preacher folded his hands on his knees and gazed coolly at the lawyer.

"No. My estate, if you wish to know, consists of some cotton land here in Union County and Mecklenburg County and that is the estate—not quite seven hundred acres in Union County and a thousand would be a lot of the land in Mecklenburg County."

"And what do you do with all the money you make from that land?"

Reverend McIlwaine's tone took on an edge. "I have not got the money from what I sold—eleven-cent cotton don't bring it. I sold the land and have notes and mortgages on the land. I would like to sell you all I have for half of two or three hundred thousand dollars. I would like to sell it to you for seventy-five thousand dollars." He settled back in the chair serenely and smiled. "If you are in a trading humor, I would like to make terms with you."

Clark changed the subject.

"You say you live in Pensacola. How often have you visited this section recently?"

"I have made two trips from Florida up here in this trial. I am summoned up here and I come."

"On these trips, have you been down in the Marvin section calling on all the witnesses?"

"No. This matter comes up in that community, and you could not go down there without the matter coming up. Occasionally, I have been expressing my opinion here, as have a good many others. I would be glad for you to call my attention to anything I said, if I have a right to express an opinion. I was in the barbershop expressing my opinion of the case, and so were many others. I have spent probably three or four days down in Marvin. I would interest myself to inquire what the condition was, the present status of the case. I certainly expressed my opinion about it."

"Have you been around talking to witnesses on my side of the case and trying to get them to agree with you?"

"No."

"What about Harriet Taylor?"

Reverend McIlwaine chuckled. "Yes, I have talked with Mrs. Taylor. I met Mrs. Taylor in Charlotte and saw that she was full of this matter. She could not keep quiet, and what could I do but talk to her? Mrs. Taylor is a caution. Mrs. Taylor came down to the hotel and I went to the hotel where she was stopping. She had not relieved herself at all. She was just as fresh as when she left Charlotte."

"Why do you want to throw off on Mrs. Taylor?" the lawyer demanded.

"I don't." The preacher grinned. "I told about her because you asked me if I talked to her. When I met her in Charlotte, she brought it up, and I did not bring up the matter until she did."

Clark tried another tack. "Doctor, I believe when you asked Miss Maggie for this money for the church, this five hundred dollars, she told you she was a very poor woman."

"I have no recollection of anything of that sort, because she knew I knew better. There were seventy-five bales of cotton lying out there in the yard. Probably some years she got more than that. I never stopped to count them."

"Wasn't she always talking about how poor she was?"

"I would not say that. I have probably heard her complain—most of us do."

"Do you recollect ever hearing her complain of taxes?"

"No."

"What else would you do on these visits, what else would you talk about?"

"Well, I suppose you know that we ministers hold prayer when asked to do so. We hold worship in the home. That is customary."

"After you had prayer with her, then she would see the light and contribute to the church, is that right?"

Reverend McIlwaine scowled and gripped the rail in front of his chair.

"I repudiate any such low motive as that right now."

17

PREACHERS

Her refusal to let me have the thousand dollars is a proof of thrift and stinginess, too.

—REV. GEORGE F. ROBERTSON, 1921

April 5, 1921

Outside the courtroom, on the first cloudy day of the trial, Steve Walkup announced that he would sue Maggie Ross' estate for one thousand dollars or more, no matter the outcome of the cousins' case. Steve said he had done odd jobs for the Rosses for more than twenty years, in addition to the sharecropping he had done on their land. They had never paid him for driving their buggy or weeding their flowers or building their fires. He figured the work was worth between twenty-five and fifty dollars a year, much more than the two hundred dollars they had left in the will.

"He is a genuine 'white man's negro,' being courteous, friendly and honest to the core," the *Journal* observed. "He has never been in trouble and claims to have been devoted to his late mistresses. Steve has some strong friends among the prominent white citizens of the Marvin community, all of whom are eager to see him receive a comfortable share of the Ross estate."

Inside the courtroom, it was Rev. George Atkinson's turn on the witness stand. His elaborate sentences, flowery with long practice preaching and persuading potential donors, enthralled the room with sincerity, as if the witness stand were a pulpit.

"My father used to preach up there years ago and I used to go up with him when I was a boy, so I talked to her first about the community, the old citizens I knew, and then I came right down to the point and told them how we wanted to wipe out this debt on the school in Albemarle and I asked them if they couldn't contribute, and they did not see their way to contribute," he said, recalling his first visit. "I do not remember the conversation exactly, but know they talked intelligently. I went up there after that, I went up there again after I left Albemarle and went to Salisbury. I went there between the summer of 1916 and 1918. I saw Miss Maggie at that time. I stayed an hour or more at that time. I had one of the graduates of the school with me and was talking to her about the work. I asked her to make a contribution. I believe it was somewhere between three and five thousand dollars." He subsided and put a finger to his lips. "Don't remember exactly," he mused. "I struck as hard as I could." He shook his head and resumed his tone: "Anyway, it was over one thousand dollars, but she did not give me anything."

"From the conversation you had with her at that time, did you form an opinion as to the condition of her mind?"

"Yes. She was perfectly sane."

The minister gave more detail of his moneyraising tactics on cross-examination.

"I stated my case to Miss Sallie and Miss Maggie. They did not give a cent so far as I know."

"Did they tell you they were not able to contribute?"

"No."

"You said you 'struck as hard as you could.'"

Reverend Atkinson nodded with a wry smile. "I have had so much experience in raising money that I do not go too far."

"You have interviewed a great many people in attempting to raise money?"

"Yes."

"How many of those were in North Carolina?"

The preacher looked down as if suddenly saddened.

"A few."

"How many times were you successful?"

"Some of my efforts were successful and some were not successful. It is impossible for a man interviewing so many people to remember the details of so many conversations."

"How would you feel, say, to find out that someone who turned you down had left thousands of dollars to other charitable institutions?"

The preacher shrugged vaguely. "When I go out and another fellow succeeds where I fail, I don't feel bad. Of course, every man feels his own work is the best and I feel like mine is the best, but I don't think I have done the only good work." He stopped, but when the lawyer stood still he went on. "Mine is a work that ought to appeal to every right thinking person. I went up there and put this up to Miss Maggie. I told her we were educating the poor girls of North Carolina. I showed her a plan of my work and a catalog of our school and described the work we were doing."

"And asked her to give you from three to five thousand dollars and she did not give you a cent?"

"And she is not the only one, no. I have seen a number of people right here in town and elsewhere that would not give me anything. I went to the richest man in the United States who had millions in the bank and he had interests in North Carolina. I got the same result in Salisbury, got some of the richest people in Salisbury living there who see our work who haven't given us anything either. Miss Maggie Ross did not give me anything. I have met a whole lot of people who have got money who won't give anything. If I get ten percent of what I go after, I am doing fine. I have got a whole lot in Charlotte who don't give anything. Sometimes, if I get fifty percent, I think that is fine. I am sorry to say that most of the contributions have come from good friends in the North and I would not be able to say that more than three percent have subscribed around here."

Rev. Bobby McIlwaine, Billy's brother, had more luck getting money from Miss Maggie—more by way of being an old family friend than a man of the cloth.

"Really, a Ross was never known to have anything but a clear mind—that family," he testified. "I had a little business transaction with her after I returned to Union County. Less than a year before her death I borrowed some money from her—five hundred dollars. I called at her home and told her what I wanted and she told me I could get the money. I asked first for two hundred fifty dollars, and she told me I could get it and I did not return to receive the money at the time she had indicated, and when I came she said she had had it, had the money for me, but as I did not come at the time she appointed, she had spent a part of it. Then, having renewed the request and doubled the amount, five hundred, she told me that she did not know if she had that much in the bank at Waxhaw, but for me to see Mr. Hudson and if he said she had that much, I could have it. I saw him and got it and paid it back in less than half the time the note was drawn for."

He told the lawyers from both sides details of the search for the will after Maggie died. Where Reverend Atkinson's rolling eloquence mesmerized the listeners, Preacher Bobby's folksy answers made them smile.

"You say you found thousands of dollars up there in gold," the cross-examiner said. "Yet she told you she didn't have two hundred fifty dollars in the house when you came for the loan. Why did she not give you gold?"

"It is easily explained, in my judgment. I will give you my opinion about it. It appears to me to be just as reasonable to ask why she would not give me her gold teeth and sold them and got the money, or her gold watch or brooch. I mean by that that she loved that gold like she did her gold watch. It was gold coin. It had a value in this way. It seems to have come down from her grandfather. It was an heirloom of the family; that is my impression. There is some sentiment that attaches to it—the same sentiments that are attached to a gold watch or gold earrings attached to that gold which had been in the family so long."

"Even so, why do you think she was constantly telling people how poor she was?"

"She had a peculiarity, just as any of the balance of us have. Though she did not show it, she was excellently posted as to what she had."

"So she was lying?"

"I do not mean to intimate she would tell a falsehood about her property. She was claiming to be poor, just as thousands of other people raised poor—they never get rich if they have a million dollars. It is a hard matter to change them. This particular lady did not always claim to be poor. I don't know as she generally did, just as she was disposed. She did not talk about her property. She was extremely modest along that line. It was owing to what you were on as to how she talked. If you were talking business to her and got on a proposition that appealed to her, she would respond according to her ability at times—for instance, the building of the church. I know something about it. I was along, but did not have as much to do with it as my brother."

The cross-examiner had heard that Mittie was in the house after the funeral and demanded that the men hand over the money they had found. Rev. McIlwaine said he didn't see her there.

Charles Parks, a neighbor of Maggie's who now lived in Albemarle, recalled selling lumber to her for tenant houses, although Dick Hudson handled most of the transactions.

"When Miss Sallie was living, she sorter had charge of things down there," he explained. "She was the leading personality and did most of the talking, and as long as Miss Sallie lived, she transacted the business herself."

Baxter Clegg Ashcraft, son of a Confederate major and a schoolteacher, cut a diminutive but distinguished figure on the witness stand. He had been the first student enrolled in the North Carolina College of Agriculture and Mechanic Arts, but he was too frail to farm. He bought the *Enquirer* in Monroe from Watt J. Boylin in 1893 and, as its editor, became a leading citizen of Monroe. He and Mary Blair had married seven years later, but they had no children. He was on the school board for a while, and Governor Bickett had appointed him to the exemption board during the war. He devoted himself to the Confederate veterans as secretary and treasurer of their Camp Walkup organization, especially making sure that they received decent burials. His thinning white hair made his small, mostly bald, head seem spherical, but his carefully combed white goatee brought his chin to a proper point above his stiff white collar.

"I knew the Rosses, Miss Maggie and Miss Sallie Ross," he told the court. "I have been knowing them about twenty-eight years. They were in my office about once a year or oftener. I have had conversations with them. The subjects of my conversations with Miss Maggie Ross were very commonplace. I don't remember but one subject that we usually discussed. I usually asked about the farming operations. How the farming was progressing, whatever season of the year it might have been, and about whether they had sold their cotton and what the price of cotton might be. I knew they raised a great deal of cotton."

"Can you tell us the details of any of your conversations, Mr. Aschraft?"

"The only one I positively remember was after the death of their brother, Dennis Ross. It was a conversation as a friend to friend. She came into my office about two or three weeks after her brother's death, that was in 1896. Two or three weeks after her brother's death, she was in my office and called my attention to the fact that her brother had died. She gave me some facts and arranged for a contribution about it. Miss Sallie paid for it. This was an obituary. I had written up the death of her brother. He was given what we call the news obituary, and this was an obituary the minister had written and they said they wanted to pay me for it. They thanked me about what I had said about their brother's death. Miss Sallie subscribed to the paper after the death of her brother Dennis. She had it sent to Bob Ross. Miss Maggie took the paper herself. After the death of Miss Sallie, the subscription to the Rosses ceased at the expiration of that year and then Miss Maggie subscribed for it."

"She came to your office and subscribed in person?"

"No. I had a solicitor in that section and she subscribed through him and through Mr. Hudson."

Rev. George F. Robertson, who lived in Pineville and preached at Banks Presbyterian, had known Maggie for only her last two years, and he seemed vaguely embarrassed at this limited contact. He was neither the silver-tongued fundraiser like Reverend Atkinson nor the down-home neighbor like Reverend McIlwaine.

"I saw her very often, and especially when she was sick," he said. "I never went in that I did not sit down and talk with her, and on two occasions at least, maybe others, I did what you call spending the day with her, ate dinner with her. I did not see anything that indicated any weakness of mind in a woman not educated. She was a woman of good, ordinary common sense."

"What was the content of your conversations?"

"I tried to get her to contribute for the field, quite a large amount, to buy an automobile for the field work. I suggested to her that she was financially able to buy the car, and we would put her name on it, *The Maggie Ross Home Mission Car*, and she said that she had put her money in bonds, and I said 'Just give me a bond,' and she gave excuses like everybody else, she had some tenant houses to build and some to repair. I still insisted that she give me a bond, but she would not do it. I gathered she was positively not in favor of the *The Maggie Ross Home Mission Car* at her expense."

"To your knowledge, did she contribute to the church?"

"I heard her say once or twice that she or her sister had given a piano to the church. It was in the church. Had a metal tablet on it with an inscription in memory of Sallie Ross when I went there. That was the only piano there or that has been there to my knowledge."

"But she would not contribute for the automobile?"

The preacher shook his head as if still disappointed. "I remember one bitter cold day, I spent some time with her, and she spoke about the discomforts of traveling, and I don't know whether she or I suggested it, but if she suggested it, I cordially seconded it. I sat there and after awhile, I don't know how long I talked with her, some little time, and when I rose to leave, she said 'Just wait a minute,' and she disappeared and went upstairs and presently she came back and said 'I am going to give you this. Let them folks over there give you a lap robe.' She gave me a ten dollar bill." He grimaced.

"Rev. Robertson, what other thing did you discuss with Miss Maggie?"

"She spoke very frequently and very grateful about the kindness of her friends and neighbors. A number of times she said she had the best neighbors in the world; that they were as good as gold. She seemed to be mindful of them."

"Any in particular?"

"I don't remember that she expressed herself in regard to any one person. She generally talked about neighborhood matters, church matters and chickens and cotton and farming, and such things as would interest an ordinary farmer's wife. She was not a married woman, but she lived in a farming community."

"Did you ever see her read or write?"

"I found her sometimes reading the papers, not in the act of reading, but the papers were there and she would say she had been reading. I don't remember especially the names of the papers—looked like the county papers, I suppose, the Waxhaw paper. I don't remember positively I ever saw the Presbyterian *Standard* there."

"Why do you think she would leave money to the Presbyterian institutions mentioned in the will?"

"She knew about the Barium Springs Orphanage. She could not be half Presbyterian and not know about it. She knew about it without a doubt. She knew about the Presbyterian Hospital. Every Presbyterian in this whole country, miles from that, does. Every once in a while the preachers talk about it."

Rev. Robertson seemed eager to say more about *The Maggie Ross Home Mission Car* on cross-examination.

"The automobile was to be used by me as minister in charge of that field, visiting, going over the field. I think her refusal to donate that automobile is proof of thrift, her ability to hold on to her money, and sometimes it requires intelligence to hold on to money."

"Do you think it takes special intelligence to hold on to money?"

"It depends on who is around. It does not take any especial intelligence to hold on to money when I am around with some missions." Many in the audience chuckled, and for once Judge Ray did not reach for his gavel.

"What do you mean, Rev. Robertson?"

The preacher set his chin. "I mean her refusal to let me have the thousand dollars is a proof of thrift and stinginess, too. I think that thrift is more of the head than of the heart. I think that stinginess and thrift both entered into it. By thrift I mean conservatism and carefulness with regard to one's personal interests. I was trying to get her to do something against her own personal interest. I thought she ought to get the automobile. I answered your question from her standpoint. If I had not thought she ought to get the automobile, I would not have gone to her. I thought if she would get the automobile, it would do a great deal of good there and thought I could accomplish a great deal more in home missions. It is evident that home missions is just as important as foreign missions. She told me that she wasn't able to give me the thousand dollars. I was very desirous to appeal to her when she said she didn't have the money and when she said she didn't have the money in the bank. I knew she wasn't telling the truth. I knew she did have the money."

"Did you know how much she had in the bank?"

"No, but she had the name of having a large amount of money in the bank. When she refused to give me a bond, I saw she was not interested in the home mission automobile."

"Did she tell you she had willed two thousand dollars to the home mission board or to the Presbyterian Hospital?"

"No."

"Did she tell you she wasn't going to leave anything to missions?"

"No."

"Did she say anything to you about having willed the Presbyterian Hospital any property?"

"No. She did not say anything about her will at all; that wasn't involved in my proposition." His eyes wandered beyond the lawyer. "I would have been interested to know about it."

18

FRANK CRANE

It appears that early in life, these old women were neglected by their kin.

—E. T. CANSLER, 1921

April 5, 1921

No witness had known Maggie Ross better than Frank Crane. He was a boy when he met the Rosses—he and his father once spent the night in their home on the Burleyson land—and he had lived in sight of their house for twenty-five years. He told the court about laying off the road for Bob Ross soon after the women moved to Marvin and about Elias Crane's visit just two years before Maggie died.

Frank Crane

"I went up to Miss Maggie's house with an uncle of mine from Texas. He came up here and he was at my house and went up in the evening and when he went in Miss Maggie came out in the hall of the house and I asked her if she know who this was and she said 'Mr. So-and-so, isn't it?' and I said 'No, this is Elias Crane, and she ran and grabbed him and kissed him and hugged him and said 'Don't tell your wife when you go back that I hugged and kissed you,' and she said Jackie was remembered in her will."

"Who is Jackie Crane?"

"His daughter. She is married now."

"Miss Maggie told him that his daughter Jackie was remembered in her will?"

"Yes."

"She is the Margaret Jackson Crane, daughter of Elias Crane, who is referred to in the bequest 'I give and bequeath to Margaret Jackson Crane, daughter of Elias Crane, five hundred dollars'?"

"Yes."

"How long had Elias Crane been away from North Carolina?"

"Some twenty-one years when she saw him. About twenty-four years now."

Mostly Crane talked about the normal comings and goings along the road.

"I lived on the same side of the street and next door to them; nothing but the church and the cotton house separated my house from them," he explained. "The church and the cotton house were to the back and I could see from my house across to theirs. I have been ginning for them for twelve years, and then I have a store. I borrowed money from Miss Maggie for several years. The most I have borrowed was five hundred dollars and from that on down to two hundred. The first was two hundred and the next five hundred and less since then."

"Did you borrow money from them very often?"

"Yes. Very often I borrowed two hundred to two-fifty for a year at a time. I would very often go up there and borrow five, ten or twenty dollars."

"Was this from Miss Maggie or Miss Sallie?"

"I have borrowed from both of them. The last two hundred and two-fifty, that was from Miss Maggie. She let me have it without any trouble."

"How frequently would you say you saw them during the years you have known them?"

"I can't state how often, but I have seen them very often. I don't know that there was a week that passed that I didn't see them. They would send for me sometimes when they had business with me. They sold different things. There was a vineyard in the back of the house that I had a half interest in, and we had some transactions backwards and forwards about that and the upshot of it was I was sent for to go to the house. I would very often sit down and talk with Miss Maggie at length sometimes when I would go up there. We were sometimes holding cotton and she would talk about that. I have bought seed cotton from them, and they have traded at my store a good deal and such things."

"Do you remember Mr. Adams and Mr. Redwine coming up there to prepare the wills?"

"Yes, I remember the occasion, but can't tell the year."

On cross-examination, Crane described Miss Jennie's work for Maggie.

"The last three or four loans were from Miss Maggie," he recalled. "I think my stepdaughter, Jennie Helms, drew up the notes and when they came due Jennie got up the interest. Jennie sometimes read and wrote Miss Maggie's letters for her. I never saw Miss Maggie write a letter. My daughter attended to correspondence for her some."

"Did you ever see Miss Maggie making any calculation or doing any figuring?"

"No."

"Did Miss Maggie pay your stepdaughter for her services."

"Not really. She once gave her five dollars. My stepdaughter used to go up and wait on her during her sickness and the sickness of her brother and sister. She went there and rendered very valuable services. She was up there a great deal and was there during Miss Maggie's last sickness."

"Was your daughter left anything in the will?"

"No."

"What was your business relationship to the Rosses?"

"When I rented, I rented from them and paid the rent to them. I was to pay two bales of cotton for the place, weighing five hundred pounds each, and they kept the cotton until they got ready to sell, and the bale was to weigh five hundred pounds, and when we weighed it, it was a little under five hundred pounds and they came down there to see me about it. I was around up there a good deal and they told me the weight of one bale of cotton was a hundred pounds short, and I went to see about it, and saw that a mistake had been made, the wrong bale had been carried there, and gave them the money. I think Mr. Ed Yarbrough was the one that took the bale of cotton down there."

"In your experience, who was handling the business?"

"I think Miss Sallie mostly transacted the business. She was the elder. Miss Maggie therefore looked up to and deferred to her. After Dennis died, Mr. Hudson handled a good deal of their money, and they handled a little bit."

"Did you ever see Miss Maggie draw a check on a bank?"

"No."

"Did you ever see her draw a note?"

"No."

"Did you ever see her write a letter?"

"No."

The propounders' lawyer came back to read the list of caveators.

"Did you ever see James B. Parker visiting up there?"

"No."

"Lela W. Harrington?"

"No."

"John W. Dees?"

"I know Mr. Dees over here"—he gestured across the courtroom and averted his eyes. "Know him well, he has been up there in my store a good deal. He was up there one day and I wasn't at home and did not get my dinner and I told them to give him dinner. That was since the will and since the death of Miss Maggie. Mr. Dees has been up there frequently since Miss Maggie was buried. He was along when the lawyers took depositions in my house." He paused and looked at the lawyer. "I never did see him visiting the Rosses during their life."

Neither had he seen Lester S. Helms, Louisa May Love, R. S. Doster, Ruth McLellan, Mr. Sandy Smith, Mary Hargett, or Manifred Deese.

"I never saw Manifred Deese until after this came up, after Miss Maggie was buried. I never saw him up there before she died."

Neither had he seen Sarah E. Parker, the heirs of Alexander Phifer, Etta S. Hargett, Julia Nelson, Raymond S. Dees, or Julia Killough.

"They did not visit their cousin up there. I never saw Julia Killough, nor any of these people. I wouldn't know them if I would see them. I never saw any strangers around. They did not come around there. I never saw anybody around that I did not know who they were."

"Mrs. P. L. Jones?"

"She lived in that neighborhood, but I never did see her at the house. She lived just a mile and a quarter from my store and they traded at my store. I never did see her at the house."

Had he ever seen Mr. M. E. Kiker, Mr. J. H. Helms, F. P. Helms, J. H. Tomberlin, Melba Kiker, Melissa Crook, Mrs. M. C. Broom, or Mrs. W. W. Horn from Monroe?

"No. I can't say that I know them."

"Mrs. T. S. Ezzell?"

"There is one right there I know that never did any calling," he said, again gesturing across the courtroom that had grown so silent it seemed hollow. "She lives right close to them. I never did see her there. She is one of the caveators and lives something like a mile or a mile and a quarter from them."

But he had not seen C. G. Parker, Henry Davis, Mack Davis, Mrs. Mildred Parker, Lillie Irby, Mrs. Bertha Lowrence, or Mrs. Ben Reader.

"No. I have never seen any of the Readers up there."

"Not Mrs. Ida Ann Reader?"

"No."

What about Mrs. Alice Helms, Walter Bass, Bertha Bass Griffin, Mattie Bass Suthers?

"No. I never heard any names of that kind."

"Did you ever hear Miss Maggie talk about any of these parties whose names I have called?"

"No."

"Have you ever seen any of her relatives visit her?"

"There are some Gribbles that live in Charlotte that come down there along right about the time of her death, but I don't know them. There were Gribbles at the funeral. She is buried there near the house. I saw the Gribbles at the burial, I don't know just which ones though."

"Mrs. Edna Stikeleather?"

"No. I never heard Miss Maggie talk about any Stikeleathers."

"Peter Ross?"

"I have not seen Peter Ross around there. He used to run his store right over there. He is sitting in the courtroom now. He may have been up there, but I have not seen him there."

"Joe C. Ross?"

"I never did see Joe C. Ross there. He lives in that neighborhood there and traded in the store, but I didn't see him up there."

"G. W. Ross?"

"I have seen G. W. Ross there. When he was buying that land in South Carolina, he went backwards and forwards. He bought a piece of land in South Carolina which he now owns and I have seen him up there."

"N. A. Ross, the gentleman sitting over there next to the attorney?"

"I have never seen him up there to my recollection."

"Lucy Ross?"

"No."

"Carrie Killough?"

"No."

"Julia Alexander Morrison?"

"No"

"Maggie Garrison?"

"I have seen Maggie Garrison there. She is the one that they give five hundred dollars to in the will."

"Mrs. Ed L. Reader?"

"No."

"James R. Davis?"

"No."

"W. B. Tomberlin? Mrs. D. K. Fincher? Mrs. Odessa Harkey? C. B. Griffin? Mrs. E. G. Griffin? Julia Owens? James W. Walters? Julia Walters?"

"No, no, no, no, no, no, no, no," like the staccato of a marching drumbeat.

"Mattie Cook?"

"No."

"Mrs. Horton?"

"No."

"Mrs. J. H. Winchester?"

"I know Mrs. J. H. Winchester, but I never did see her there. She is a schoolteacher, used to teach, married a Winchester. She lives in the same township."

"B. L. Dees?"

"No."

"E. G. Dees?"

"No."

"Clifford R. Craig?"

"No."

"James T. Ross? Mrs. Ida Craig? A. S. Martin? W. C. Martin? Will Rogers? C. B. Rogers? G. E. Rogers? S. L. Rogers? C. M. Rogers? W. D. Rogers?"

"No, no, no, no, no, no, no, no, no, no," like the popping of so many firecrackers in the hushed room.

"J. G. Rogers or Mary Rogers Pierce?"

"No. I have never heard Miss Maggie speaking about these Rogers. I don't know what kin they were to her."

"Not Flossie Rogers Haywood?"

"No."

Nor had he seen any of the Morrises—E. P., R. N., or Bessie.

"W. D. Craig? Owen Presley? Homer Presley? C. B. Presley? Mary Hargett? John Manus? Jane Lee Manus? Harry Manus? Brad Manus? Carr Manus? Franklin Manus?"

"No, no, no, no, no, no, no, no, no, no, no, no," like so many rifle blasts in the silence.

"Blanche Smith?"

"No."

"S. C. Ross?"

"I know him. He lives in Charlotte, I think. I never saw him there."

The long list was finished, and an empty silence hung in the crowded courtroom for a heavy moment. Some of the guilty cousins shifted in their seats and stared away from both the witness and the somber jury. The lawyer quietly asked Crane to recall who on the roll he *had* seen at Miss Maggie's house.

"Of all the caveators that have been called over, I have seen none there except the Gribbles and Mr. George Ross at the time he was buying the land," the neighbor answered. "It was during Miss Sallie's lifetime that I saw Mr. George Ross there. I may have seen him since. I can't swear to that."

The agitated cross-examiner tried to snap the wistful air.

"Do you know all those people, Mr. Crane?" he demanded.

"No, I don't know the most of the names that were called to me."

"Then how can you be sure they did not visit their cousins?"

"I would have known it if I had seen any strangers around there. Strangers came around there sometimes. My house is nearer up on the road and the church and the cotton house are back just about on a line with Miss Maggie Ross' house. My store is farther to the east. I stay there most of the day. A road runs out west leading to Charlotte. I don't pretend to tell the jury that I saw everybody that came from that direction, where they came and where they stopped. Their kin people visited them very little."

"Do you have an unobstructed view of the house?"

"There is a very little rise between my house and the Ross house. There are some trees, but you can see the house."

"Whom on the list do you know?"

"I know the Gribbles that lived in Charlotte and they visited frequently just before Miss Maggie's death. My son took Miss Maggie up there when Bob Gribble died. She went to his funeral. I know Mr. Edwards that married a Gribble. I met him in Marvin a time or two about the time of the burial. He was down there a time or two."

"Are you saying you know everybody that went to the Ross house?"

"No. I do not pretend to say that. I was not at home all the time."

"Do you know John W. Dees?"

"Yes. He was constable in my township. I have seen him in the family often. It has been years since he was constable. He has been living in Mecklenburg some ten or twelve years. I think I saw him up there one time, in the lifetime of Miss Sallie."

Judge Ray called a lunch recess. When the afternoon session opened, the propounders rested their case, leaving the loneliness of Maggie Ross to echo in the jurors' minds.

19

HARRIET TAYLOR

I don't think that she understood what she was doing when she willed me the five hundred dollars, because if she had done what she ought to have done, she would have given me two thousand.

—HARRIET TAYLOR, 1921

April 5–6, 1921

Seventy-six-year-old "Cousin Hettie" took the stand first for the caveators as the sunlight shifted from the eastern windows. She had watched the Rosses about as long, and about as closely, as Frank Crane, but her account painted a very different kind of life.

"I met the family in 1871," she said. "I last saw her two weeks before she died. I saw her quite often. We moved on our place in 1888. I called Mrs. Susan Ross 'Aunt' and Sallie and Maggie 'Cousin.' From the time we lived there in 1888 I did not see much of Miss Maggie from then on except at church and around until 1892. They moved to Marvin and we lived just across the road from them. They lived right across the road from us for two years, until about 1894, then we moved just in hollering distance over on the Ardrey place. We lived there a year and about three months. Then we moved to Mr. Bill McIlwaine's place about a mile from them. We saw them frequently and waited on them in sickness. I broke up housekeeping and lived with my children."

"But you continued to relate to the Rosses?"

She nodded. "I was present when Dennis died. I nursed them. I attended to them as an infant in their sickness. I washed and dressed them. Sometimes I have been with them two weeks at a time, sometimes as much as three weeks at a time and sometimes a month. Once I stayed there six weeks. I would go to see Miss Maggie frequently, and I would stay there three weeks at a time."

"Why did you go down there?"

"Because she would send for me."

"Tell us what you remember about Miss Maggie in 1907."

"She was sixty-eight years of age. Her health was not good at that time. She was a woman who had to take medicine every night. She would take pills. She would take them for constipation. She was a delicate woman. She would take Native Herbs. She was a lean woman. She wore a band to support her stomach. She said her liver was bad. She was a melancholy kind of woman, would have melancholy spells."

The woman's voice warbled and her head bobbed knowingly as she cataloged Maggie's troubles.

"How often would she have these spells?"

"Sometimes as often as three times a week. Sometimes she would have them once a week and sometimes once every two or three weeks, and sometimes twice a week."

"Can you describe for us how she would behave during these spells?"

"She would sit for hours and not speak a word. She would generally have these spells when she heard something that would disturb her among the colored people. These spells would last a day or two sometimes. She would sit and twirl her thumbs, stroke her chin and stare out of the window into space."

"Tell us about the last time you were with her."

"She said 'I feel like if I had everything I had out there in the cotton patch I would burn it up.'"

"How would you describe Miss Maggie's memory?"

"Her memory was not very good. If she would hear anything she could never tell again just like it was. She could tell what had happened when she was a child better than she could tell things that had happened in recent years. She could talk about cows and chickens and things like that, but she could not carry on a connected conversation."

"Did you ever see her transact any business?"

"No. Prior to Miss Sallie's death, Miss Sallie transacted all the business. Mr. Hudson helped Miss Sallie. After Miss Sallie's death Mr. Hudson took charge. Miss Maggie had but very little education. She could read a little, but she could not write a letter. She could read writing if it was very plain. She could not count money—only by giving her time, and then sometimes she would not get it right. She would say 'Hettie, is that right?' and sometimes it would lack five cents and sometimes it would be right. She knew silver money."

"Do you think she knew the value of money?"

"I do not know whether she knew the value of it or not. She always made out like she was very poor. She would not buy all she wanted to eat. The cook would come in and tell her that she had nothing to cook, and she would say that she was too poor to buy anything. She could not carry on a connected conversation."

The same sentence, Cansler observed quietly: "She could not carry on a connected conversation."

"What did you notice about her relationship with her sister?"

"Miss Sallie and Miss Maggie would have their difficulties. During Miss Sallie's lifetime she conducted the business. Miss Sallie took the lead. Miss Maggie would tell Miss Sallie to let her have her money and let her have control of it, and Miss Sallie would very often say 'I will not do it, you hadn't got sense enough to take care of it.' She said she would give it to her when she got ready. Miss Maggie did not get control of the money that belonged to them to my knowledge. Miss Sallie handled the money as long as she lived."

"What about after Miss Sallie died?"

"After Cousin Sallie died, Cousin Maggie kept up her assessment to the church, what she was assessed to pay, from the time Sallie died on up to the year before Maggie died, and she said that she was not going to keep it up, she had paid just all she was going to, she was not able to pay it, but Mr. Dick Hudson came and him and her talked and she paid it."

"What else did you notice about her relationship with Mr. Hudson?"

"When he came to see her on business they would go in a room, nobody else would be present, and they would talk privately. I would be there when Mr. Hudson would come over, but they would go in this room, in the living room."

"Did you have an opportunity to observe the relationship between Miss Maggie and Mittie Bell Houston?"

"Yes."

"Tell us, if you know, about what they would do over there, what Mittie Bell would do and say?"

Taylor's eyes flashed. "If she wanted anything she got it."

The propounders moved to strike this answer, and Judge Ray agreed. But as Cansler settled into his seat, an understanding began to take shape in his mind. The caveators' lawyer started over.

"Did you ever hear Mittie Belle ask Miss Maggie for money?"

"Yes."

"Did Miss Maggie give her the money?"

"Sometimes she would give it to her and sometimes she wouldn't, and Mittie Bell would get mad about it and go home, and then is when Miss Maggie would get all disturbed about it, and as soon as she come in, why she would say to tell Mittie Bell to come back, I want to see her, and she would come back and get what she wanted. She got the money."

"What else did she get?"

"She would come and get butter, eggs, meat and flour and anything she wanted. I don't know of a thing she asked for and did not get it, only when she would ask for money sometimes she would not get it and she would have Mittie Bell sent for a day or two afterwards and give it to her."

"Did you observe Mittie Bell Houston living in the house with them before her marriage?"

"Yes. When there was no one else around there, she lived as a white child in the house." Judge Ray reached for his gavel, and the courtroom murmur subsided. "When there was company there, they put her back in the kitchen, she was kept there with her head tied up and if strangers came around she would come out like a servant, when the preachers were there. She slept in a bed sometimes and sometimes in the bed with Miss Maggie."

"Do you know how often she has slept with Miss Maggie?"

"No. I can't tell you whether it was regularly or an occasional thing."

"Did you ever see Mittie do any work around there after she was married?"

"No, except if she wanted to bake custards when she wanted them herself. Miss Maggie and I did the cooking. Miss Maggie said she wanted to educate her, but she would not stay in school to be educated."

Taylor told about Mittie's going to Livingstone, about the baby that Dr. Potts delivered, about Maggie's spell of grippe, about Florence's birth, about the preacher's vists.

"I have heard her say several times that she would not pay nothing for education, and once upon a time I opened a book and found something from the Salisbury Institute there, that Mr. Atkinson sent there, and I said 'What is the Salisbury Institute?' and she said 'Mr. Atkinson had been here wanting me to give some money for it, but I did not give him any, I would not give him any to save his life.' I was there when the gentlemen came around to get money for Elizabeth College. They talked to her and read. They was nice men. I can't remember their names. They did not get any."

The lawyer showed her a picture of Mittie Bell, Miss Sallie, Miss Maggie and Taylor's mother. She took the photograph and squinted.

"That is really better than Miss Maggie looked." She handed the picture back.

The long light was coming in the western windows, and the east was in shadow. Judge Ray gaveled adjournment. The propounders' cross-examination started Wednesday with the photograph.

"Tell us about your Grandmother Taylor here in the picture."

"She was a nice old lady. I always thought a heap of her."

"What about Miss Sallie?"

"Miss Sallie was a nice lady."

"And Miss Maggie? How does she seem in the picture?"

"I can't see anything wrong with Miss Maggie."

"Can you identify Mittie Belle in the picture?"

"The little negro is standing back behind them, but I do not want my picture took with a negro."

"But your grandmother had her picture taken with them."

Taylor's eyes narrowed on the lawyer. "My taste is more refined than Grandma Taylor and Miss Sallie and Miss Maggie."

"But you said they were all nice women."

"They were."

"Does Mitte Bell look stuck up to you in this picture?"

"I don't know whether she does or not. I do not want my picture taken with her."

"Why, Mrs. Taylor?"

"I do not like negroes—only in a certain way."

"What way is that."

"If a darky was to get in trouble and I was right close by, close enough to assist him, I would assist him, but as to these other things, I am above it. I have always thought that."

"Yet you have slept in the bed with Mittie Bell."

Taylor shifted in her chair and straightened her back. She had to find some way to cling to her dignity despite this public display of a distasteful part of her past. "I slept with Cousin Maggie next to me and Mittie Bell on the opposite side, yes. Wasn't nary bed in the house for me. They would make up a pallet for Mittie Bell when I would go up there and then after I would lay down Mittie Bell would come whimpering and crying and say she was afraid and she would crawl in on the side with Cousin Maggie, but she would not get in on the side I was on."

"Why did you stand for that?"

"I had promised Cousin Sallie on her deathbed to look after Cousin Maggie. Cousin Sallie would not allow her to eat at the table when she was there." Her eyes were uplifted and she afforded herself a smile.

"You still called her 'Cousin Maggie' and let Mittie Bell get in bed with her?"

"Yes. Sometimes Cousin Maggie would make her go back lay down on the pallet. That was the only bed in that room. I was very much opposed to sleeping in the same bed with that little negro."

"Why didn't you go and sleep in the bedroom across the hall?"

"Because Cousin Maggie said 'Cousin Harriet, I don't want you to leave me, I want you to sleep in the same room with me.'"

"How old was Mittie Bell at that time?"

"Mittie Bell was about nine years old."

"But I thought you said Mittie Bell never slept in the bed with Miss Maggie as long as Miss Sallie lived."

"No." Taylor shifted in her seat and averted her eyes. "I said that Miss Sallie did not let her eat at the table when she was there before she died, and I said when she was little, about nine year old, when she slept with her, that could not possibly be after Cousin Sallie died. Mittie Bell would sleep in the same bed with Miss Maggie while Miss Sallie was living. Miss Sallie knew about it, and she would tell Cousin Maggie not to be such a fool about that little negro."

"Now, didn't you tell me a while ago, Mrs. Taylor, that the only reason that you stayed there and took care of Miss Maggie when she was letting that little negro eat at the same table and sleep in the same bed with her was because you had promised Cousin Sallie on her deathbed that you would take care of her—didn't you tell me that a while ago?"

The woman cast her eyes to the judge as the color rose in her powdered cheeks. "He might have made me tell it that way, but I didn't mean it that way!" She turned back to the lawyer. "There is not much difference in sleeping in the same bed with a negro and sleeping in the same room with them." She looked so distraught the lawyer changed the subject.

"Let's get back to relationship with Miss Maggie. What was her condition when you met her in 1871?"

"I don't know."

"Did she look like she does in the picture, or did she look younger?"

"She looked like she does in her picture now."

"How much sense would you say she had then?"

"I don't know. I never met them any only at church and about until we moved on the place in 1888."

"How old was she when you first met her?"

"I don't know."

"What was the condition of her mind then?"

"Not very good. She had a little sense. She was like a heap of us—she needed more than she had." She shifted in her seat, still miserable. "I can't tell you how much sense she had. She did not have the sense people that are educated have. I never did think she was smart. From the first time I ever got well acquainted with her, she was not bright. She was not bright back there when she was thirty-eight years old. She couldn't carry on a conversation with any sense."

"What about her condition along about the time Dennis died?"

"Both of these old ladies were bedridden lots of the time. My children were all married and I stayed a good deal with Miss Maggie and Miss Sallie and waited on them in sickness."

"Did they pay you?"

"They did not pay me much. I waited on them many a night and never slept a wink, and they would say to me that they would pay me. They were feeble, so I did for them. They would say 'We got it fixed so you will get pay for every bit of your work.' Miss Maggie said they had it fixed up to give me some of their money. They paid me, for twenty-three years, sixty dollars. They were pretty stingy."

"But they left you five hundred dollars in the will."

"I reckon they did," she mused. "It looks like they wanted to give that to me." She fixed her eyes on the lawyer. "I don't think that she understood what she was doing when she willed me the five hundred dollars, because if she had done what she ought to have done, she would have given me two thousand."

"You still expect to get more, don't you, Mrs. Taylor?" He picked up a piece of paper. "You swore in your deposition as follows: 'I have the intention of presenting a bill for what is due me in case the will should be broken.' Is that correct?"

Taylor set her chin and squinted at the man. "I think I deserve it."

"Did Miss Maggie think she couldn't afford it?"

"She was always complaining about poverty. She kept her money in a little trunk upstairs, and kept the keys in her pocket. When she went to bed at night she kept them between the pillowcase and her pillow. I have been upstairs and got money out of the trunk and brought it down to give to Mittie Bell. One time she gave a ten-dollar bill to a negro man. She paid me thirty dollars after Cousin Sallie died. In all they paid me sixty dollars. I had been there three months at the time she paid me the thirty dollars."

She stiffened her back, folded her gloved hands in her lap, and lifted her head to meet the lawyer's eyes. The story was out, the secrets she had swallowed for all these years, and she felt her reputation was scattered on the floor around her. But she would not look down. She was, by God, above all that. Cansler returned to his seat with his suspicions confirmed.

20

COUSIN MARGARET AND THE COOK

It was so lonesome up there I couldn't stand it.

—HARRIET GRIER, 1921

April 6, 1921

Taylor's testimony stretched into Wednesday morning, then her daughter Margaret Garrison Moore, who had been in Florida for five months before the trial, echoed the stories of an addled, feeble Maggie dominated by her older sister and Mittie Bell.

"I have known Miss Maggie Ross ever since I can remember," she said. "I lived in Lancaster County, South Carolina, until I was thirteen, and at that time we moved to the Ross farm. That was in 1888."

"Did you have sufficient opportunity to observe her?"

"Yes, I ran around the house and carried them in stove wood and lived in the house with them."

"Where were you living in 1907?"

"I was living in Charlotte."

"Were you in touch with the Rosses at that time?"

"Yes. After I moved to Charlotte, I visited them in their home. I did their sewing for them in the spring and fall. I visited them for new sewing, and they visited me. The last time she ever visited me, Miss Maggie, was in 1916. After Miss Sallie's death, I did Miss Maggie's sewing. I always made their clothes whenever I was called on to do so. Sometimes when I was there I would sweep their house and get dinner."

"Can you identify this photograph?"

Moore glanced at the picture. "That was taken in the year 1898 or in the spring of 1899. It is very much like Miss Mag. She was a very delicate-looking woman with lots of wrinkles."

"Tell us your observations of Miss Maggie."

The witness settled sideways into a relaxed pose, draped an arm across the chair back, and crossed her legs negligently.

"She was a very delicate woman. I have seen her sit for hours and pull her chin and gaze into open space. She wouldn't eat during those spells, and she would act as if she didn't know what was happening. She was very melancholy. She would seem lost for hours and twirl her thumbs. One might speak to her and she wouldn't hear and she would act this way for a few minutes and then again she would act like that for a long time. I have seen her have as many as three a week. Between her spells of melancholy, she would appear cheerful."

"Did you ever hear her talk about money?"

"I have heard Miss Maggie say she was not worth anything, and was not able to give anything to charity, orphanages or church. I have heard her say she did not believe in mission work."

Unlike her warbling mother, Moore spoke in a blunt, arch tone and kept shifting her mascara-dark eyes to the jury box.

"What was her general mental condition?"

"She didn't remember very good. She would start to tell something and get mixed up in it and start off on something else. She had very little education. She could read a little, and she might have been able to write her name. I never saw her do any business in my life. She could not make calculations."

"Did you have an occasion to see her in the fall of 1907?"

"I was down there and she went out of the house and came back and sat down. She was nervous and fretted and worried and at last she spoke. She said 'Sallie, I'll not fix another pound of butter for that man.' Miss Sallie asked why, and Miss Maggie says 'He's going to give me eighteen cents next week.' Cousin Sallie began to chuckle and laugh and said she was only getting fifteen cents now. Cousin Sallie turned to me and says 'I told you she didn't have a darned bit of sense.' I went over and sat down in Miss Maggie's lap and explained the matter to her. I explained that she was getting three cents more than she had been. Maggie said 'Sallie thinks I ain't got no sense.'"

"How was her memory?"

Moore shrugged, rolled her eyes around the room, and tightened her red lips into a small pout.

"Cousin Maggie was very absent-minded. I would give her a little Christmas gift, and she would put it away and I would ask her if she got it and she would say yes, but she could not tell me where it was. She would be hunting for her glasses and they would be on her forehead all the time. I have told her things and she would try to repeat them in my presence to other people and could not do it. She could not carry on a connected conversation."

Just like her mother—same sentence: "She could not carry on a connected conversation."

"Did you have opportunity to observe the relations between Miss Sallie and Miss Maggie?"

"Yes. I would go there to sew. Miss Sallie would always tell Miss Maggie what to do and she would do it. Miss Maggie was just like a child. When Miss Maggie would say she was going to have her dress first, and Miss Sallie would say she was going to have her dress first, then Miss Maggie would give in. During the twenty years, more or less, that I knew these old ladies, Miss Sallie would tell Miss Maggie to go bring her a drink of water and she would do it, to bring kindling for the fire and she would do that. Miss Sallie was the stronger minded of the two. I have never seen Miss Maggie refuse to do anything that Miss Sallie ordered her to do."

"Did you have an opportunity to observe her relationship with Mr. R. A. Hudson?"

"Yes. I have been there several times when Mr. Hudson was there."

"Did you ever hear Mr. Hudson issue any orders to Miss Maggie?"

"I never heard him speak to either one except in a respectful manner. He would come and sit and talk to us all awhile, and then he would say 'Mrs. Moore, will you please excuse Miss Maggie, I can always explain business better to her by myself.' I was never present when their business was transacted."

The crowd enjoyed a rare chuckle when Moore described the enlarged photograph, prominently displayed in the Ross sitting room, of Governor Bickett's son, William Yarborough Bickett, riding his goat "Billy." She remembered going to Livingstone College with Maggie and Mittie, seeing Dr. Potts come when Mittie came home pregnant, driving Maggie to visit Bob Gribble's family, taking Maggie to the dentist, meeting Maggie in Charlotte with Billy McIlwaine and Mrs. King and Mrs. Hood to buy a piano.

"After the church was finished, I asked Miss Maggie if the piano had been placed. This was between 1911 and 1913. She told Mittie to get the key from Steve Walkup and we would go look at the piano. Mittie said Miss Maggie had got a piano for the church and now she had to get her one. Maggie told her she had the organ. Maggie said she reckoned she would have to buy Mittie's piano. Miss Sallie gave me a ring in 1907. Miss Maggie was present. I heard a conversation between Mittie Belle and Miss Sallie in the presence of Miss Maggie. This happened in December 1907. I was visiting them, and Cousin Sallie went out and came back with something in her hand. She always called me Cousin Mag, and she said 'Cousin Mag, here are some things I value more than anything on earth and I want you take care of them.' There were two pins and a ring. Mittie said 'Miss Sallie, you told me you were going to give that ring to me' and Miss Sallie said 'I will make Mag give you hers.'"

The lawyer introduced the ring and pin into evidence.

"Did she give you any other gifts?"

"In 1913, I was visiting Miss Maggie and she gave me two candlesticks. Mittie Bell was present at the time, and Mittie Bell says 'Miss Maggie, you promised me those candlesticks' and Maggie came over and took one out of my hand."

"By the way, do you know if Miss Sallie did make Miss Maggie give her ring to Mittie?"

"I have seen Miss Maggie's ring on Mittie's finger since Maggie's death." She stole a glance toward the black quadrant.

"What other opportunities did you have to observe the relationship between Miss Maggie and Mittie?"

"They would be at my house in Charlotte and we would go up town to shop and Mittie would see things she wanted and Miss Maggie would give her the money to buy them with. I have seen her get other things from Miss Maggie besides money. After Miss Sallie's death, when Mittie got married and she would come back, she would always want something to carry home with her such as butter, eggs, chickens and the like, and Miss Maggie would give them to her. I have seen Mittie wear Miss Maggie's underwear and ribbons and shoes. I have heard her ask for Miss Maggie's handkerchiefs and Miss Maggie would tell her that she had handkerchiefs of her own, but she would use Miss Maggie's. In 1913 or 1914, Miss Maggie and Mittie came to my house and Miss Maggie had a red ribbon on her neck, and I told her she must not wear it up street. She said Mittie dressed her and she must wear it." She put a gloved hand to her mouth as if hiding a giggle.

"Did you observe their relationship after Florence was born?"

"Florence Tucker was born in early fall in 1907. I was spending some time with Miss Maggie after this baby was born, and Mittie came down with her baby, Florence Tucker, and when it needed attention she would put it in Miss Maggie's lap and ask her to attend to it. I would object to this and Mittie would say that Miss Maggie knew more about babies than she did. Then Miss Mag would dress it."

"Did you ever see Mittie doing work around the house?"

"Never in my life."

"Did you ever see Bob doing work around the house?"

"No. He never lived in the house with these old ladies after he married that I know of. He lived on the old Burleyson place.

"Were you present when Miss Sallie died?"

"Yes."

"Would you describe what you saw?"

"Miss Maggie was all nervous and wrought up and she imagined she saw a white bird. She said 'Oh, there comes a beautiful white bird after my sister.' She said she saw angels."

"Did you see angels, Mrs. Moore?"

"No, I did not see any angels."

The cross-examining attorney showed her the group photo that her mother had identified.

"That was taken in the spring of 1898 and was taken by a traveling photographer," she recalled. "The house is the one in which they lived."

"Does Mittie look like in the picture that she was a very dominating child or a determined little negro?"

"No."

"Did you know that Judge Frank Osborne would rub his chin and stare into space?"

Moore put on the pout again. "No."

"Would you think that an elderly person who had lost a near relative, looking off that way would indicate weakness?"

"Yes."

"What if trouble caused them to act that way? Would you think it would indicate weakness?"

"No."

"Do you know of anything to cause more trouble than to lose a brother and sister and to have no one else to lean on for guidance and support?"

"No. I would consider that cause for sorrow."

"Would you think it unnatural for one who had lost their relations to break down and cry once in a while?"

"Yes, it would be unnatural. That would indicate some weakness of mind."

"Do you think that the fact that Miss Mag had to take purgative every night had anything to do with her mental condition?"

"Yes, I think that had something to do with her mental capacity."

"Can you tell me anything that she ever tried to tell you and couldn't?"

"In the year 1906, we went down to Waxhaw to make some purchase for the family and came back, and she was telling something about some cotton that she had heard down at Waxhaw and she couldn't tell it right and I would have to put in every few minutes and help her get it straight. It was about a storm that had damaged the cotton crops a few nights before that."

The lawyer excused her, and she skipped lightly from the stand, giving a glance and a parting smile to the jurors.

Harriet Grier, the only black person who took the stand during the trial, recounted the ways she had observed Mittie dominate Maggie. She detailed Maggie's last hours and gave more examples of Maggie's lack of business sense.

"When she would go to pay me, if I took out nothing, she would give it to me correct, or if even dollars, she would pay it. If I took out fractions, she could not pay it correct and would go get Miss Jennie Helms to figure it for her. One time she gave me ten dollars to go to Waxhaw and get some things like coffee, sugar and such like, and when I came back she could not figure it all up and told me to take it down to Miss Jennie and get her to fix it. When I brought the paper back, she just looked at it and said it was all right."

"Did you ever see Miss Mag figure or write any?"

"No. Mr. Hudson attended to her business."

"Who did the work around the house?"

"Amos McIlwaine and Steve Walkup."

"Not Bob Ross?"

"Bob Ross did not do any work around there. I seen him haul some wood there once or twice during the ten years I was there, but that is all. He did not live in the house with them but lived about two miles away from them. Miss Maggie told me that she gave him all he made. Miss Maggie said she give Tom and Mittie all they made and then partly kept them up."

Aunt Harriet held firm on cross-examination.

"Would you say Miss Mag was a Christian?"

"I can't say that. She was a church member. Preachers would come there and pray and she would get down on her knees. I can't recognize Miss Mag as a Christian."

She defended the steady increases in salary that she had demanded across the years.

"I told her I would not stay for less than ten dollars. Then I went to twelve dollars and she said that was an enormous price, and she would give it if I wouldn't stay for less. She said she would give it rather than let me go. It got so lonely up there that I told her I would have to leave and she asked me what I would stay for. She said she would give me fifteen dollars if I would stay on, but it got so lonely I decided to leave and she gave me twenty dollars."

"So lonely up there," Cansler noted. "Did you take advantage of that old woman?"

"No, sir." Aunt Harriet shook her head and cast sad eyes at the lawyer. "It was so lonesome up there I couldn't stand it. Clothes were going up and my dresses and aprons cost more."

The caveators' lawyer came back to stress Mittie's mistreatment of Maggie.

"I said that Mittie Bell pulled Miss Mag's nose and ears, and Miss Mag was crying and saying 'Oh Mittie, quit.'"

"Was Mittie angry?" the propounders' lawyer asked on re-cross-examination.

"Mittie was laughing when she pulled Miss Mag's nose and ears."

21

VISITORS

From my observations of her, my opinion is that she did not have sense enough to make a will.

—J. W. HALL AND OTHERS, 1921

April 7, 1921

Henry Banks Stephens had rented land from the Rosses for nineteen years, almost half his life. The fall after Maggie died, he and his wife, Mary, bought a farm from the Traywicks and moved out to Providence Road near Weddington. He delivered, in breathless sentences before the unaccustomed audience, more stories of Maggie's inept dealings.

"I delivered a bale of cotton up there one morning and I asked her how she was and she said she was torn all to pieces, and I asked her why and she said last night she had seven bales of cotton out in the yard and this morning she didn't have but six. We went out and counted them and there were seven bales there."

"Can you describe your business dealings with her?"

"If I overpaid my rent in cotton and there was some money coming to me, she would ask me to make the calculation, or if I owed her some difference in the rent she would ask me to make the calculation. One time I overpaid my rent and she asked me to figure out the difference and it come to thirteen dollars fifty-six cents, and she said it was all right and she got up and went to the door and turned around and said 'what did you say it was?' and I told her. She went upstairs and come back and counted out thirty-six dollars fifty cents. I told her what was due me and handed the difference back to her and I says 'that belongs to you' and she said 'oh, I ain't got no sense nohow.'"

Banks's brother, Oscar Stephens, who had been on the Rosses' land for ten years, testified more briefly about his business dealings: "I paid most of my rent to Bob Ross. He is a colored man on their place. He lived at the old Burleyson place."

Noah Helms, who made the contract with Dick Hudson when he renovated the old Banks Church for Miss Maggie, would not testify to her mental condition. R. L. White, Harriet Taylor's son who had mostly seen the Ross women at church, told another story about Maggie's inability to make change.

"I traded cows with her one time," he said. "She was to give me eighteen dollars to boot. She gave me a twenty-dollar bill and I handed her a two-dollar bill and she said that wasn't right."

"Was there anyone else present?"

"No. Mr. Hudson was brought in and he told her it was right and attempted to explain. She said she could not understand it that way."

Like the caveators' other witnesses, he testified that she did not have sufficient mental capacity to make a will. Cross-examination started with questions about White's family connections.

"I am a half brother to Mrs. Margaret Moore, and a son of Mrs. Harriet Taylor."

"Is the witness J. W. Hall your brother-in-law?"

"No."

"Does your mother live with Mr. Hall's family?"

"No. She visits frequently as they are good friends. He lives a half a mile away from me."

"Is there any other member of your family here to testify in this case?"

"No."

"Did you tell Rev. R. J. McIlwaine that your mother and sister were lying around up at Miss Mag's trying to get her to give them her property?"

"No."

A lie, he was sure. But he changed the subject.

"When did the cow trade about which you testified take place?"

"About two years after Miss Sallie's death."

"Did you know prior to the cow trade that Mr. Hudson attended to her business?"

"Yes. She came to me to make the trade."

"Did you know she did not have sense enough to make the trade or know the value of the cow?"

"She accepted my terms."

The caveators' lawyer asked him to clarify the swap.

"I traded her a cow with a young calf that I gave twenty-five dollars for that morning for a heifer that never would find a calf."

"And Mr. Hudson was there?"

"Yes."

"And he did not object to the trade."

"No."

Hall, White's neighbor, based his opinion on weekly visits to buy chickens, butter, and eggs at Maggie's home during the four years before she died. "Aunt Harriet Grier, the colored woman with Miss Mag, would come out and settle with me," he remembered. "Occasionally Miss Mag would come out."

The propounders returned to the Taylor connection.

"Mrs. Harriet Taylor is a frequent visitor at my house, and a close friend of the family," Hall said. "She has a son, Mr. White, who lives down in my neighborhood. I am not related to them."

Lafayette A. Gallant lived at Steele Creek in Mecklenburg County until he married Billy McIlwaine's sister Margaret in 1886 and moved to the McIlwaine land in Sharon Township, just across the creek from the Rosses' homeplace. He helped the family when Dennis was injured, and he ran a store near their house. In 1898, he moved to Charlotte, transferring his membership from Banks Presbyterian to Second Presbyterian in the city. He still visited Marvin regularly, and he would see Maggie sometimes when she visited the Garrisons.

"The first time I ever saw Miss Mag, she didn't have the appearance of being a very strong woman," he said slowly, perched on the edge of the witness chair as if he felt proud but wary. "She was sick off and on. I have seen her in bed."

"What sort of memory did Miss Mag have, Mr. Gallant?"

Judge Ray sustained the propounders' objection. The caveators excepted, explaining that they proposed to show she had a poor memory.

"I never saw Miss Mag attend to any business," Gallant said.

"Who attended to her business during the twelve years that you lived near Marvin?"

"Mr. Hudson."

"Do you know whether Miss Mag could read or write?"

"No. I have never seen her write, read anything or make any calculation. During the time I knew Miss Mag, she didn't have a very strong mind. Miss Sallie had the stronger mind by far."

The propounders tried to raise questions about the witness himself.

"Do you have health problems, Mr. Gallant?"

"There is nothing the matter with my health except that I am nervous." He shook his head as slowly as he spoke.

"Do you sit on the front seat at the Courthouse in Charlotte to get caught on the jury?"

"No."

"What is your regular business?"

"I have got no regular business."

"Didn't your brother-in-law help educate your children?"

"No. He did help educate one son, but my son is paying it back. My brother-in-law has been very liberal with his poor kin. I was out working on my farm like a negro at that time. That was fifteen years ago."

"Have you had a regular job since then?"

"No."

"Is it true that you bob up as a witness in all will cases?"

"No."

"Is it true that you have been involved in attempting to break a will before?"

"I had an aunt in Charlotte and she made a will and left most of her estate to her niece and nephew. I never tried to get lawyers to bust it."

"Do you think Miss Mag was an idiot?"

"No."

"What about Miss Sallie?"

"Miss Sallie was a strong-minded woman."

"Do you think that Miss Mag had as much sense as you have?"

"No."

"What about Miss Sallie?"

"She was a shrewd woman. I wouldn't say that she was much of a trader. She inherited most of her property and held on to it. If Miss Sallie had your education, she would have had more sense than you. If Miss Mag had had the chance of an education, I don't think she could have taken it in."

The caveators' lawyer gave Gallant a chance to cast himself in a better light.

"I married Dr. W. E. McIlwaine's sister. I have a son in Charlotte who is a physician. He was in the Army and was in France about thirteen months. He got a D.S.C. over there. He is my oldest son, and then I have two other sons who work at Belk Brothers."

"Mr. Gallant, do you have any interest in this case."

"None whatever. I was subpoenaed to come down here and I tried to get excused."

George Washington Ross was the only blood-kin caveator who took the witness stand. He was also the only Ross relative on the list who could talk about a relationship with the women. At sixty-six, he made an appealing witness—gray-haired distinguished, easygoing, thoughtful, even fun-loving—a softer face for the jury than the driven, determined John Wesley Dees, who led the caveat. He was the grinning guy, more than six feet tall, towering over the sisters in the 1898 photograph, tangible evidence of an exception to Crane's damning list of cousins who shunned them. Farmer, sometime storekeeper, confidante of many, regular at the Weddington dances in the old days before his wife, Susan, died, he lent a dignity to his side that the likes of Lafayette Gallant and Harriet Taylor and Margaret Garrison and Banks Stevens lacked. He appeared comfortable but serious on the stand.

"I knew Miss Mag all my life," he said. "I knew of her but didn't become so well acquainted with her until I was about twenty-one years old. Prior to 1898, I lived at the McIlwaine old place about one and a half miles of the Rosses. Later I moved to the Billy Ardrey place, about a half mile from them. Then I moved to South Carolina."

"You bought land in South Carolina from your cousins?"

He nodded. "Miss Sallie and Mr. Hudson had the papers drawn up."

"Did you ever know of Miss Mag attending to any business?"

"No, but Miss Sallie told me that they attended to their own business as far as they could."

"Was Miss Maggie there?"

"Miss Mag was present, but she didn't have anything to say."

"Did Miss Sallie conduct all their business?"

"She said they employed Mr. Hudson to attend to what they could not do."

The lawyer showed him a photograph of Maggie.

"That does not look like Miss Mag at that time. She looked much older."

He looked at the 1898 picture.

"That does not look much like her, as she is fleshier in the picture than she was in person. She was not a stout woman and didn't appear to look stout."

"How would you describe her health, Mr. Ross?"

"When I knew her she was always complaining."

"Did you see her often?"

"I visited her. She visited me a few times. After Miss Sallie died, I went to see her once or maybe twice or three times a year. She never did talk much."

"Have you seen Mittie Bell at the house?"

"Yes."

"Bob Ross?"

"Bob would come to the door."

"How would you describe her health?"

"One time I went there and when she met me she called me 'Cousin George' and she was wiping her eyes and she sat there awhile and said she didn't know what she would do if it wasn't for her butter and eggs. She sat there a pretty good while and worked with her fingers and gazed out of the window."

"Did you ever see her read or write?"

"No. I don't think she had any education. Miss Sallie was the stronger-minded woman."

"How would you describe your relationship?"

"We were on friendly terms—called each other 'cousin.'"

"Was there ever any friction between you?"

"No."

The propounders' attorney referred to Maggie's statement to Aunt Harriet—she was going to leave her property to the ones that help make it—in cross-examining George Ross.

"I do not come in that class 'who helped make their property,'" he admitted. "I paid a fair price for the property. I never helped make their property. I owed some on this property until 1912. I took their deed for the land. I finished paying Miss Mag for the land after Miss Sallie died. Mr. Hudson gave me receipts."

"How were you related to Miss Mag?"

"She was my second cousin."

"Do you know how they acquired the land in question?"

"They inherited this land from their brother."

"Did Miss Mag ever say to you that she thought you were hanging around up there trying to get some of their property?"

"No."

He stepped from his chair with a nod to both tables of lawyers.

W. S. Garrison met the Rosses about the time he married Margaret Taylor in 1894. They quit farming and moved to Charlotte from Marvin about 1910, but their marriage deteriorated and they soon separated.

He worked as a streetcar conductor before going into the fire insurance business. They had been divorced three years, but as fellow heirs testifying on the cousins' side they were cordial in the courtroom.

"When I was living in the Marvin section, Mittie Bell Houston was living in the house with Miss Mag and Miss Sallie," he told the caveators' lawyer.

"Did you ever see Bob Ross there?"

"Yes. We were living across the street from the Ross women at that time and I remember seeing Bob Ross in the front room dressing one morning about eight or nine o'clock."

"Now, what was the condition of Miss Mag's mind?"

Judge Ray sustained the propounders' objection, and the caveators complained that they proposed to show she had a weak and feeble mind.

"Mr. Garrison, would you describe Miss Mag's health at the time you knew her?"

"She was in very feeble health. She would be sick. According to my way of thinking, she was a feeble-minded woman."

Cansler questioned his frequent visits to Miss Maggie, considering he thought she lacked mental capacity.

"Yes, I would go to see this feeble-minded old woman," Garrison shot back. "I love to visit insane asylums." He shook his head and settled back. "She was not strong-minded."

"What is the basis of your opinion, Mr. Garrison?"

"Just my general observation and conversations and all those things. It's not what she said that caused me to think like that, but what she didn't say."

"Did she know you when you went to see her?"

"Yes."

"Did she have as much sense as you have?"

"Probably."

"Could you make a will like the one we have heard?"

"Possibly."

"Is your opinion based on the fact that she willed most of her property to negroes?"

"No. She could have given Mittie Bell and Bob a home and this thing would never have come up."

S. H. Fincher, who built tenant houses for the Rosses, described Hudson's control of the business, but he did the caveators no good.

"Miss Mag had ordered some shingles from Waxhaw, and they were no good, and I didn't use them," he said on cross-examination. "Later, Miss Mag came down there and told me she was glad I didn't use them, and that I was right in not using them."

"What did you think of her mental capacity?"

"I have stated that her mind was good so far as I know."

22

DR. POTTS

Miss Sallie said that they were awfully sorry that it happened; that they had tried to raise Mittie Bell right, and for me not to say anything about it and they would pay me for it.

—DR. ROBERT MARCELLUS POTTS, 1921

April 7, 1921

The clerk then read the deposition of Dr. Robert Marcellus Potts, forty-nine, who had practiced medicine in Marvin in 1897 and 1898 and kept many of his patients—and his membership in Banks Presbyterian Church—when he moved to Rock Hill and to Fort Mill. He had started treating the Ross women when Sallie was ill in 1902 and first treated Maggie in 1906.

"She was rather delicate, nervous disposition, frail woman, inclined to be nervous. She had a tendency to be despondent or pessimistic, looking on the dark side of things. This was from 1906 until her death. Rather pessimistic."

"Did you ever call to see Mittie Bell Ross as a physician?"

"Yes. Mittie Bell was at Miss Sallie and Miss Maggie Ross' home."

"When was this?"

"My recollection is that it was in 1905."

"What was the purpose of the visit?"

"I was called to deliver Mittie Bell Ross of a child."

The languishing crowd in the courtroom bristled as the hair rises on a spooked cat.

"Was this your first call to see Mittie Bell?"

"No. Prior to this, my recollection is that Miss Sallie Ross called me in to examine Mittie Bell and see what was the trouble."

"Was Miss Maggie Ross there at that time?"

"Yes, according to my recollection."

"What did you discover?"

"I made an examination of Mittie Bell and found that she was pregnant."

The alert audience murmured low, and Judge Ray fingered his gavel.

"Where did you make this examination?"

"Upstairs in the Misses Ross' house."

"Did you report the result of your examination to the Ross women?"

"Yes."

"And what happened on the later visit?"

"I delivered Mittie Bell of a child."

"Where did this happen?"

"It was in the sitting room where Miss Maggie sleeps."

"Were you paid for your services?"

"Yes."

"Who paid you?"

"Miss Sallie."

"To your knowledge, was Mittie Bell married at that time?"

"No. The circumstances showed that Mittie Bell was single. I had never heard of her being married."

The murmur rose across the room. Here, at last, was the sensational evidence the paper had promised, damning even in the clerk's matter-of-fact monotone.

"When did this occur, Dr. Potts?"

"Mittie Bell was delivered of this child between the tenth of August, 1905, and the seventeenth of October, 1905, as my recollection is refreshed by examination of my records."

"And what was the reaction of the Ross women at the birth of this child?"

"Miss Sallie said that they were awfully sorry that it happened; that they had tried to raise Mittie Bell right, and for me not to say anything about it and they would pay me for it."

Judge Ray tapped his gavel and the angry buzz subsided almost as soon as it began, but the shuffling in the seats continued. The clerk droned on, reciting the scandalous words as if they were a grocery list.

"Was Miss Maggie present at the birth of this child?"

"My recollection is that Miss Maggie was in the house at the time the child was born, but was not actually in the room when the child was delivered."

"Was Miss Maggie present when Miss Sallie asked you not to say anything about the birth and they would pay you for it?"

"Yes, according to my recollection. Miss Maggie was generally present. She was in the house."

"Cross examination by the propounders," the clerk read.

"Dr. Potts, who paid your accounts against Miss Maggie Ross?"

"She did."

"So, as far as your business was concerned, you found her competent to look after her affairs?"

"Yes. I would tell her how much my bill was, and she would pay it."

"Did she show any signs of being 'off' in any way?"

"No."

"Mentally defective in any way?"

"No."

"How much mental capacity would you say she had in the year 1907?"

"I don't know. I saw nothing wrong with her mental capacity."

"Did you ever test her mental capacity?"

"No."

"Did you talk business affairs with her?"

"No. She would tell me her troubles in ordinary conversation."

"She could carry on an intelligent conversation?"

"Yes."

"She didn't talk like anyone off in her mind?"

"No, I saw no evidence of her being off in her mind."

"Dr. Potts, in your visits to the Ross home did you see any evidence of any influence exercised by Mittie Bell Houston over either Miss Maggie or Miss Sallie Ross?"

"No."

"Re-direct examination by caveators."

"Dr. Potts, would you describe your relationship with Maggie Ross as personal or professional?"

"Mostly, I looked after the health of the Ross women. Would drop in sometimes in passing. I and my wife would sometimes call to see them. I never had occasion to discuss anything with them except their health, their bills to me and the weather. Only ordinary conversation."

"Never discussed business with her?"

"Nothing except personal bills. I discussed such matters as come up in ordinary conversation."

"Could Miss Maggie read and write?"

"I don't know whether she could or not."

"Did you ever hear Miss Maggie discuss business matters?"

"No."

"What did you mean when you said you considered Miss Maggie competent?"

"I meant that I did not know what her mental capacity was. I considered her competent to discuss ordinary things."

"You said Mittie Bell had the bastard young one in the sitting room of Miss Maggie's dwelling house, is that correct?"

"Yes."

"Was that because of undue influence?"

"I can't say whether it was or not."

"In your conversations and visits and associations with Miss Maggie Ross, did you ever see her do anything or show anything to indicate that she was weak minded?"

"No. She did complain to me of being absent-minded during the last one or two years."

"Re-direct examination by the caveators."

"Can you tell us the mental condition of Miss Maggie Ross in the year 1907?"

"I haven't an opinion satisfactory to myself about that."

"Re-cross examination by the propounders."

"Why do you state that you have not an opinion satisfactory to yourself about the mental condition of Miss Maggie Ross?"

"The reason is that I didn't know but little about her."

23

BOARDERS

You could just look at her and tell that
she was mentally defective.
—DR. W. H. CROWELL, 1921

April 7–8, 1921

Dr. Samuel Howard Ezzell was the older half-brother of Rep. Earle Ezzell and, from a third marriage of their father, half-brother to Thomas Sanford Ezzell, who had married Ann Davis, a Ross cousin—the one, as Crane had pointed out, who lived nearby and never visited Miss Maggie. Dr. Ezzell, at forty-seven, had recently gone back into farming after doctoring for years. After Dennis died he stayed in the Rosses' home for a few weeks to get the farm records in order. He moved to Van Wyck, in Lancaster County, in 1901, married Brenda Thompson in 1906, and moved to Waxhaw to practice medicine.

"A time or two when I was working on the books, I asked Miss Mag about some little item when she would be in the room, but I never got any information from her," he recalled. "She was always complaining. She was always sick, but not sick enough to be confined to bed. She had a kind of sickly appearance. She was gloomy all the time. She was always in a pessimistic mood."

"Did you observe her after you lived in the house?"

"In 1896, her mental condition was kindly weak, and as she grew older it grew weaker. She was in bad health when I was living at Van Wyck, and I would call on her several times."

"Have you discussed this opinion of Miss Maggie with anyone?" the cross-examiner asked.

"No, unless I discussed it with my family."

"Did the fact that she willed her property to negroes affect or determine your opinion?"

"No."

Dr. W. H. Crowell, age fifty-four, lived with the Rosses around the time he married, before Dennis died. He was from Mecklenburg County, where he had graduated from Davidson College. He had studied at the University of Berlin, the University of Virginia, and the University of Maryland, with an internship at the Lying-In Hospital in New York for his specialty in obstetrics. He had come, he said, one hundred seventy-five miles from Whiteville, North Carolina—an exaggeration, whispered folks who knew it was more like one hundred thirty miles—to testify for the caveators.

"When I was there boarding, Miss Mag complained a great deal, but I don't think I ever prescribed for her," he told the lawyer. "She was thin and did not look like she was well or healthy. She would get kindly melancholy and would cry and twist her fingers when she had these gloomy spells. I considered her weak minded." The lawyer showed him the group picture. "That is a very good picture of Miss Mag."

"What was your experience in her ability to transact business?"

"I recall one time that I wanted some money changed, and I gave it to Miss Mag. She couldn't get it correct and called Miss Sallie to help her."

"What did you observe about her memory?"

"She could remember better things that happened year ago, better than she could in recent years."

Judge Ray banged his gavel. Cross-examination would have to wait for tomorrow.

The farmers knew that the steady buildup of clouds for three days, with the wind coming from the northeast, would eventually break the long spell of pleasant days. The sun had warmed Monroe into the mid-seventies ever since a light frost on Saturday. The clouds managed only a drizzle at their deepest on Friday, but they made it the darkest day inside the courtroom so far.

"I was at the University of Maryland three years," Dr. Crowell began when he resumed the witness stand Friday to answer Cansler's questions. "Then I went to the University of Virginia. I came back to Marvin and married in 1896. I spent four or five months courting and wasn't thinking much about Miss Mag and Miss Sallie." He flashed a smile.

"Did you ever sit down and have a conversation with them?"

"Sometimes. They were ignorant people and would talk about ghosts and things, and didn't talk much about their business."

"How did Miss Mag appear in those days?"

"She looked older than she really was."

"Did you see her do any foolish things?"

"No. But she believed in ghosts and talked about them."

"Have you ever seen a ghost?"

"No."

"Did you believe in ghosts as a boy?"

"No."

Cansler widened his eyes, deepened his voice, and fluttered his hands on each side of his face like a Halloween ghoul.

"Did the goose flesh not ever rise up when you would pass a graveyard at night?"

"No."

The lawyer showed him the group picture again. "Do you think this picture shows a want of sense?"

"No."

"Does it show that she was not educated?"

"No."

"Do you suppose she knew she was having the photo taken?"

"I suppose so."

"What makes you think Miss Mag was insane?"

"She could remember things that happened in her younger days better than she could in recent years, and that is an evidence of insanity, and a lot of older people are that way. It is evidence of senile decay."

"Did you ever know Miss Mag to make any trades?"

"No."

"Did you ever know her to throw away money on anyone?"

"No."

"Why do you think she did not know the value of money?"

"When I wanted my ten dollar bill changed, she could not do it."

"Do you think Miss Mag knew the value of five hundred dollars?"

"No. Her inability to make this change for me, and the fact that she was not sure about it, is evidence of her not knowing the value of money."

"Do you think your ability to judge her mental capacity is better than the ordinary observer's?"

"Yes. I know more now as a physician than I did then. You could just look at her and tell that she was mentally defective."

"So she was not attractive, but you took your bride in her home to board."

"Yes, but I did not think she was an attractive companion for my wife."

"What did you study in college, Dr. Crowell?"

"I studied the mind."

"Did you try to establish a hospital in Charlotte for the use of Twilight Sleep?"

"Yes, but it fell through."

"Do you think Miss Mag had enough sense to establish a hospital?"

"No."

24

ALIENISTS

If the evidence set forth in the hypothetical question are true, this would lead me to believe that Miss Mag Ross was feeble-minded, and that she had the mental condition of a normal child of seven or eight years perhaps.

—DR. J. K. HALL, 1921

April 8, 1921

The caveators hired three alienists, doctors specializing in mental and nervous conditions, to testify about Maggie's mind. They had never met her, but they qualified before the court as expert witnesses. Dr. J. K. Hall, forty-one years old, born in Iredell County, educated at Chapel Hill and Jefferson Medical College, once on staff at the State Hospital at Morganton, became president of the Westbrook Sanatorium in Richmond in 1911. By the time he testified, he had treated several thousand patients suffering with nervous and mental diseases. Dr. Albert Anderson, sixty-one years old, born in Wake County and educated in medicine at the University of Virginia, had been practicing since 1888. He went to Dix Hill in Raleigh in 1913 and was superintendent of the state mental hospital. Dr. Isaac Taylor, born in New Bern and educated at Princeton and Chapel Hill, worked at Broughton before he started Broad Oak Sanitorium, a private alternative to the state-run hospital, in Morganton in 1901. Each of the experts, on the witness stand for sworn testimony, was asked this hypothetical question fashioned from the evidence the caveators had collected:

> If the jury should find from the evidence that in the years 1907 and 1909 Miss Maggie Ross was an unmarried woman living with her unmarried sister, Miss Sallie Ross, who was eight years her senior, and who transacted her business and managed her affairs for her, in Union County in the little village of Marvin; that she was frail and delicate and in 1898 had the appearance shown in the photograph introduced in evidence by the caveators; that in 1907 she was about 68 years of age and in 1909 was about 70 years of age; that she was in poor health, having spells of sickness once a year or oftener, which caused her to be confined to her bed for weeks at a time; that she suffered from rheumatism and catarrh of the stomach and also from displacement of some internal organ which necessitated the wearing of a truss; that she suffered from chronic constipation for which she took laxative medicine every night; that some time prior thereto she had an attack of la grippe; that she was frequently unable to sleep at night; that she was nervous, melancholy, despondent and pessimistic with a tendency to look on the dark side of things; that she was subject to frequent crying spells and to spells when she would sit twirling her thumbs or fingers or pulling her chin and staring vacantly into space, oblivious of her surroundings, during which she would pay no attention even when spoken to; that she imagined that she was poor, when as a matter of fact she had thousands of dollars on deposit in the bank and several thousand dollars in gold and paper money in her house; that before her death in 1920, she imagined that she was unable to buy necessary medicine, although at the time she owned property worth around one hundred thousand dollars; that she imagined that she had to live off of the proceeds of her butter and eggs although she had the rents from about fourteen hundred acres of land; that in 1909, on the occasion of the death of her sister, she imagined that she saw angels and that she saw a white bird come for her sister; that she was absent minded; that her memory was poor; and that she had better recollection of the events which occurred in her childhood than those which occurred only a short while before; that she was unable to carry on a connected conversation or to repeat correctly a conversation which she had heard only a short while before;
>
> That she had never been a bright woman and had very little education; that she could scarcely read and was not known to have written any letters, drawn any checks or to have done any other sort of writing; that she was unable to make simple calculations; that on one occasion she was greatly upset because she believed that a bale of cotton had been stolen, asserting that she had seven bales the evening before, and that one was gone, whereas there were seven then at the time she believed there was only six; that on another occasion she was complaining because a merchant who had been paying her fifteen cents for butter had offered her eighteen cents for same, thinking that eighteen cents was less than

fifteen; that she was unable to settle with her servant if the servant had taken up a part of her wages so that the remainder due was not even money; that she was unable to calculate balances due on rent and would forget what the rental contract was from Spring to Fall; that on one occasion she swapped cows and was to pay eighteen dollars to boot, and upon giving a twenty dollar bill, could not tell how much change she ought to get back; that she did not transact business but allowed her sister to transact same; that after the death of that sister she had her business transacted by R. A. Hudson;

That she lived on terms of social equality with a negro girl, allowing the negro girl to eat at the same table with her and to sleep in the same bed; that she went with the negro father of the negro girl to Salisbury to visit her while she was a student in the negro school at that place; that after the negro girl had become pregnant with an illegitimate child and she had been told this fact by a physician, she allowed the negro girl to continue to live in her house and to give birth to the child in her own bedroom; that she allowed the negro woman to pull her nose and ears, to wear her clothes, underclothing and shoes and take other liberties; that she would nurse the children of the negro woman and would allow the negro woman to order her to clean her negro baby;

That in the year 1907 she signed a paper writing purporting to will a large estate consisting of her half interest in about fourteen hundred acres and a large amount of personal property, including a large amount of money in banks; that in this paper writing she left nothing to a cousin who lived nearby and who was poor and needy and who had rendered valuable service to her, and for whom she had expressed affection, and ignored also her white friends and neighbors who had helped her and whom she had described as the kindest neighbors in the world, and ignored also the white tenants on her lands and left the larger part of her property to the negro woman and her father, although she had said that she intended to leave her property to those who had made it, whereas the negro woman and her father had not made the property but had lived on the land rent free and had been partly supported by her; that at the time the paper was alleged to be executed, Miss Mag Ross was crying aloud and did not say anything with regard to the paper, have you an opinion satisfactory to yourself as to the mental condition of Miss Maggie Ross on November 20th, 1907, when the alleged will was alleged to have been executed and on September 9th, 1909, when the alleged codicil is alleged to have been executed?

"Have you come to a conclusion, Dr. Hall?" the caveators' lawyer asked.

"I have. My opinion is that she was feeble-minded all her life, and that in the later years of her life, she had mental decay. If the jury find as true the facts stated in the hypothetical question, in my opinion she did not have sufficient mental capacity to make a will and codicil."

"Describe mental decay and feeble-mindedness to the jury and describe their symptoms."

The propounders objected. Judge Ray sustained the objection, and the jury was sent away for the testimony.

"Feeble-mindedness is that state in an adult where he has the mind of a child. If the evidence set forth in the hypothetical question are true, this would lead me to believe that Miss Mag Ross was feeble-minded, and that she had the mental condition of a normal child of seven or eight years perhaps. One of the characteristics of old age is the decay of the physical body, but that's nature and unavoidable. The tendency is for the minds of feeble-minded people to begin to break earlier than the mind of a sane-minded person."

The jury came back.

"Please state what facts stated in the hypothetical question in your opinion show that Miss Maggie Ross was feeble-minded or suffering from mental decay."

Judge Ray sustained the propounders' objection. The caveators said they wanted Dr. Hall to show how he had formed his opinion.

"He has already testified that Miss Maggie did not have sufficient mind to make a will," the judge answered. "I do not propose to let the doctor make a speech."

"Why did you come here as a witness, Dr. Hall?" Cansler asked on cross-examination.

"Mr. Stack wrote to me and asked me if I would come and testify. I had some of the information in this hypothetical question before I came here. Mr. Stack just wrote me a very brief statement as to this case. I did not have sufficient information when I came to form a belief as to her mental condition. I wrote Mr. Stack that in my opinion, if she was weak-minded to a sufficient degree, that I could testify as to why she would make such a disposition of her property."

"Do you know what the laws of North Carolina require of a man who makes a will?"

"I have an opinion. I know of people who can comply with the provisions of the law. I have testified in several trials as to the question of people's minds. I testified in the Foster Parsons case at Rockingham and in several other murder cases."

"Is crime necessarily the result of the want of mental capacity?"

"No."

The next day's *Charlotte Observer* reported: "The witness and Attorney Cansler on cross-examination had an interested and deep discussion on the difference between inferior mentality and moral depravity." The topic then turned to superstition.

"Is there great significance attached to the fact that Miss Mag believed in ghosts?"

"Yes. I know a man who thinks he can talk to his son who was killed in France. He is mentally wrong."

"Do you attach any importance to the picture in forming an opinion as to her mental condition?"

"No."

"Is it possible for a physician to treat her twenty years and find out nothing about her mental capacity."

Dr. Hall hesitated before he answered "Yes," and Cansler was finished.

"Did you know Mr. Cansler got Gov. Bickett to do for Ed Alexander what you tried to get the jury to do in the first place?" Stack asked the witness on re-direct examination.

"Yes. I have heard Mr. Cansler used my evidence for commutation."

Everyone in the courtroom knew that sensational story from six months before. Ed Alexander, the son of a famous Iredell County family, had killed Jim Rayle. His family asked Cansler to represent him, but he refused because he thought Alexander was guilty. Dr. Hall testified that he was absolutely sure Alexander was insane, but a jury convicted him of murder, he was sentenced to death, and the state Supreme Court had upheld the sentence although four justices agreed that he was insane. Cansler read the record and decided the young man was not responsible for the crime. On a Sunday afternoon in October, he and his friend Heriot Clarkson—at their own initiative and for no fee—drove to Lumberton to ask Governor Bickett for mercy. "The state would commit a crime to execute this man," Cansler said, and the governor commuted the sentence.

At the same time, Governor Bickett commuted the death sentence of another Iredell County man, a black man named Ralph Connor. Connor's brother, in a fight with a deputy sheriff, was shot and lying helpless on the ground when Connor rushed up, enraged, and shot the deputy twice. Only two black ministers in Raleigh asked the governor for mercy for Connor, and his lawyer gave up seeking support.

"On the question of premeditation I am convinced that, under the circumstances of this case, Connor was less capable of deliberation and premeditation than was Alexander," Governor Bickett wrote. "Back of Alexander stretches centuries of civilization, during which his ancestors had been taught self-control. A little back of Connor lies the jungle and centuries of savagery, during which the ancestors of Connor were taught to slay any man who would dare to take them prisoners, and the man who killed the most was the leader of the tribe. Shall the negro be held to a higher measure of responsibility than the white man? Not while I am Governor of North Carolina. I believe with all my soul in white supremacy, but it must be white in soul as well as in skin, and at the State's mercy-seat there is no color line."

Stack continued his redirect. "What might feeble-mindedness have to do with being influenced?"

"In my opinion, a woman who is feeble-minded and who is suffering from senile decay would be much easier influenced than a woman under different circumstances," Dr. Hall said.

Dr. Anderson, the caveators' next witness, agreed.

"If the jury finds as a fact the evidence set forth in the hypothetical question, my opinion is that Miss Mag Ross did not have sufficient mind to make a will in 1907 or a codicil thereto in 1909," he said.

"Have you read the will?"

"Yes."

"If the evidence set forth in this hypothetical question is true, would Miss Mag have been easily influenced by Miss Sallie?"

"Yes."

"Do you know how much mental capacity it takes to make a will?" Cansler asked on cross-examination.

"Yes. I began studying about what it takes to make a will the day Mr. Stack first wrote me in regard to this case, which was sometime in February, I think. The letter Mr. Stack wrote me did not contain all the facts set forth in the hypothetical question."

"What did he say?"

"He told me that she had a bad memory."

"Is that alone evidence of insanity?"

"No. However, it is some evidence of insanity. He also wrote me that she could not carry on a connected conversation."

There it was again: "She could not carry on a connected conversation." The same sentence from a third witness.

"Would that be a symptom of insanity?"

"Not unless I knew how disconnected it was."

"What symptoms convince you that she was insane?"

"The fact that Miss Mag said she had no money when she had plenty is evidence of insanity. The fact that she said she saw angels and a white bird coming after her sister is an important symptom."

"What about Elijah?" Cansler demanded, flipping open a black leather-bound Bible. "Didn't he see angels sent to protect him? Does that mean he was crazy?"

"Yes, I know about Elijah," the doctor replied coolly. "God inspired him, but not Miss Mag. She is not in the same class."

The caveators recalled Dr. S. H. Ezzell to tell more about Miss Maggie's superstition.

"I helped dress Dennis at his death," he recalled. "We needed some underclothing for him, and Miss Sallie directed us where to find it. And Miss Mag said 'Get good warm underclothing and put on him, for you know he was powerful cold natured.' She always called him *Dee*nis."

"Was Miss Sallie present at this event?" the propounders wondered.

"Yes."

"Did she object to Dennis' warm underclothing?"

"No."

"What do you think about Miss Sallie's mental capacity?"

"She had good, hard sense."

"Is that when you decided that Miss Mag was insane?"

"I don't know, but it struck me as absurd."

"Why?"

"Because Dennis's character was not good in the community. I thought he was going to hell, and if Miss Mag had said 'put on thin underclothing,' I would not have thought anything about it."

"What do you mean, 'his character was not good in the community'?"

"It was rumored in the community that he would steal his sisters' money. He was tried when a boy for murdering a negro baby."

"Was he convicted?"

"No. He was acquitted."

Cansler changed the subject. "Is it true that you tried to get Dr. Potts to testify that Maggie did not have mental capacity to make a will?"

After a long pause, Dr. Ezzell admitted: "Yes. A few days after this litigation came up, I saw Dr. Potts and talked to him about breaking this will."

"Why? Was it because she left Dr. Nisbet a thousand dollars and nothing to you or to him?"

"No!"

"What is your interest in this case?"

The doctor leaned toward the lawyer in earnest. "None. I have no interest in this case, I swear!"

He told the caveators' lawyer on redirect examination that he had happened by Dr. Potts' house off the Charlotte and Columbia highway one day when he was taking two patients to Charlotte.

Dr. Anderson returned to the stand to continue his cross-examination as the afternoon shadows lengthened.

"What about Sir Oliver Lodge?" Cansler suggested. "He says he can communicate with the dead."

"Sir Oliver Lodge is mistaken when he says he can communicate with the dead."

"What about people who believe in ghosts? Are they insane?"

"Belief in ghosts is not a symptom of insanity."

"Then what makes you conclude that Miss Maggie was insane?"

"Mr. Stack wrote me about the negro being born in Miss Mag's room. Moral depravity alone is not sufficient to break a will, but it is evidence of insanity in Miss Mag."

"Would a white man who lives in the state of adultery with a negro woman be crazy?"

"No. But white women letting a negro girl have a baby in their house after they know about it is strong proof of an abnormal condition of their mind. It is worse than a white man living in adultery with a negro woman."

25

DOCTORS, NEIGHBOR, AND KIN

They lived with negroes and I considered myself above them.

—AMANDA HOWARD, 1921

April 9, 1921

The wind changed for the first time in the trial, blowing from the southwest and pushing the temperature to eighty-five degrees on Saturday. The bright heat baked the courtroom where the final alienist, Dr. Taylor, took the stand and answered the same hypothetical question. The caveators had decided not to call a fourth alienist, Dr. Davidson of Charlotte, as they once had planned.

"Do you have an opinion as to her mental condition?" Parker asked Dr. Taylor.

"Yes. If the jury should find these facts to be true, I would say she was feeble-minded and would not have sufficient mental capacity to make a will and would have been easily influenced by her sister."

J. C. M. Vann conducted the cross-examination.

"Do you think you know more than the ordinary man about the mind?"

"Yes."

"Do you think it is a general rule that crazy folks cannot make a will?"

"Yes."

"When did you make up your mind or opinion as to Miss Mag's mind?"

"Not until after I came here. I formed my opinion after I talked to Captain Clark."

A local doctor, H. D. Stewart of Monroe, qualified as an expert to answer the same question. Dr. Stewart, who studied medicine at the University of Maryland and started practicing medicine in 1900, had been an army captain in the recent war and had cared for people with mental and nervous disorders.

"I think I have had sufficient experience to diagnose a case of senile dementia, if I had sufficient history of the case," he said. "If all these things are true, then my opinion is that she would be deficient mentally. She would not have sufficient mental capacity to know her property without instructions or the effect of the disposition of her property, etc."

"Did you know the late H. B. Adams," Cansler asked.

"Yes."

Cansler composed his own hypothetical questions:

If the jury finds as a fact that Miss Maggie and Miss Sallie Ross sent for Mr. Adams to go up to their home and that he went in company with Mr. R. B. Redwine; and that after they got there, Miss Sallie Ross informed Mr. Adams and Mr. Redwine that they had sent for Mr. Adams to draw their wills and that Miss Sallie stated to Mr. Redwine that in view of the fact that his uncle taught them, she wanted Mr. Redwine to be her executor, and that Miss Maggie then said she wanted Mr. R. A. Hudson to be her executor, and that then Mr. Adams sat down at the table in the sitting room in company with Miss Maggie and Miss Sallie and Mr. Redwine, and Miss Sallie Ross, in the presence of these parties, stated to Mr. Adams how they wanted their property disposed of and that he took notes of the statement that Miss Sallie Ross made to him in the presence of Miss Maggie Ross, and that thereafter he drew the wills of each of them and sent them to them, stating in a letter that if there was anything in the wills contrary to the way they wished them to be, to let him know and he would make the correction, sending at the same time duplicate wills, asking them to please sign and return the copies to him; that the wills were executed in duplicate in the presence of three witnesses, and that two of these witnesses have come into court and testified that in their opinion Miss Mag Ross knew the nature and character of her property, who were the natural objects of her bounty, and how she was disposing of the same, and that after the wills were so executed, the duplicates were returned to Mr. Adams and were found in his safe after his death, would your opinion be that Miss Mag had sufficient mental capacity to make this will?

"Yes."

"Assuming the jury find as true that Miss Sallie died on July 1909, and that after her death Miss Maggie Ross came to Monroe, in company with Mr. R. A. Hudson, and went to the office of Mr. Adams, who prepared this codicil to her original will, and that after the codicil was prepared by Mr. Adams, Mr. Sutton and Mr. Ezzell were called in, and at the request of Mr. Adams and in the presence of Miss Maggie Ross, witnessed the execution of that codicil, would your opinion be that she had sufficient mental capacity to make the codicil?"

"Yes—that is, if I confine myself to the facts stated in this question and ignore the facts stated in the hypothetical question of the caveators."

So it was with the war of words. From one life emerged one set of facts, none of them seriously in dispute. The propounders did not deny that Mittie had her baby in Maggie's bed; the caveators did not deny her name on the will and the codicil. But the stories composed from those facts, their narration and their meaning, could not be further apart. Twelve white men would have to decide which to accept.

The caveators came back with another question.

If the jury find as a fact that Miss Sallie and Miss Maggie Ross were two maiden ladies living in the little village of Marvin, and that Miss Sallie was eight years older than Miss Maggie, and that when Mr. Adams and Mr. Redwine went up there to see them, that Miss Sallie did most of the talking, and that Mr. Adams, after he had drawn their wills, sent them to Miss Maggie and Miss Sallie, and that Miss Sallie sent for these gentlemen to act as witnesses, and that when these witnesses arrived, Miss Sallie brought in the wills, and that she was crying some and that Miss Maggie was crying out loud, and that Miss Sallie asked the witnesses to sign as witnesses, and that Miss Maggie didn't say anything until the witnesses went to leave, considering these facts, as well as the facts set forth in the hypothetical question, to be true, what would your opinion be?

"She did not have sufficient mental capacity to make a will."

Amanda Winchester Howard of Waxhaw, widow of Robert Fulton Howard, took the stand for the caveators. She said Maggie didn't have enough sense to make a will, but the cross-examiner brought to light that their only contact had been brief conversations at church. He introduced in evidence the two deeds by which the Howards had sold their land to Susan Ross.

"How could you tell Miss Maggie did not have right good sense? By looking at her?"

"No."

"Why did you not associate with the Rosses?"

"They lived with negroes and I considered myself above them."

Claud P. Edwards of Charlotte, whose wife Sue Gribble Edwards was a caveator, said he didn't think Maggie could make a will. Sue did not make the trip from Charlotte.

"When we would go down to see Miss Mag she would always come to the gate to meet us and take us to the house and she would appear to be very glad to see us," Edwards said. "And she would always have to kiss everybody as they came in and kiss them when we left, and we usually left her crying when we went away, and insisting on our coming back. I first began to visit the Rosses in 1904. My wife and I would drive down through the country and spend the day. Miss Sallie treated us very cordially and seemed to think as much of us as Miss Maggie did. Mrs. Gribble usually accompanied us. It was a nice drive down there, and we would get there about one o'clock and stay until five or six. I don't think I took more than two meals in their home before Miss Sallie's death. They fed us very well. After 1915, my wife and I got to going down there more frequently because we had an automobile to go in, which was a better way to go. When we would go, we did not notify Miss Mag of our coming, and as a rule Aunt Harriet was not there and we knew that Miss Mag was too weak to cook so we took our lunch with us."

"Did you approve of her keeping negroes in the house?"

"No."

"Did you have any conversations with her about business?"

"We did not talk about business when we were there."

"What did you talk about?"

"I remember talking to her about the war one time. She asked me something about the war, and after the war had been over six months, she asked me how the war was getting along."

"How would you describe her condition?"

"She appeared to be lonely. After 1915, we would go down sometimes every two weeks and sometimes we would wait longer than that. She gave me the picture of Robert Gribble after his death and had me to give it to his family. She talked intelligently about it—there was nothing unusual or unnatural about it. She would weep when we would start to leave, and I thought that was a little unnatural. She would insist on us coming back and would say that we had a way to come and she did not."

"Do you still say she did not have ordinary sense?"

"Yes."

"What experience did you have that led you to believe she did not have ordinary sense," the caveators' attorney asked.

"On one occasion when I was going to Charlotte with her to take the picture, my wife's brother asked Miss Mag how much land she had and she said 'Lord, I don't know.'"

"Do you know how much money you have?" Cansler asked.

"Yes, I know exactly how much money I have in the bank. I have one thousand thirty dollars in the bank."

"Can you tell me how much you have in your pocket?"

"No."

It was one o'clock in the afternoon. Judge Ray adjourned court until 9:30 A.M. Monday and sent the jurors home to be with their families for the weekend. Rev. Bobby McIlwaine was scheduled to preach at Altan Presbyterian at 11 A.M. Sunday and at Bethany Presbyterian at 3 P.M.

26

NEWS

The evidence has been sensational at times,
tending to show deplorable conditions in the
Ross home where the negroes were admitted to
absolute social equality.

—THE *CHARLOTTE OBSERVER*, 1921

April 9–10, 1921

On the front page of that afternoon's *Charlotte News*, the jurors saw a courtroom story more sensational than any testimony they had heard all week, a hastily filed report of the shocking verdict in Georgia that morning:

WILLIAMS FOUND GUILTY AND WILL BE IMPRISONED
Georgia Farmer Convicted of Death of Negroes on
His Farm While in Condition of Peonage.

Covington, Ga., April 9—John W. Williams, accused of the murder of eleven of his negro farm hands to halt a federal investigation of peonage, was found guilty of murder by a jury in Newton county superior court here today and sentenced to life imprisonment.

Judge John R. Hutcheson had the defendant stand up and after reading to him the verdict added "And the verdict of the jury is the sentence of the court."

The defendant, who had been cheerful before the jury came in, received the verdict outwardly calm, but when his wife and daughters began to sob almost audibly he seemed to be making a desperate effort to hide emotion.

Motion for a new trial was immediately filed and hearing on the motion set for April 30 at Decatur, Ga., before Judge John B. Hutcheson who presided at the trial.

The verdict of murder with recommendation for mercy, which under Georgia law automatically carries a life sentence, was read exactly 18 hours after the case went to the jury, and was calmly received by Williams. A moment later, as his wife and children began to sob almost inaudibly he seemed to be struggling to restrain his own emotions. Just after court adjournment the man's two daughters became hysterical and were led from the room by friends.

Williams appeared more affected by his family's suffering than he had been by the verdict. He was on trial charged specifically with the murder of one of the negroes found drowned in Newton county. Clyde Manning, negro farm boss for Williams and jointly indicted with him, testified that on Williams' order he and another negro, afterwards killed, had done the killings.

Williams had maintained a cheerful attitude during the trial and had stoutly maintained his innocence, although having admitted he might be temporarily guilty of peonage, as he said he had paid fines for negroes and let them work out the debt.

Sentence was formally passed within a few moments after the verdict was announced. Judge Hutcheson restated the verdict as read by T. R. Starr, a farmer and foreman of the jury, and added: "And the verdict is the sentence of the court."

The verdict was not in exact form, but in open court both sides agreed that it was legal by supreme court decisions and that no exception would be taken.

The motion for a new trial was made on the grounds that the verdict was "contrary to the evidence, contrary to the law and without evidence to support it."

The jury was composed of seven farmers, the others being merchants, clerks and a barber. Most of the jurors were young men, six of them serving on a jury for the first time.

The case went to trial last Tuesday, one day being taken up with arguments for postponement and selection of a jury. The state took little more than a day to present its evidence, while the defense relied mostly on the unsworn statement of Williams.

Never had any of them heard of a southern jury convicting a white man of murdering a black man. They spared him the death penalty but put a leading planter in prison for life.

It was, as newspapers had reported since about the time the Ross trial began, an unheard-of crime. On April 1, the *Journal* reported on page two that two more bodies had been recovered from the Alcovy River near Monticello, Georgia, bringing to eleven the total connected to the federal investigation of peonage. Williams was suspected of holding indebted workers against their will, then killing them to keep investigators from gathering more information. The story ran under the headline

PLANTER KILLED ELEVEN MEN TO CONCEAL CRIME
Mutilated Corpses of Eleven Negroes
Removed from Shallow Graves
and the Alcovy River
STRUCK TO OVER HEAD WITH AXE

Monticello, Ga., March 27—Inquests were held today over three bodies found buried on the Williams' plantation; two found on the Campbell plantation, also operated by Williams and three taken form the Alcovy river. Three other bodies were taken from the Yellow river two weeks ago.

The bodies found today were chained together and weighted down with sacks of stone and iron attached to the head and feet.

A coroner's jury investigating the deaths of five negroes whose bodies were found buried and the two found in the river, fixed the responsibility in each case. In two instances at least, the jury found that negroes were forced to dig their own graves.

The bodies were disinterred, placed in coffins and buried late today in the Jasper county pauper's cemetery, the county paying the expense.

The coroner's jury conducted the inquest by numbers. The first inquest was over John Williams, same name as the plantation owner, whose grave was dug by himself. The jury was informed that the negro was sent to a pasture in a ravine not far from a creek to dig a post hole. After digging that hole Manning's confession shows that he struck Williams over the head with an axe, pushed the body into the hole and covered it up.

Johnny Green was number two. He was sent to the same pasture to bring cows back to the stable. Manning says that he killed Green in the same way, but had to dig the grave.

Willie Givens was referred to as number three. He was killed on his way to a country store, in the same ravine, but Charles Chisholm was named as the negro who killed Givens.

The jury traveled four miles across the country to the Campbell plantation, also operated by Williams. Fletcher Smith, body number four, was found there. Smith was sent to dig a well and when he had dug deep enough to receive his body Manning's confession, as repeated to the jury, showed that he killed him with an axe and then covered up the hole.

The coroner's jury decided that Clyde Manning killed John Williams and Johnny Green, with plantation owner John S. Williams implicated;

Manning was responsible for Fletcher Smith and "Big John"; Charley Chisholm killed Willie Givens; Manning, Chisholm, and Williams were responsible for the deaths of "Little Bit" and John Brown; and "Charley Chisholm met his death at the hands of Clyde Manning and John S. Williams." During his three-hour testimony at the trial, Manning said he participated in the killings because Williams told him "It's their neck or yours."

Sunday morning's *Charlotte Observer* provided a more developed front-page story. Williams, who had been taken to jail in Atlanta, was convicted of killing one of the eleven, Lindsey Peterson, the first in an expected series of trials. Peterson was bound to Willie Preston with a trace chain around their necks, with a sack holding a hundred pounds of rocks, and thrown into the river.

"They were stubborn and a-beggin'," Manning testified, "and me an' Charlie rolled 'em over the banister of the bridge." Planter Sullivan had driven Peterson, Preston, Manning, Charlie Chisholm, and Harry Price to the bridge. When Price, bearing weights, saw his fate, he told Manning "Don't throw me over, I'll get over," then cried "Lord have mercy" and flung himself into the water. Williams had been indicted for murder in connection with all three deaths, although his defense claimed the deaths of Peterson and Preston were one event.

In the same column, the *Observer* carried another report, from Monticello, Ga., announcing that prosecutors would seek indictments against Williams, three of his sons, and Manning on charges of murdering a total of fourteen black people, and indictments of six or seven other people on charges of lynching a black man named Eugene Hamilton.

"The law-abiding citizens will show to the world they believe in law enforcement," Solicitor General Doyle Campbell said. "A number of citizens are involved and we have evidence sufficient to indict six or seven. We have the lynchers on the run and will clean up the county."

Next to the reports from Georgia, the *Observer* ran its Monroe correspondent's summary of the trial over Maggie's will:

"When superior court adjourned here this afternoon the Ross will case had consumed nine days, with no prospect of the end in sight. The caveators still have a number of witnesses to put up, and the propounders in rebuttal will offer several dozen witnesses." After summarizing the history of the case, he continued:

> Over 100 witnesses had been subpoenaed, including many who had moved away from the Marvin community to other states. After proving execution of the will by the three witnesses who signed it at the time Miss Maggie Ross did, the propounders sought to show that the will was valid by putting up a number of witnesses who testified to the mental capacity of both Sallie and Maggie Ross. Several of these witnesses, including the pastor of the church to which Maggie belonged, declared that she was not only mentally competent to make a will but was a shrewd business woman. Others testified that while most of her affairs were managed by R. A. Hudson as agent, she frequently transacted matters of business in an intelligent manner and sometimes discussed such questions as selling cotton, farm work, etc., with her neighbors.
>
> The caveators are seeking to show by many witnesses that Miss Maggie Ross was mentally and physically weak; that she transacted no business, Miss Sallie Ross doing all of this prior to her death and R. A. Hudson since that time; that she was moody, suffering frequent spells of melancholia and abstraction; that she was dominated by her sister and intimidated by the negro woman, Mittie Bell Houston; that at the time the will was signed she was crying loudly and never did specifically assent to it, and that therefore the will of Maggie Ross should be set aside and the estate which it seeks to devise should revert to the heirs-at-law, the same being the caveators and others of like relationship.
>
> The evidence has been sensational at times, tending to show deplorable conditions in the Ross home where the negroes were admitted to absolute social equality. The propounders are seeking to show that this was the full consent of Maggie Ross who had a natural affection for the negroes and for this reason allowed them the privileges they took and bequeathed the property to them, while the caveators contend that it was against Maggie's will but that she did not have mental force or will power sufficient to combat the conditions. The hypothetical question propounded to the expert witnesses embodies the principal contentions of the caveators which they have introduced evidence to prove but which are denied in toto by the propounders.
>
> Added interest attaches to the case because of the array of legal counsel involved. . . . Many points of law have been threshed out in lengthy debate by counsel, and almost every will case ever before the state Supreme Court has been referred to as authority for the points advocated. Frequent comment is heard upon the brilliance and careful attitude of Judge Bis Ray, who is presiding over the court.

27

CAVEATORS REST

I thought I was better than the Rosses, because they would eat and sleep with negroes. I never associated with negroes. They would not be here if everybody thought like I do about 'em.

—J. W. BAKER, 1921

April 11, 1921

John J. Parker showed up for court on Monday amid a buzz that he was in line for a federal court appointment. Judge Jeter C. Pritchard died in Asheville on Sunday, and everyone expected another North Carolinian to get his seat on the Fourth District Circuit of Appeals. With a Republican in the White House, the appointment would make a fitting consolation for the valiant gubernatorial candidate, and even Democrats in his home state could support the move. The gossip around the courthouse and the Law Building across the street shifted, for the moment, from the sensational trial under way (and the threat of frost from a fast-moving cold front) to the sensational lawyer on the cousins' side.

"Mr. Parker, it was pointed out, is a young man, and if named, would have long years of service before him," the *Journal* observed. "He is also a man of wide experience and a lawyer of no mean ability and should wear the ermine of the judicial office with dignity and honor, his friends say. Democrats and Republicans alike in Charlotte will be united to bring pressure to bear on the White House to have the Union County man named. Although no definite plans have been formulated as yet, it was insinuated that steps will be taken shortly to have Mr. Parker's name presented to the President for recommendation to the judgeship."

Inside the courtroom, Parker's witness J. W. Baker was first on the stand that morning. "I have known Miss Mag Ross about twenty-three years," he said. "I lived in a half a mile of her and saw her frequently and visited in her home several times."

"Can you tell us about the most recent occasion when you were with her?"

"I was present when one of her mules got hurt. I was going by there and the mule got hurt in the stable. I stopped and had a conversation with her, and she said that anything like that affected her mind, and she hadn't had her right mind in years and years."

"Did you see her much when Miss Sallie was alive?"

"I used to go there and play the violin."

"What did you observe about Miss Maggie on those occasions?"

"I lived in a half a mile of them, but every time I would go back, Miss Sallie would have to tell Miss Mag who I was, as she would not know me."

"What day did the mule get hung," Cansler asked when he took the witness.

"I don't know, but it was a week or two before she died."

"How did she appear at the time?"

"She was feeble."

"How did you happen to converse with her?"

"I was just going along the road with another fellow, Boyce Bartlett."

"Why was Miss Maggie outdoors?"

"She knew the mule had been hung, and she came out to the barn to see about it."

"What did she say?"

"She said she heard it knocking and that anything like that unnerved her and affected her mind, and that she had not had her right mind for years and years."

"Did she know who you were?"

"No."

"Had you been there recently?"

"No, I hadn't been there in a long time."

"How did she address you?"

"She just said 'Howdy do.'"

"Do you think everyone who has seen you and doesn't remember you is weak-minded?"

"No."

"Why did you think that of the Rosses?"

"I thought I was better than the Rosses."

"Why?"

"Because they would eat and sleep with negroes."

"So you never associated with negroes?"

"No. They would not be here if everybody thought like I do about 'em."

J. S. DeLaney testified that the women had given him fifty cents apiece when he stopped by to raise some money for missions. Miss Sallie went and got the money.

"How often did you go there for missionary money?" Cansler asked.

"Twice."

"Do you know what church they belonged to when you were there?"

"I don't think they belonged to any church at that time."

"Who gave you the missionary money?"

"Miss Sallie gave me fifty cents for herself and fifty cents for Miss Mag."

"Did you see them another time after that?"

"Yes, before I was married. I was on my way to church and came by there after sundown one night. As I came by there, one of them, I don't remember which, was out at the gate. I spoke and she spoke and they asked me to 'light.' I told them I was going to church. I stopped and they said for me to hold on, that they would bring me something, and she brought me a waiter of tea cakes and a glass of wine. I do not know which of the girls it was."

Cansler turned the conversation to DeLaney's son, E. S. DeLaney, a lawyer who lived in Charlotte.

"Do you know that he has been up in that part of the country ever since they started to contest the will, going from house to house trying to get witnesses to testify that Miss Mag didn't have sense enough to make a will?"

"No, I don't know that."

"Have you seen him up there in that section?"

"Yes, but he never talked to me about the will. I asked him nothing about this."

"Do you how much sense it takes to make a will?"

"No. I have no idea."

That was the last of the caveators' witnesses. They announced they would rest, but they reserved the right to introduce a few character witnesses.

The clerk read aloud Jonathan Burleyson's will, the deed of Jonathan Burleyson to Dennis Clay Ross, the deed of S. H. Walkup as executor to John Burleyson and Dennis Clay Ross, the deeds between Dennis and his grandmother Sarah Burleyson, and the deed of Maggie's sale to Doc and Tirzah Coan.

28

PROPOUNDERS REPLY

Gentlemen of the jury, this evidence is admitted solely on the issue of mental capacity and is not to be taken or considered by you upon the issue of undue influence, and is not to be taken or considered by you directly or indirectly as proof of the facts the statement of the conversation contains, but solely as evidence bearing upon the question of the mental capacity of Miss Maggie Ross to make the will offered for probate.

—JUDGE J. BIS RAY, 1921

April 11–12, 1921

To many in the courtroom, the caveators had done their job. The birth and burial of the bastard black baby was established. Equally established for many—why should the jury think differently?—was that event's proof of moral degeneracy, hence mental decay, hence Maggie's incompetence to make a will. How could Cansler and company defend the indefensible? Their own witnesses, so far from challenging the description of social equality in that house, seemed to substantiate the facts while pressing for a different conclusion. But on what grounds could anyone conclude that a southern woman who behaved that way was anything but crazy?

The propounders, seeking to undo the refrain that Maggie couldn't carry on a "connected conversation," started with the deposition of Mrs. C. C. McIlwaine, a neighbor lady beyond reproach who knew Maggie about thirty years and went to church with her. "I think Miss Mag was intelligent enough," she said. "In the course of our acquaintance we just talked of general things. She talked sometime about business affairs."

"Did you have many conversations with Miss Maggie about business affairs," the cross-examiner asked.

"No."

"Can you recall any particular conversations about a particular business matter?"

"Yes, but it is a family affair and I would prefer not to discuss it."

The lawyer changed the subject.

"Did Mr. Dees ever visit them?"

"No. I stated on direct examination that I never knew of Mr. Dees visiting them and waiting on them in their sickness."

"Did you ever know of Bob Ross visiting them and waiting on them in their sickness?"

"No. I saw him come to the door and ask her how she was."

"What about Rosa Howie?"

"No."

"Florence Tucker Houston?"

"No."

"Alice Ross?"

"No."

"Tom Houston?"

"No."

His counter to Frank Crane's recital finished, the lawyer continued: "Do you know why she should have cut out her kin people and left her property to negroes?"

"No."

Mrs. McIlwaine's twenty-three-year-old granddaughter, Mary Howie, took the stand after the deposition to recall her childhood relations with Miss Maggie.

"I never had many conversations with her," she said.

"Did you talk with her enough and see her enough to form an opinion satisfactory to yourself as to the condition of her mind?"

"Yes. I think she was of sound mind at the time I knew her."

"Did you ever spend the day or night at the home of Miss Maggie Ross?" the cross-examiner asked.

"No."

"Did she visit you at your house?"

"No, but she did visit my grandmother."

"How often?"

"Something like three or four afternoons, and once she spent the day. She spent several hours in the afternoons. On these occasions, I was present only a small part of the time."

"As a matter of fact, you know very little about the mental condition of Miss Maggie Ross, isn't that right?" Parker pressed.

"Yes."

"Then what do you mean when you state that you think she was probably of sound mind?"

"I simply mean that I never saw her do anything startling or extraordinary."

Bill Pierce, who had been caught in the barber shop a week earlier, said that he had seen Maggie eight or ten times in his childhood when he lived four miles from them. "I went up there on one occasion with my father to buy some pigs. Miss Sallie and Miss Maggie were both present, and they 'hemmed and hawed' about the price, and so my father left and didn't buy any pigs. I was just a boy at this time."

W. A. Rogers told about taking Maggie to a dance in 1882, when she was twice his age. From his experience as a contractor working for them after Dennis died, he thought she was all right mentally.

T. W. Taylor, sixty-six years old, remembered a conversation at the Coans' house with Maggie after he had come back from three years out West. "We sat there awhile and she came out on the porch and sat and talked a good while and asked me all about my boys and asked all about how they were getting along. Just sat and talked like two people would.

Asked me about my brother. She called my brothers by name. They had left and gone west about eighteen years before that. One of them had lived with her on her plantation. She asked me about my son Walter. She asked me about Grace, my son's wife, and asked me how many children she had. She called Grace by name. She asked me about Jim, my other son, and where he lived. She asked me why it was my wife didn't like to stay out west, and I told her it was because she didn't like the water out there."

The tenants J. E. Crane, Ambrose Yarbrough, Ed Yarbrough, and Henry Stephenson testified next for Miss Maggie. J. E. Crane told about getting a bale knocked off the rent, about selling fifty-five bushels of corn to Maggie for cash at a dollar a bushel, about buying a wagon for her in Fort Mill, about her building a new house for him when he got married. Ambrose Yarbrough told about his new house: "There was a tree there and Miss Mag said not to build too close to it, she didn't want it cut and it would make a good shade for the porch."

"Did you ever see Mittie Bell or Bob up there working," the cross-examiner asked.

"No. I have seen Mittie pass my house going up that way. Miss Mag would go up to Bob Ross's and spend the day."

Ed Yarbrough, fifty years old, told about paying rent, including Maggie's making change for the difference in what was owed, and about building houses for her. "I bought a lot of stuff for her and sold a right smart for her," he said. "I would bring back a bill and we would settle up. I told her I wanted to buy the Watson place and she told me she couldn't sell any land, that her business was fixed up and it would break into her and her sister's business to sell it."

"Did John Dees come to see you about this matter?"

"Yes."

"When?"

"Last October."

"Did you ever see him visiting Miss Mag?"

"No."

"What did he say to you about this case?"

"He started the story about Mittie's baby and I went over and asked Steve Walkup if it was so and he said it was."

Henry Stephenson told about selling beef and mutton to Maggie: "She always wanted roast." He also remembered the day in 1901—he was fourteen or fifteen years old—when his father, William John Stephenson, sent him to get the Rosses' papers that would help the surveyor locate a corner of the property. "We finally decided that the point had been done away with and we went to see Miss Mag and Miss Sallie about it. The next morning, Miss Mag came down and we showed her where the distance ran out and she called my father and told him that corner, as she remembered it, was beyond a cluster of twigs, about thirty feet away. We cut out the right of way and found the corner. There was no trouble after that in finding the balance of the corners. The next morning we surveyed the other side, and Miss Maggie said she wanted to be there for she knew where the lines were. She stayed with us until it commenced to rain."

J. H. Boyte, sixty-one-years old and the surveyor for the City of Monroe, confirmed the story. It happened when he was the elected county surveyor. He also remembered going to the sisters' home for payment for a surveying job. "Miss Sallie said 'Now you must be as reasonable as you can, as we are poor and can't hardly raise the money,' " he recalled. "I told them what my charges were and she says to Miss Mag, 'I think that's reasonable, and you see if you can't find the money and settle.' "

"Do you remember anything Miss Mag said that day?"

"No, but the day I did the surveying and she was alone, we talked all down the line."

Judge Ray recessed for the evening.

Dr. Olin Nisbet, fifty-four years old, opened the tenth day of testimony with a detailed description of how he had treated Maggie and Sallie before and after he moved to Charlotte in 1901.

"Did you see Miss Maggie after Miss Sallie's death?" Cansler asked.

"Yes, several months later. She came in my office and spoke to me and said she had been to Charlotte shopping and she wanted to come in and speak to me and tell me about her sister's death, and she came back into my consulting room and she told me about Miss Sallie's death."

"Did she tell you anything else?"

"She also said they had made their wills together and had taken care of Bob and Mittie Bell and that they had remembered some of their friends."

The caveators objected to the comment about the will. Judge Ray overruled the objection but cautioned the jury: "Gentlemen of the jury, this evidence is admitted solely on the issue of mental capacity and is not to be taken or considered by you upon the issue of undue influence, and is not to be taken or considered by you directly or indirectly as proof of the facts the statement of the conversation contains, but solely as evidence bearing upon the question of the mental capacity of Miss Maggie Ross to make the will offered for probate." The same exchange went on through Dr. Nisbet's testimony.

"Had you ever heard them talk about Bob and Mittie Bell in this way before?"

"One time when I was at their home, during the time that I lived at Waxhaw, I heard them say that Bob had been a house-boy and had grown up around the house and that they had practically raised Mittie Bell and that they were going to see that they were taken care of."

Objection, overruled, caution.

"Did you ever hear them talk about leaving money to the hospital?"

"During the time that Miss Sallie was a patient at the Presbyterian Hospital, I made my usual morning visit to Miss Sallie, and during that visit we were talking about the Presbyterian Hospital and Miss Sallie said that it was rather noisy. And I said 'Miss Sallie, you have plenty of money and why not give some of it to the Presbyterian Hospital?' And she said 'I hadn't thought about that. Maybe I will.'"

Objection, overruled, caution.

"Would you tell us again about your conversation when Miss Maggie came to see you after Miss Sallie's death?"

"She said she had been down shopping and wanted to come up and speak to me and also wanted to tell me about Miss Sallie's death.

I took her back in my reception room and she told me during that time that she and Miss Sallie had made their wills together and that they had taken care of Bob and Mittie, and remembered some of their friends."

Objection, overruled, caution.

The cross-examiner got the doctor to endorse the professional reputation of the alienists, asked if he'd treated Mittie Bell (he hadn't) and pressed him on his own opinion of Maggie's mental state.

"I am not an expert on mental diseases. I specialize in the stomach and bowels."

"Could chronic constipation occur with senile dementia?"

"Yes."

The lawyer showed him the group picture and asked him to describe his treatment of the sisters at that time.

"When I was living in Waxhaw, in 1898, and would go to their home to treat Miss Sallie, Miss Mag would follow me to the door and ask me how Miss Sallie was getting along, and I would give her instructions about giving medicine to her sister."

The next witness, Doc Coan, described selling cows and pigs and a mule to Miss Maggie, and buying corn and cotton seed and land from her. In a deposition, his bedridden wife, Tirzah, spoke of their friendship and care for each other in sickness.

"Did you ever know her to do anything or hear her say anything which would indicate that she did not have a good mind?"

The caveators objected but were overruled.

"No, I thought her mind was perfectly good."

"How often did you see each other during the year 1907?"

"There wasn't but a few days but what she was down, and she was down to see me six weeks before she died and told me she would be back in a short time to see me again."

"During all these conversations, from the time you first knew her until her death, did you ever see her do anything or hear her say anything that would indicate that she was not a woman of sound mind?"

Objection, overruled.

"In my opinion, she had sufficient mind to know the property she owned and what she wanted to do with it."

"Did she talk to you about her kin people?"

"She told me she had mighty few kin people. She named some of them. The time before last she was there, she was talking about the Gribbles and what kin they were to her and she said to me 'You are the same kin they are to me.'" Tirzah explained her own suffering: "I have had rheumatism and been past walking now nearly nine years and my nerves have given away and I can't use myself. I have not been away from this house but once in nearly nine years."

The cross-examiner picked up on her health.

"I had a spell about twenty-five years ago and for just a short while—three months or something like—and then I got able to do my work. I never was very stout, though able to do my work up to about ten years ago. I was able to do my work and go around over the place fifteen years ago. I have no children to help me any."

"Did Miss Maggie know of your afflicted condition?"

"Yes, and she visited me often."

"But she didn't name you in her will. Did she ever talk to you about her will?"

"She told me to make myself easy and that I would not suffer."

"And that made you think she would remember you in her will?"

"Yes. Miss Sallie mentioned it to me, but I didn't know that she just spoke it in that way."

"How did she speak?"

"She told me one day that she thought almost of me as if I were her sister."

"Did she tell you that she was going to will most of her property to Mittie Bell and her kin people?"

"No."

"Did either Miss Sallie or Miss Maggie leave the impression on you that they were going to leave you this place where you are living?"

"No, for we expected to pay them for it and did pay them every cent they asked. We gave her thirty dollars per acre and it came to seven hundred thirty-five dollars and I reckon you can see where she signed her name."

"Did she ever mention who she was going to will her property to?"

"No. She just told me she had a right to dispose of the property as she saw fit."

"Did she tell you at that time that she had already made a contract with her sister Sallie to will this property to be sold for the purpose of paying off legacies?"

"No."

"Did Miss Maggie Ross have a sound mind?"

"As far as I can judge. And if it was her will to put her property where she has put it, it is all right with me. I believe she had a sound mind and you might talk until night, I think her mind was all right. Many a person has a sound mind and puts her property where people thinks it looks silly. I think she acted right and just in doing what she did. If it was her will, it is my pleasure for it to be that way."

Stitt Howie told another story of Maggie's precise knowledge of her property lines, this one just two years before she died. "I asked for a plot of the Helms tract," he said. "She went upstairs and got it and handed it to me. We ran the tract and I returned the plot. Later we returned to establish a corner, about a hundred yards back of the house, and we couldn't locate the corner. I went up there and asked for the plot or papers in this tract and she couldn't find them, said probably Mr. Hudson had them and she would go out and find the corner for us; that she thought the corner was near a certain row and we later located it in another row fifteen or twenty feet away."

The cross-examiner focused on Dick Hudson's role. Howie happened to know, because he was treasurer at Banks Presbyterian, that Hudson paid Miss Maggie's dues of twenty-five or fifty dollars a year. He also testified that Hudson, an elder at Banks, had called and tried to get him to join the lawsuit because the church was involved.

Ed Stephenson, Henry Stephenson's thirty-one-year-old brother, told about selling beef and corn to Maggie without Hudson's involvement. "I would kill about every week during the fall of the year. I knew the part she wanted. She paid me for it. I sold her a lot of corn about three years ago—twenty-seven and a half bushels at a dollar thirty-five per bushel. I weighed the corn before leaving home. She sent Steve to tell me she wanted the corn. I drove up with it and she had Steve to unload it. She asked me if I had weighed it and I told her it weighed eleven hundred pounds. She told me to come in and count it up and I told her the amount and she went upstairs and brought the money down and give it to me. It come to a little over thirty-seven dollars."

Fannie Forbis, the sixty-year-old neighbor who received two hundred dollars in the will, said she carried on ordinary conversations during their frequent visits. "She never talked to me very much about her property. She knew what property she had, but she was no woman to talk about her property—not any more than was necessary about it."

"Have you ever heard her say anything against her tenants?"

"No. She seemed to like them all."

"Did you talk about Mrs. Taylor?"

"Yes, Mrs. Taylor was there often. She would come and stay two or three weeks at a time. Well, Mrs. Taylor came there and stayed when she got ready. I never heard Miss Mag say anything, but once and she said Mrs. Taylor was too inquisitive and wanted to know what was in her will and she wasn't going to tell."

Jim Crane, Frank's son who was in his forties, told about taking Maggie to the circus when he was twenty-four or twenty-five. "She wanted to go by the old home place," he recalled. "She seemed to enjoy the circus and talked to me about the animals. Miss Mag paid all the expenses."

W. H. Collins told how she rescued Will Body from losing his goods. Professor R. N. Nisbet told about buying the acre for the school. Both thought she had sense enough to make the will. J. M. Niven, who had been on the Board of County Commissioners with Dick Hudson, told how Maggie covered Bob's expenses. She shopped at his store fourteen or fifteen years, about once a month. "I waited on her myself usually. She would pay me with money out of her purse. She was a careful buyer. She was more careful about her shoes than anything else."

29

R. A. HUDSON

I think Tom Houston's account is in that book. . . . He was called by the Marvin people "Miss Mag's son-in-law."

—R. A. HUDSON, 1921

April 12–13, 1921

R. A. Hudson took the stand Tuesday afternoon and stayed through most of Wednesday. He told how he became the women's agent after Dennis died, how Maggie raised his pay after Sallie died, how he and Robert McIlwaine found the wills after Maggie died. He also told what he knew about the will before he read it, recalling the afternoon when he found them debating whether to give all of the money to Richard or some to Harry Hood. The caveators objected. Judge Ray overruled them but gave the jury the same caution he had given about Dr. Nisbet's testimony.

R. A. Hudson

"Richard was twelve or fourteen years old at that time," Hudson said. "They seemed to be very much attached to Richard and my grandson Harry Hood."

"Did they say any more to you about their wills at the time?"

"No. Later on, they were talking about their wills and asked me who would make good witnesses to their wills and I told them any of their neighbors, and I suggested Mr. Ezzell, Mr. McIlwaine, Mr. Crane or Mr. Sutton."

Objection, overruled, caution.

"Did you ever have any other conversation with them about the wills?"

"No. The first time I saw Miss Mag's will was when I was bringing her down to make the codicil to it. I did not read the will at that time."

Objection, overruled.

"Miss Mag on going home told me what she had done. She said that Mr. Adams told her it was not necessary to probate Miss Sallie's will and that she had made a codicil to her will, cutting out Alice Ross, divorced wife of Bob Ross, and giving me one thousand dollars. She said she and Miss Sallie had never paid me anything and they were going to give me that."

Objection, overruled, caution.

"How long have you been doing work of this kind for Miss Mag?"

"Ever since the death of Miss Sallie. I have not told lots of other little things. She would send for me every two or three weeks. I made a charge against the estate of five hundred dollars. This has been paid to me. That is all I received for my services during the year 1920. Mr. Redwine paid me that. I never collected anything from Miss Mag for the use of my automobile and buggy. I lived there three and a half miles from her and seventeen miles from Charlotte. I took her to Charlotte often and I would come to Monroe for her, and I would go to Waxhaw monthly to pay her hands' accounts for her. She never furnished any conveyance. I'd use my own conveyance."

"Were you involved in the trade Miss Mag and Mr. Coan made for some property?"

"Yes. She sent for me to come and make a deed and see it run off."

"Did she tell you the price she got for it?"

"Yes, and I told her she was offered a plenty for it."

"What other opportunities did you have to observe her business sense?"

"Another time, Mr. J. N. Price came by and asked me to ride by Miss Mag's with him. He went over there to try to get a contribution for his church and she told him she didn't have any money right then and she didn't contribute anything."

"Did you ever have a talk at any time with Mittie Bell in regard to getting Miss Sallie and Miss Maggie to devise her or bequeath to her any of their property?"

"No."

"Did you ever at any time have a conversation with Bob Ross in regard to using your influence to get Miss Maggie to pay him or to give to him or to will to him the property at their death?"

"No."

"Did you ever discuss with Bob Ross or Mittie Bell Houston or any other of the legatees anything about Miss Mag and Miss Sallie's wills?"

"No."

"Did you ever mention to Miss Mag or Miss Sallie anything about them giving any of the legatees anything?"

"No."

"Did you ever use your influence in getting them to make this will?"

"No."

Objection, overruled, except.

"Have you tried to get witnesses in this case?"

"No."

"Have you busied yourself with hunting evidence?"

"No."

"Have you been present at the taking of any of the depositions?"

"No."

Parker's cross-examination fixed on Hudson's influence over the women.

"How long were you confidential adviser for the Ross women?"

"More than twenty years."

"Would they charge rent without consulting you?"

"Yes."

"Did Ed Yarborough come to you about his rent being increased?"

"He may have. Some tenants did."

"What would you tell tenants when they would come to you about rent increases?"

"I would tell them to go on and the rent would not be raised."

"Did Mr. Coan complain about his rent?"

"Yes. That was in Miss Sallie's lifetime."

"Do you know Ed Hoey?"

"Yes. He is a cotton buyer in Charlotte."

"Do you remember selling him cotton for the Ross women?"

"Yes, one time."

"Do you remember Miss Maggie going to him in 1905 and complaining to him."

"No."

"Do you remember going to him and telling him they had no sense?"

"No."

"Did you have an influence with them?"

"Yes. They would follow my advice. I would advise them about the rents of their land and I advised them about the collection of their rents. I paid their supply bills for them for their tenants. I gave the checks myself. Whatever they asked me about I would advise them. I looked after the buildings on their place and would make the contracts for building the houses. They believed what I told them and followed my advice."

"So you did have an influence over them?"

"Yes. I was in a position to see what was going on around the place."

"For example?"

"I knew that Mittie Bell and Bob were paying no rent and that they were getting into debt to the estate. I knew that Tom Houston was about eighteen hundred dollars in debt to the estate. Tom is Mittie's husband."

"Did Miss Maggie ever tell you that Florence was sleeping with her?"

"No."

"Did you ever see Miss Mag taking care of the baby?"

"No."

"Did you ever tell Miss Mag not to be so familiar with those negroes?"

"No."

"Did you know about Miss Mag going to see Mittie Bell at college?"

"No."

"Did you know that they were eating at the same table with the negroes?"

"No."

"What legacies did your family receive from the will?"

"My son was left one thousand dollars in this will and my grandson, Harry Hood, was left five hundred and my wife Sallie Hudson was left five hundred."

"Did they ever perform any services for Miss Mag?"

"No."

"Do you know Margaret Jackson Crane?"

"No. She has been out of that community for several years."

"Why did you pay yourself out of the estate after the caveat was filed?"

"I paid out several bequests the day the account was filed and I gave myself five hundred dollars."

"We allege in our bill of particulars that you went and tried to get the church to come into this action. Is that true?"

"Yes. I wanted the church to come in."

"Did you go to the Methodists and try to get them to come in?"

"No."

"You had a subpoena to bring all the papers and books of Miss Mag that you had. Are these all you had?"

"Yes."

The attorney picked up a ledger. "When did you first see this book?"

"I think in 1900."

"Where did the book come from?"

"I suppose Miss Maggie or Miss Sallie bought it."

"Can you explain why the first eighteen pages are cut out?"

"No."

"Can you explain why the tops of pages twenty-three, twenty-four, twenty-five and twenty-six are out of the book?"

"No."

"The index shows page twenty-three to be R. A. Hudson's account," the caveators' attorney pointed out, showing him the book. "And what is page fourteen?"

"R. A. Hudson & Co.'s account," Hudson read.

"And page fourteen is gone?"

"Yes."

"Who wrote this book, Mr. Hudson?"

"I wrote most of the book myself."

"And the latter part of the index is gone?"

"Yes."

"Do you know how it got out?"

"No."

"Whose handwriting is in this book?"

"All of it is mine."

"Can you explain the missing pages?"

"This may be one of the old books I had in the store and cut these pages out so I could use it for Miss Mag's and Miss Sallie's account. I may have taken it over to them."

"Is Tom Houston's account in that book?"

"I think Tom Houston's account is in that book."

"You told Mr. Cansler he was Mittie Bell Houston's husband, is that correct?"

Hudson nodded. "He was called by the Marvin people 'Miss Mag's son-in-law.'"

Parker paused and looked around the room. Stack was bent over a pad on his table, smothering a smile. Sikes fidgeted. Cansler's calm, narrowed eyes gave the impression of dozing. "Miss Mag's son-in-law," he echoed. Some of the women in the audience were leaning toward their husbands, whispering behind their fans. Some of the jurors were watching him. Some were still staring at Hudson.

"How much does he owe the estate?"

"About eighteen hundred dollars. I told Miss Mag he was eating her up."

"Would you read this figure for us under Bob Ross's account?"

"One thousand three hundred sixty-seven dollars and eighty-two cents."

"One thousand three hundred sixty-seven dollars and eighty-two cents," Parker repeated.

Hudson looked up at the lawyer. "That's what he owes the estate. I let him have this by order of Miss Mag. I filed this account as doubtful because Miss Mag never intended for him to pay it back. I charged it for my own information to see what all he was getting."

The temperature reached twenty-six degrees in Union County on the night of April 12, one of the latest killing frosts the county had known. By Wednesday morning, the wind had turned to the southwest and the ascending sun was driving the temperatures back into the mid-seventies. When court convened, Judge Ray announced that he intended to declare a mistrial if the lawyers did not wrap up the case by Saturday night. The pace quickened. Hudson returned to the stand, and Cansler gave him a chance to account for the missing pages.

"In the book I kept for the Ross women the first eighteen pages are gone," he explained. "The index in this book refers to page eighteen as being the account of the Morrow, Heath Company. I did business with them, and when I took the book to the Rosses I just tore my accounts out. All those that are torn out were some I had started and I just tore them out when I took the book to them."

"When you sold cotton for the Ross women, what did you do with the money, Mr. Hudson?"

"I would do whatever they told me to do with it. I never checked on their money except when they ordered me to, or for their use."

"Did you keep records of the sales of the cotton?"

"No."

"Did you ever at any time use any of their money?"

"No, except what I borrowed from them, and I always paid that back with interest."

"Did you feel that you were solvent?"

"Yes."

"You borrowed money from them?"

"I gave Miss Mag a little mortgage one time, but it was never registered."

"What property did you own at the time?"

"I had six hundred acres of land worth around fifty dollars per acre."

"Who made out the return on the estate as executor?"

"When we got ready to make out these statements, Mr. Redwine did the writing."

"Did you pay out any further legacies after you were served with notice by the caveators?"

"No. Well, we paid out some little accounts afterwards. We paid out Mr. Crane's account and some other little ones."

"Why did you go ahead, Mr. Hudson, and cash those checks after notice of caveat was served on you?"

Judge Ray sustained the propounders' objection and sent the jury out to take the answer.

"I couldn't tell you why I paid those small accounts or cashed those checks after notice of caveat had been served on me."

"When were these accounts paid?"

"A month or two after this caveat was filed."

"Did you consult anyone about paying these accounts before paying them?"

"Yes. Mr. Vann."

Judge Ray ordered the jury to return. The propounders called to the stand—in turn, W. W. Fowler, H. B. Clark, W. L. Hemby, J. P. Simpson, and Carl Wolfe—to ask them one question: "Would you say the general character of Mr. Hudson is good?" They answered alike: "Yes."

30

CHARACTER WITNESSES

All I know about Miss Maggie is that I have known her since she was about ten years old and have been a neighbor to her all my life, and she was a good Christian woman and able to attend to her own business.

—SAMUEL DICKEY HOWIE, 1921

April 13, 1921

Dr. William Robert McCain's mother, Mary Walker McCain, a girlhood friend of Maggie's, hired Aunt Harriet to cook for her after Maggie died. The propounders called the doctor, who lived with her in the old homeplace, to testify because he had treated the sisters and people in their household since 1899, beginning with a call to see a sick cow.

"Did you meet Miss Maggie on that trip?"

"Yes, but I did not speak to her."

"Were you their regular physician?"

"No, but I went over there to see Miss Mag, perhaps three or four times."

"On what other occasions were you called to the house?"

"I have been called over there to see Aunt Harriet Taylor. I was her family physician, and she would call for me. Then I called to see

Aunt Harriet Grier a time or two while she stayed there. Then I treated Florence Tucker Houston, Bob Ross's granddaughter."

"Did you have an opportunity to converse with Miss Mag on those trips?"

"Yes. She and my mother were girls together and I would sit awhile and talk with her."

"When were you there to see Mrs. Taylor?"

"During the flu epidemic."

"From your observation of Miss Maggie, do you have an opinion satisfactory to yourself as to her mental condition?"

"Yes. In my opinion, she had sufficient mental capacity to make a will."

"Who was Miss Mag's regular physician?" Parker asked.

"Dr. Nisbet of Waxhaw, until he moved to Charlotte."

"Why were you usually called to Miss Mag's place?"

"To see the tenants."

"How many times did you call to see Miss Mag?"

"Four times, I think."

"And how long was each of these visits?"

"About thirty minutes—the usual professional call."

"What did you talk about when you were there?"

"Generally, about her condition."

"And you went to see Miss Mag's adopted granddaughter, Florence Tucker Houston?"

"Yes." The forty-seven-year-old doctor rubbed his hands together and scowled as if remembering a foul taste. His eye caught Parker's. "She called her her precious little darling." He stared at the floor. "She told me to do the best I could for her and she would pay it."

Cansler returned.

"You were subpoenaed by the caveators in this case, is that correct?"

"Yes, but I was excused by them."

"What did you think when you observed Miss Maggie's attitude toward her adopted granddaughter, Florence Tucker Houston?" Cansler asked, choosing Parker's inflammatory phrase on purpose.

Dr. McCain glared at the lawyer. "I felt like taking a baseball bat and knocking the old lady in the head with it."

Cansler ignored the tone. "Where did you examine Florence?"

"When I went there to see this little negro, she was in their bed. A single bed."

"Did she require medical attention?"

"She was mighty sick."

"How old was she?"

"Three or four."

W. D. S. Clark, sixty-nine years old, had seen Maggie plowing her family's fields when she was twenty and he was nine or ten. He'd seen her only twice since then, once when his house burned and they gave him some sheets and pillows and once in passing a few years later. He thought her mind was good, but he admitted to the cross-examiner that they had talked only twice.

Capt. W. C. Heath was an important witness for the propounders, even though he had never known Maggie Ross. Born the year after the war, he had earned the honorary military title because of his work for Confederate veterans. He was educated at The Citadel in Charleston and managed Heath-Lee Hardware Company until 1896, when he took over Monroe Cotton Mill as secretary-treasurer. He had been chairman of the Board of Governors of the Southern Cotton Spinners' Association. His opinion mattered.

"How would you describe the general character of R. A. Hudson?" John Sikes asked him.

"Good." Capt. Heath nodded.

"H. B. Adams?"

"He was a lawyer of ability, a Christian and a man of the highest type."

"R. B. Redwine?"

"His character is good."

Sallie Hudson remembered her lifelong friendship with Miss Maggie, especially her role in the lonely years after Miss Sallie died. "I would spend the day with her once in awhile and she would come over and spend the day with me," she said.

"Did she ever talk about Miss Sallie?"

"No. She would talk about her chickens, garden and sewing and such things, just things an ordinary woman would talk about."

"Did she go to church regularly?"

"Yes, until the last few years of her life."

"Did you ever discuss business with Miss Maggie?" the caveators asked.

"Never in my life."

"Were you in her home when the will was brought out?"

"Yes."

"Was it read?"

"No. It was too dark. The Gribbles were there and wanted it read."

"Did the Gribbles see Miss Maggie before she died?"

"No. She was dead when the Gribbles came."

Hudson's daughter, Pearl Hood, now living in Monroe, recalled a trip to the mountains with the Rosses when she was eleven years old, before Dennis died. "I went with them and Mr. Charlie Parks on a trip up to Rutherfordton, Asheville and around," she said. "They took Bob Ross along to wait on them. I had the time of my life."

"Did you have any business dealings with Miss Mag after Miss Sallie's death?"

"I rented land from her up to this year."

"Did you do the contracting yourself?"

"Yes. I rented just a little corner that joined us. I was to pay her three hundred pounds of lint cotton, and I paid it in check and money sometimes."

"To whom did you make out the checks?"

"If I paid by check, I made it out to Miss Maggie Ross."

"When you got them back, were they endorsed by her?"

"As far as I know."

"Did you pay her in check last year?"

"No, I paid her corn instead of cotton. I sold cotton at twenty-eight cents per pound and the corn at the rate of two dollars per bushel. My son delivered the corn to her."

"Did Miss Maggie make the calculations on your rent?" the caveators' lawyer asked.

"No, I made the calculations myself."

"Did you ever see Miss Maggie write a check in her life?"

"No."

"Can you swear that the checks you gave her were endorsed by her?"

"Well, no. I just supposed they were."

"Did you ever see her transact business with anyone else?"

"No."

The clerk read the deposition of Samuel Dickey Howie, C. C. McIlwaine's fifty-six-year-old son-in-law who moved to Florida from Waxhaw in February 1907 and moved back, to Fort Mill, in 1918.

"Why, I am satisfied her mind was good," he said. "She was a lady of good mind and memory and able to sell her own property if she was so minded to do."

"Did she ever talk to you about her kin folks?"

"If Miss Mag had any kin folks, I don't think she ever realized it. Her relations were very distant and didn't live anywhere near her and never visited her so far as I know."

"Do you know any of her kin folks?"

"No. I might know some folks claiming kin with her now, but so far as their being kin to her I never knew it nor heard of it."

"What did you mean in saying that she was of sound mind?"

"I simply mean to state that I never saw her do any act that was very unusual, as I might expect of a person in an insane asylum. All I know about Miss Maggie is that I have known her since she was about ten years old and have been a neighbor to her all my life, and she was a good Christian woman and able to attend to her own business."

At this point, the propounders introduced the document that had bound Bob Ross to Susan Ross:

APPLICATION FOR APPRENTICE

State and Susan Ross Vs.
Robt. Ross and Rosa Ross

Returnable Oct. 1st, 1874

Notice given to parties. Continued to Oct. 29. Oct. 30th adjudged that applicant have Robt. Ross bound to her as apprentice—Appeal craved and granted by Rosa Ross, the mother of Robert Ross—Judgment of probate court approved except, that adjudged that applicant Susan Ross pay all costs.

Testimony turned to the spinsters' correspondence with their lawyer about the will. T. C. Haigler, who had been postmaster in Waxhaw in 1907, identified the receipt to the sender of the registered letter—the duplicate wills—that the sisters (Route 3 Waxhaw, the Marvin route) sent to H. B. Adams at Monroe on November 20, 1907. The receipts became evidence. J. O. Fulenwider, the Post Office money order and registry clerk in Monroe, explained that the records for the registry were destroyed, as was routine, in 1911.

Judge Ray adjourned court for the day.

31

PROPOUNDERS REST

But for the difference in their color, I would have thought they were equals.

—J. G. PARKS, 1921

April 14, 1921

On Thursday morning Dr. H. Q. Alexander, the former president of the Farmers' Union, came first to the stand.

"I visited Miss Maggie and Miss Sallie Ross in the year 1907 eighteen times," he said. "I think each visit was made to see Miss Sallie. My receipts indicate that I prescribed for Miss Maggie during that time."

"Did you see Miss Mag on all those trips?"

"Yes, but my conversation was limited to the purpose of my call. I would just give instructions about medicine and things like that."

Parker dwelt on the illness in his cross-examination.

"Dr. Alexander, what did you treat Miss Sallie for on all those visits in 1907?"

"I do not recall. She was in bed, and I am inclined to think that she had bladder trouble."

"Doctor, is it true that Bright's disease has a tendency to weaken the mind in its last stages?"

"Yes."

"What did you treat Miss Mag for?"

"I do not know. I prescribed for her, but I do not know what for."

"Was she in bed?"

"No."

"Have you ever discussed business with Miss Maggie?"

"No."

"Then what makes you sure she had sufficient mental capacity to make a will?"

"I never noticed anything indicating that she was not all right mentally. Miss Mag's mind was not a strong mind, as compared with that of her sister."

Cansler rose to clarify: "Doctor, when you say 'not a strong mind,' do you mean a weak mind?"

"Miss Sallie had a mind above the average for opportunity. Miss Maggie's mind compared with Miss Sallie's may be called weak."

The propounders then called Rev. Bobby McIlwaine back to the stand.

"Do you know Mr. R. L. White?"

"Yes."

"Did you have a conversation with him in regard to Mrs. Garrison and Mrs. Taylor?"

"Yes. He said he believed his sister Mrs. Garrison had stayed around the Rosses and courted the old ladies in order to get the old women to give them their property."

The caveators ignored that testimony in their cross-examination.

"Rev. McIlwaine, where did you stay last summer?"

"In the Ross home."

"Did you pay rent?"

"No. I made repairs around there and charged nothing for them."

"How did this arrangement come about?"

"Mr. Hudson, the executor, put me in charge of the Ross house. When coming from the funeral and coming to Monroe later with Mr. Hudson, I mentioned the fact that I wasn't strong and would like to stay out in the country during the summer, and I thought of the Ross home being vacant, and Mr. Redwine said it belonged to Banks Church under the will. I saw the trustees and Mr. Redwine said for me to take possession."

"Rev. McIlwaine, what is your interest in this case?"

"I was put up among the first witnesses. I have been in court ever since trying to do my duty and see justice done. I am serving the church at large to see the church get its money under the will as the old women wanted it."

J. G. Parks, who had managed the Belk store in Waxhaw where Miss Maggie shopped from 1902 to 1911, had gone on to Concord to be part of the retailer's Parks-Belk store. He had seen Maggie handle money.

"She was a shrewd trader," he said. "She knew a bargain when she saw it. She said they were poor and did not have much money. She said they could not go in style and ride in automobiles like some people but had to use their money to live on."

"Who transacted Miss Mag's important business?" Parker asked.

"Mr. Hudson. He paid her accounts."

"Did she do her own shopping?"

"She would buy articles in the store."

"Did Mittie Bell shop there?"

"Yes, she would come there and buy things."

"Did you have an opportunity to observe her relationship with Miss Mag?"

"Yes. But for the difference in their color, I would have thought they were equals. Miss Mag would object to buying things of high prices. Mittie would pout and Miss Maggie would say she would have to buy it to keep Mittie from pouting. Mittie Bell would buy anything she wanted, no matter if it was high priced, and Miss Maggie would pay for it. Mittie would pick out dresses for Miss Mag and Miss Mag would often buy them. I knew if I got Mittie to liking something that I would get to sell it."

"Mr. Parks, do you think Miss Maggie's mind was as strong as Miss Sallie's?"

"No. She would have a general idea of her property but not as much as Miss Sallie would have. She left most of her business to Miss Sallie to transact."

Cansler rose again. "Did she know the negroes to whom the bequests were made?"

"Yes."

"Do you think she could have made a will?"

"My impression is that she would have left the matter of making a will to Miss Sallie."

Ernest Crane, Frank's son, said he had seen Bob Ross go in at the back door and do work around the place, hauling corn, wood, and hay to her, but he did not see Maggie doing business except at his family's store. "Miss Mag stayed in the house most of the time," he told the cross-examiner, adding that his half-sister Jennie Helms often did her calculations.

John A. Kell remembered a conversation when she had told him she would invest in land because she expected twice the return of bank deposits. "But she said she was getting old and did not want any more land, and that she had everything fixed and wanted nothing more." He also told about taking George Atkinson to Maggie's house to ask for money. "She said people were always asking for money for charitable purposes, but she had everything fixed and could not help them."

Oscar Potts, who lived over the line in Lancaster County, said he had seen Maggie forty or fifty times in the forty years he'd known her, mostly at church although she had spent the day at his house. He always thought she had sense enough to make a will. "If I had known she slept with a negro woman," he told Parker, "I would change my mind."

J. N. Price told of going with Hudson to ask Miss Maggie for money to build Siler Presbyterian Church. "She said she could not help me just then," he recalled. "She said she had income tax to pay and had bought Liberty Bonds and stamps and her taxes had to be paid. Mr. Hudson seemed to approve of this."

"Did you have further contact with her?"

"I went back and I think I wrote her a letter. Then I was there on the Sunday before Armistice Day. My family were with me in the car, but I went in and talked to her alone. I told her I had come again to see her about the church money. She asked me about the churches in that section and the old people in that section. She said at that time she had not sold her cotton, but she might help us later."

Just before noon, the propounders rested their case.

32

SIKES AND PARKER

Show the world by your verdict that a negro can get justice in the court.

—JOHN SIKES, 1921

April 14–15, 1921

Mayor John Sikes at age forty, married to his own Maggie for fourteen years and father of four children, cut an earnest figure with his soft eyes and high-domed forehead that reached to a thin layer of dark hair on the back half of his head. His thin, tight lips were set between a jutting nose and an equally jutting chin. He could be calm, but passionate. He began his address after lunch, reminding the jurors that they had promised, just two weeks before, that they had no prejudice against a white woman's leaving property to negroes. He pointed out that, whereas the caveators had brought strangers from Richmond and Morganton and Raleigh, the propounders had put forty-five of Miss Maggie's neighbors and acquaintances, good Marvin folk, on the stand to testify to her sound

John C. Sikes

mind. He rehearsed the story of Bob's being taken by Sheriff Griffin from his mother's arms at age two, apprenticed to Susan Ross, brought up in the home where he worked without pay. He said he hoped that no one would try to set aside a written instrument of his, as the cousins were trying to set aside Maggie's.

"Gentlemen!" he exhorted the jurors. "When opposing counsel shout 'nigger!' I want you to accord to Bob Ross that same kindly, tender feeling that you would me or any other white man. If I had been bound to them, and had tilled their soil, drove their teams and operated their cotton gin, I'd feel that I was a proper object of their bounty rather than those relatives, most of whom never darkened the doors of Sallie and Maggie Ross' house. Show the world by your verdict that a negro can get justice in the court. Don't deprive Bob Ross of that which is his due."

Sikes called the jurors to imagine the sisters sitting in their own home, telling Adams what disposition they wanted to make of their property; to see Sallie turning to R. B. Redwine, who was also present, saying: "Years ago your uncle taught me to read and write, and I want you to act as my executor"; to see Maggie interrupting eagerly: "I know who I want for my executor. I want R. A. Hudson."

"If she knew how to select such a competent executor, didn't she have sense enough to make a will?" he asked. "R. B. Redwine, a man of long legal experience, knows how much mental capacity it takes to make a will. He swore that Maggie Ross was competent to make a will, and no one dares attempt to impeach his character."

The mayor said there was no evidence to show that the negroes had used undue influence and that Hudson was unaware of the contents of the will until after the death of Maggie Ross. "And it's a reflection on the memory of the late H. B. Adams to say that he went up there to draw a will for mental incompetents."

He read aloud the codicil to the will, pointing out that Maggie knew Alice's adultery meant she "forfeited all claims to our charity." "This shows that she was not the moral degenerate she was got up to be by the caveators," he argued.

People who expected to benefit by the will have hatched up this scheme to cheat Bob Ross and Mittie Bell Houston out of their rights, and if you decide to break this will you will be a party to the act. George Sutton declared that he would have considered Maggie Ross sane if she had left her property to white people. He admitted that he wanted the will broke because it was for the best interests of the churches and community. Yet by seeking to pollute the fountainhead of justice, they do a worse injury to their church! Mr. Sutton never heard of her being insane until the will was read. Mr. Ezzell, one of the remaining two witnesses to the will, said she had sense enough to make a will; Charlie McIlwaine knew them all his life, and he says they were competent to make a will. Dr. McIlwaine, who has known them since the war, and who is a man of high intelligence, says Maggie Ross was a woman of good business judgment and that she had the capacity to make a will. Dr. Atkinson, Rev. R. J. McIlwaine, and Rev. Mr. Robertson gave similar testimony. Their neighbor, Frank Crane, says they told him many years ago that they intended leaving their home place to Bob Ross.

The caveators claim Maggie Ross didn't know the extent or nature of her property. Mr. John Boyte, a surveyor, testified to you that she located a corner boundary on her fourteen-hundred-acre tract of land after he failed to do so with his surveying instruments!

These alienists answered long, weighty hypothetical questions, but Dr. Nisbet, who knew her personally, had been her physician, says she was of sound mind.

He leaned on the rail in front of the jury box and spoke to them as if in confidence, cutting his eyes toward Parker and Stack. "When a lawyer has a bad case he gets Dr. Hall, Dr. Anderson and Dr. Taylor, unearths some foolish things the defendant has done during his lifetime, and propounds to them hypothetical questions expecting, and usually receiving, a favorable answer. Their evidence should be given little consideration. An Illinois Supreme Court judge, in handing down a decision on a will case, says the testimony of alienists is of very little value and should be considered by the jury with caution." He backed away and raised his voice to fill the room. "An imbecile? She traded horses and cows, sold land and gave money to churches!"

The lawyer paced in front of the jury box and glanced toward the empty witness stand.

Tirzah Coan, the poor rheumatic, helpless woman—with her mind clear as a bell—who will soon face her Maker, says Maggie Ross was competent to dispose of her property. There's a good, Christian woman who won't answer for what some connected with this case will have to. She wants to see the bequests contained in her cousin's will carried out although she has more claim on the bounty of Maggie Ross than any of the others who are seeking to have this will broken.

Dr. McCain, who has no love for negroes in his heart, and who would like to see the will broken, admits Maggie was of sound mind. George Ross is the only cousin seeking to break the will who has had the courage to come into court and declare Maggie Ross to have been mentally incompetent to make a will. Where are the other caveators? There is nothing wrong with the mind of Maggie Ross, gentlemen. The "wrong" is the manner in which they disposed of their property.

Sikes, tracing his fingers through the air, concluded with a dramatic demonstration of how the hand of Maggie Ross, now cold in death, had scrawled her signature across that paper representing her will. Then he spread out his arms in front of the jurors.

"I implore you. Permit her bequests to be carried out!"

John J. Parker—no stranger to the charge of shouting "nigger!"—countered that the cousins were Miss Maggie's natural heirs and deserved to see her natural will done.

"I hope," he answered Mayor Sikes, "that if I ever become weak in body and mind, and designing people take advantage of my disability, that my friends will come into court and cry out against the injustice perpetrated against me!"

You must decide three issues, Parker explained to the jury. Was the will executed according to the formalities of the law? Did Maggie Ross possess sufficient mentality to make a will? And in the making of the will was she unduly influenced by others?

"It is not a question of Bob or Mittie Bell," he said. "If you find that others used undue influence, a species of fraud, under your oath you must break the will. The duplicate wills—what Mr. Cansler was pleased to call 'mutual reciprocal wills'—are a suspicious circumstance," he argued. "If I make a will tomorrow, I can tear it up any time I see fit, but with duplicate wills, one of them reposing in the safe of an attorney, it is a different matter. I've made wills for people owning more property than the Ross women and they seem to think that one will is enough."

Parker asserted that the wills were the work of an "interested party," and as he continued he suggested who that might be: *Mr. Hudson* brought

Maggie after the death of her sister to make a codicil giving a thousand dollars to—*Mr. Hudson*! Hadn't John Parks testified that Miss Mag "would do anything *Dick Hudson* said"?

"It is strange," Parker continued, "that Mr. Redwine was not asked to draw that will. He was their attorney. He had won a case before the Supreme Court for them. Why not him instead of Mr. Adams? Because Mr. Adams was *Mr. Hudson's* lawyer."

As he ticked off the will's bequests to charitable institutions, he mocked: "Poor old soul! She left five hundred dollars for a library yet she never read a book in her life."

Even the formalities of will-signing are suspect, he suggested. "Ezzell and Sutton, two of the witnesses to the Ross will, say Maggie Ross didn't sign the will. Did she acknowledge it as her will? She did not. If you believe the witnesses, Mag was crying like her heart would break when Sutton, Ezzell and McIlwaine were at her home for the purpose of witnessing her will. Old man Charlie McIlwaine, who was a biased witness, said 'there was right much excitement' on this occasion. What was the crying about? Making a will ought to be a matter of pleasure—it should be a great satisfaction to know you are making provision for your loved ones. I can tell you. She was crying either because she didn't have sense enough to make a will or because she was being influenced by other parties to do something contrary to her wishes. Her tears were a protest against that will, not an acquiescence. If you say that was her will you'll say something she never did."

Another suspicious circumstance, Parker said, was that Sallie brought out the wills folded so that only the signature lines showed. "Why such great secrecy? Didn't Mr. Sutton ask her if they hadn't better read it? And didn't she say: 'It isn't necessary.' The law says secrecy is good evidence of undue influence. They say"—he gestured toward the propounders' table—"that their kin-people haven't a right to the property because they didn't help make it. The Ross women didn't acquire any property. They inherited it from their grandmother, mother and brother. Although they owned fourteen hundred acres of land at their death, they didn't acquire an acre after the passing of their brother, Dennis Ross. If they hadn't left a will the law would have given it to their kinsmen who are descendants of the actual owners of the land.

The propounders tell you they brought forty-odd citizens of the Marvin community to testify to the competency of the Ross women and not alienists from Richmond and Morganton. Who were these men? Jim Crane took her to the circus in Charlotte to see the animals and women in tights; while another one of their witnesses, a fellow by the name of Rogers, went with her to a dance when she was forty-six and he was but seventeen. Many of their other witnesses had tried to get money out of Miss Mag. Did they put up a witness to testify contrary to their interests? We did. Mrs. Harriet Taylor, who gets five hundred dollars under the will, says she didn't have enough sense to make a will. Her daughter, Mrs. Moore, likewise testified against her interest. Dr. Crowell, who ate at their table for twelve months, said that back in 1896 Maggie didn't have any sense.

Poor, simple-minded soul. She even realized her simplicity. She frequently called on a man by the name of Baker to come to her house and fiddle while she danced. So poor was her memory that he had to be introduced to her on each occasion. She couldn't remember the most trivial things; she couldn't repeat a conversation. There's no evidence that she ever wrote a check; she made no contracts. It was all done by His Majesty *Dick Hudson*. Every figure in her account book was made by him. Picture this aged and infirm woman with thousands of dollars in the bank telling her neighbors that she had to live on her eggs and chickens. She told Harriet Grier that she was afraid she would die in the poor house. *Dick Hudson* said she lived no better than the poorest people in the community.

Parker had not yet finished when Judge Ray recessed for the evening.

A half-inch of rain had fallen before court reopened on Friday, and the clouds hung in the sky all day. Despite the shade, the temperature rose above eighty degrees, and the crowded courtroom turned sticky for the day of oration. As Parker picked up his speech, he derided Maggie's belief in ghosts. "The age of witches has passed," he declared.

The world has become more intelligent. Children believe in ghosts. So do people of childish minds. One competent to dispense of a hundred thousand dollar estate doesn't believe in ghosts. Miss Maggie saw angels hovering over the body of her dead sister. Under her great grief she harbored these delusions. She heard the flutter of angels' wings and saw little birds flying in the room. None but the child-like hear the flutter of the angel's wings!

Her incompetency to make a will, beyond all peradventure, is shown by her association with Bob Ross and Mittie Bell Houston. Dr. McCain told you of finding her fondling a kinky-headed little negro. He said he wanted to bat her in the head with a baseball bat. But I take a more charitable view. If I should find a white Southern woman sleeping with a negro, eating at a table with one, I'd feel like supplicating God to remove the blight from her mind! Maggie's association with these negroes shows a lack of moral character. It is a blight upon the community in which she lived.

Pathetically they speak of Bob Ross. All the services they have shown that he rendered was to haul a little wood and hay upon one or two occasions. He had his land rent free; he was given money, *Mr. Hudson* having recently paid debts for him to the extent of thirteen hundred dollars. He is a modern illustration of the wisdom of Solomon: "Treat a servant like a son and you will see the day when he becomes the master." My high opinion of *Mr. Hudson* was lowered when he admitted that he acted as a business agent for a woman who acknowledged a negro as her *son-in-law*!

Do you tell me that a Southern white woman, living near the South Carolina line, would allow a negro woman to give birth to an illegitimate child in her home? Maggie Ross allowed Mittie Bell to bury her shame in her own quilts and bedclothes. She didn't say, like the Biblical character, "go and sin no more." She let her stay on. They connived to keep secret the birth of the child. They offered Dr. Potts money for his silence, thus committing a grievous offense. It is a felony to conceal the birth of a child!

Parker ended by attacking Miss Maggie and Miss Sallie for neglecting their caring kin and neighbors when they were writing their will. "Tirzah Coan, who closed the eyes of Dennis Ross when he died, who nursed them in sickness, comforted them in their grief, wasn't left anything. Jennie Helms, who did their calculating, was not remembered; nor were the Gribbles who visited her often when she was rich and when she was poor, and who were kissed on their arrival, being told by Maggie that she loved them dearly. She couldn't leave but five hundred dollars to Mrs. Taylor who was a comfort to them for many years, but she could and did leave her homeplace to Bob Ross, who had been living in luxury all of his life, and whose every wish was granted during their lifetime."

John J. Parker

33

A. M. STACK

People of intelligence don't submit to that kind of conduct unless they are under duress of other people.

—A. M. STACK, 1921

April 15, 1921

Amos Stack focused on the formalities for the first half-hour of his oration. He spoke as rapidly as he could, quoting witness after witness to convince the jury that Maggie, feeble-minded as she was, had suffered another's influence to make her will. "No one saw her sign the will," he said, referring to Sutton and Ezzell, "and so far as you know she didn't know its contents." Stack said Sallie influenced Maggie to make this "unnatural will," and Sallie was dominated by Hudson and other parties. "Witness have testified that both of them were crying like babies when the will was brought out for them to sign. That's sufficient evidence, gentlemen, that they were being forced to do something contrary to their wishes. The body of her sister had hardly gotten cold before Maggie, the poor, feeble old woman, was brought down to

A. M. Stack

Monroe to make a codicil to her will bequeathing money to the Hudson family." He was shouting now.

During the making of this codicil, Maggie sat there as dumb as a wash tub!

It is significant that the late Mr. Adams was secured to draw the will instead of Mr. Redwine, who was their attorney. Isn't it strange that those old women changed lawyers? Not for a moment would I reflect upon the name of Henry B. Adams. I studied law in his office for fifteen months and practiced in the same building for ten years with nothing but a thin partition between us. He was a lawyer of ability; he was a noble man; he was faithful to his clients, and in that will he was faithful to his client, R. A. Hudson. I resent the imputation that he conceived such a will. It was the work of another man.

Why should they ignore John Dees, whom Sallie said was the image of Dennis Ross, yet will a thousand dollars to Mr. Hudson, who admits he was but a hireling? Why did they leave nothing to Mrs. Coan, who served them in sickness and was their companion in their loneliness, yet bequeath a thousand dollars to R. A. Hudson, Jr.? Why did they overlook Miss Jennie Helms, who did their calculations for them, yet remember Harry Hood, a grandson of Mr. Hudson, to the extent of five hundred dollars? Did they render any services? Not one of the family except Mr. Hudson, Sr., and he was paid a salary.

Don't listen to the propaganda about Bob Ross being "a family negro." The records show that he was taken from his mother against her wishes. Frank Crane told you he heard her scream when they forced her to give him up, and she appealed to the Supreme Court for the possession of her own flesh and blood. Bob never did any work for Maggie Ross. He was a "dead-beat," a "sponger." Maggie once said that the land ought to go to those who made it. Surely she didn't think Bob Ross made it. She nor Sallie "made it." They inherited it from the Burleysons and from Dennis Ross, and all the attorneys for the caveators are seeking to do is to get that property for the descendants of those who made it, to see that Maggie Ross's own wish is carried out.

Stack suggested that Hudson's conniving influence on Miss Sallie shrewdly included the bequests to schools, churches, and libraries—put into the will for the purpose of "hiding his rascality."

"Witnesses testified that Mag had expressed herself as being opposed to contributing towards the education of other people's children. She refused to aid Rev. George Atkinson in his most commendable school endeavor. She had no charity in her heart for poor, struggling white girls who craved an education, but she did send that negro, Mittie Bell Houston, to college. The only known contribution she ever made to the cause of foreign missions in her life was a half a dollar. Why this change of heart? Why these thousand dollar bequests to schools, churches and hospitals? The reason is too obvious to bear mention.

"The failure of the Misses Ross to request the removal of the remains of their father, along with those of their two brothers and mother, to the cemetery plot in the Banks church, was almost a sacrilege, a desecration," he told the jury, painting a vivid picture of the old father sleeping alone.

> Leaving him there by itself showed senile decay. She willed her dead brother's watch to Bob Ross because he wanted him to have it, but Dennis Ross had been dead all these years. Why did she wait so long to carry out her dead brother's wish? For more than twenty years she paid no heed to his dying request. Maggie gave her watch to Mittie Bell; Sallie willed hers to Mrs. Hudson instead of to Mrs. Coan or Miss Helms, who were certainly more deserving of her remembrances.
>
> There's no evidence that Maggie knew how much she owned; she was even unable to return her property for taxation, and she considered herself poorer than a church mouse although she had thousands of dollars in the bank. When the preachers would come to her seeking a loan, she would order them to go to Mr. Hudson and tell him to let them have the money "if she had it in the bank." One preacher wanted five hundred dollars, and she sent him to Mr. Hudson with the same story although she had several times that amount in the house. She wasn't a liar. The propounders haven't even intimated that she was. She even let Hudson pay her preacher. The evidence on this point, gentlemen of the jury, is conclusive. She didn't have the sense to make the smallest transactions; not even the sense that my little twelve-year-old girl possesses. She calculates and pays her own church dues. I have no desire to traduce the memory of poor old Maggie Ross. I prefer to wear the mantle of charity and attribute that will to others of stronger minds; and in her feeble old age she was a fit subject for the insidious efforts of those parties.

The will, he explained, sprang from the minds of Hudson and the two negroes, Mittie Bell Houston and Bob Ross. Her inability to make change further strengthened the argument as to her lack of business ability, and he referred to the testimony of Margaret Garrison that Maggie became angry when one of her customers offered her eighteen cents for butter when he had been paying but fifteen. She couldn't understand that eighteen cents was more than fifteen. But he saved his strongest venom for her relationship with Bob and Mittie.

"They say that social equality is a matter of taste," Stack said.

It's not. Webster says taste is born of intelligence, so you must conclude, taking into consideration her association with those negroes, that she was weak-minded. She ate at the same table with negroes. She let Mittie Bell wear her silk dress to Camp Meeting. The negro girl even wore her underwear. She let negroes eat off the same stick of candy. She let Mittie Bell throw her baby into her lap with the command: "Clean it." I dare any of you jurors to tell your wife about these occurrences and then tell her that Maggie had good sense. Do you tell me that a Southern white woman would have permitted a negro to stay at her home after she had given birth to an illegitimate child? Why didn't she send her to her mother, who lived on the same place, when she learned of her condition? Was Maggie Ross intelligent? People of intelligence don't submit to that kind of conduct unless they are under duress of other people. She called Mittie Bell's baby her "little darling." Her conduct was shocking to Dr. McCain. It would be shocking to anybody, especially when she called Tom Houston, Mittie Bell's husband, her "son-in-law."

Ah, gentlemen, the truth is that Mittie Bell dominated that poor, old woman with threats. "You and your sister," she must have told Maggie more than once, "murdered my baby and if you don't buy me this, or do this, I'll report you."

Stack pointed out that the McIlwaine brothers' testimony, so vital to the propounders, was tainted because they had borrowed money from the Ross women, and their church was one of the legatees under the will. "My good friend, Rev. R. J. McIlwaine," he said, "spent last summer in the house bequeathed the Marvin Presbyterian Church, and I suppose he will do likewise this summer."

"Charity begins at home!" he shouted, lamenting Maggie's failure to remember Tirzah Coan, "who loved her like a sister, who nursed her in sickness, who closed the eyes of her brother when death came, and who was their companion. I would never think of leaving money to a church if I had a poor, decrepit cousin in need. All of the Presbyterian brethren think Miss Mag had a good mind because she left money to their church. A fool wouldn't do that, they think. She gave nothing to Dr. Potts, who attended them in their sickness, often driving through the rain and sleet in the dark hours of the night. But that Charlotte doctor got a thousand dollars."

Stack quoted from the testimony of Harriet Taylor and Margaret Moore, who had spent long visits in the sisters' house across many years; Dr. Ezzell, who once kept their books; and Dr. Crowell, who boarded with them for fourteen months, who said he never saw Maggie read a book, not even the Bible, and who considered her feeble-minded back in 1896 and 1897.

"Set aside this unnatural will obtained through the influence of others," he urged the jury. "You will go down in history for generations to come as members of the jury that decided the Ross case."

34

E. T. CANSLER

If these flimsy, half-hatched contentions of the caveators are true, you might as well blow up your court house, destroy your churches, tear up your Bibles and relax into barbarism!

—E. T. CANSLER, 1921

April 15, 1921

E. T. Cansler, rising to deliver the final argument, had an explanation for the will's leaving Nathaniel Ross's body in the Union Methodist cemetery when the others were moved to Banks: "His wife didn't want to live with him—she ordered him away—so why force them to rest in the same grave?"

The attorney took up the first of the three issues that Stack had laid out.

E. T. Cansler

Was the will executed according to the formalities required by law? The late Mr. H. B. Adams, who drew the will, was one of the leading lawyers of the state, and a man of the highest character who would

> not stoop to draw a will for a person of weak mind at the solicitation of another. But assuming for argument's sake that H. B. Adams was a corrupt man, as attorneys for the caveators infer, a tool of R. A. Hudson. He would have been doubly sure that the will was properly executed so it would stand in the courts. Sutton and Ezzell, who declared they didn't see Miss Mag sign the will, made oath that she did before the Clerk of Court when the will was probated. McIlwaine, the third witness to the will, said on the stand that she signed the will in their presence. Why this change of mind in Sutton and Ezzell? I don't know, I'm merely stating facts to you.

The rest of Cansler's argument combined the issues of Maggie's mentality and the alleged undue influence: "I am going to undertake to show you that this case is the result of the jealousy of three woman, Mrs. Taylor, Mrs. Moore and Harriet Grier, who were piqued because they were not remembered in the will after they had spent so many years in courting the good graces of the deceased Ross women. Take their evidence out of the case, and you have nothing but a shell left."

Cansler then referred to a courtroom scene from Charles Dickens's *Pickwick Papers*:

> And now, gentlemen, but one word more. Two letters have passed between these parties, letters which are admitted to be in the handwriting of the defendant, and which speak volumes indeed. These letters, too, bespeak the character of the man. They are not open, fervent, eloquent epistles, breathing nothing but the language of affectionate attachment. They are covert, sly underhanded communications, but, fortunately, far more conclusive than if couched in the most glowing language and the most poetic imagery—letters that must be viewed with a cautious and suspicious eye—letters that were evidently intended at the time, by Pickwick, to mislead and delude any third parties into whose hands they might fall. Let me read the first—"Garraway's, twelve o'clock. Dear Mrs. B.—Chops and Tomato sauce. Yours, Pickwick." Gentlemen, what does this mean? Chops and Tomato sauce! Gentlemen is the happiness of a sensitive and confiding female to be trifled away by such shallow artifices as these?

On such evidence was Mr. Pickwick convicted by a jury of trifling with Mrs. Bardell's affections and forced to pay seven hundred fifty pounds in damages. The caveators, Cansler explained, expect you as a jury to fall for the same sort of flimsy evidence. "More Chops and Tomato sauce!" became his refrain, delivered with a bow and a smile to

Parker and Stack as he wound through his oration attacking the caveators' case.

On the mentality required to make a will, Cansler said, all of the sense required by law is that a person be able to give a lawyer a skeleton or outline of her will. It is the attorney's duty to dress it in legal phraseology. Where Parker, for the "heirs at law," had told the jury over and over that the law makes the best will, Cansler accused the caveators of trying to destroy the sacred inviolability of the written testament.

Cansler called up the late Henry Adams. "He was incapable of meanness, he was incapable of violating a trust, and he knew those women had sense enough to make a will. The fact that H. B. Adams drew up that will is sufficient evidence of its validity to all who knew that splendid lawyer and citizen."

In contrast to Adams, Cansler attacked "those alienists, who were brought to Monroe from Richmond, Raleigh and Morganton by the caveators to answer long wordy hypothetical questions. Dr. Anderson has been superintendent of the insane asylum so long that a stranger at the institution would take him for a crazy man. Dr. Taylor was so confused by Vann's cross-examination that it appeared that senile decay had set in on his mind. Those doctors deal so much with crazy persons that they consider most everybody insane."

Then he turned back to Harriet Taylor and Margaret Moore—whose carbon-copy testimony that Maggie couldn't conduct a "connected conversation" had shown up in the alienists' hypothetical question—and Harriet Grier: "It's a case of the blind leading the blind, those crafty women whose names I have just called, who by their fawning blandishments and inquisitive attentions, sought to get Mag Ross's property, and who are now jealous of those negroes, being at the bottom of the case."

He skewered George Sutton's wish to break the will "for the good of the country": "An old woman living in the Marvin community all of her life, a good neighbor, a friend to everybody, yet Mr. Sutton says he never heard of her sanity being questioned until the contents of her will became known. Why should the women not leave money to negroes? People die leaving thousands for foreign missionary work in Africa, and I wouldn't be surprised if it wasn't for missionary work among negroes that DeLaney went to her for that contribution which he spoke of on the stand."

His dark eyes peered over the round, dark frames of his glasses. He leaned toward the jury, taking all of them in with those eyes.

"You've got to convict R. B. Redwine and the late H. B. Adams of participating in a fraudulent conspiracy to influence the Ross women to leave their money to those negroes before you break this will. Bob Ross, Mittie Bell Houston, Sallie Ross and Mr. R. A. Hudson were the persons using undue influence upon Maggie Ross, attorneys for the caveators say. They didn't dare come into court and charge Adams with participating in this conspiracy, contenting themselves with the imputation that he was a tool of R. A. Hudson and the negroes. Why didn't they secure R. B. Redwine, their attorney, to draw the will?" He shrugged. "It isn't considered good ethics for a lawyer to draw a will in which he is executor.

"If these flimsy, half-hatched contentions of the caveators are true, you might as well blow up your court house, destroy your churches, tear up your Bibles and relax into barbarism!"

Cansler stepped back and surveyed the empty witness chair.

"Where are those beloved cousins twice and third removed? George Ross, one of the two caveators who had the courage to come into court and attack the sanity of Maggie, stultified his testimony when he admitted that he accepted a deed to some land from her, believing her to be feeble-minded. Why didn't we produce Mittie Bell Houston? What, bring that corn-field negro up here to contradict a white woman? She would have been shot to pieces by Mr. Parker's astute cross-examination. It's not necessary for us to put negroes on the stand to win our case. We have a sufficient number of white witnesses."

Not just the ones who had testified.

I call up Sallie Ross, dead and gone. If she betrayed her sister, if she influenced her into making this will, handling her like a potter handles clay, then she's not worthy of the name "sister," and her name ought to be execrated throughout the County. But she can rest in peace, undisturbed. Maggie Ross made that will. Didn't she tell Dr. Nisbet, who wouldn't have sworn a lie for his thousand-dollar bequest, that "we've made our wills together, leaving the home place to Bob and Mittie and remembering a few of our friends"? Wouldn't you believe Dr. Nisbet, fine old gentleman that he is, in preference to Mrs. Moore, who, according to one of the boys, tried to "vamp" the jury while she was on the stand! Take the testimony of Dr. McIlwaine. He has no interest in this will except that natural to one of philanthropic impulses. He says it got out in the community that Maggie and Sallie had made a will, and he went to Maggie and asked her if she had left a house to the church? She replied affirmatively. Poor, crazy old fool! She had no memory for facts, figures or faces, yet when Dr. McIlwaine mentioned the subject to her some years later she recalled their previous conversation.

The three family physicians of Maggie Ross have pronounced her as having been sane. Dr. Alexander told you about leaving potent medicines with Mag to give to her sister who was desperately ill. Crazy, old fool! Dr. Potts unequivocally testified that she was of sound mind. Dr. Ezzell got mad when he learned that Dr. Nisbet was left a thousand dollars in the will. That's where the hell-raising started. He stopped in at Potts's and suggested that he join in testifying that Maggie Ross didn't have any sense, but Dr. Potts, I congratulate him, refused to be a party to such an act. Dr. Crowell, who lived with the Ross women back in '96 and '97, was just learning to crawl when he knew them. He was growing his first feathers, a mere fledgling; and I question his judgment since learning that he lost all he had to a German sharpster who tried to show him how he could reverse the Bible and overrule the laws of nature with "Twilight Sleep," an alleged method of painless childbirth. He undertook to remove that punishment, that ordeal, visited upon womanhood when Eve was driven from the Garden of Eden.

Hudson influenced them into making that will bequeathing their homeplace to negroes? I must say that he was liberal to give Bob and Mittie such a large slice. Break this will, gentlemen! You will do it over the mute protests of the late H. B. Adams and the late Sallie and Maggie Ross. A church refused its thousand-dollar bequest. What? Won't those immaculate spotless gentlemen who took eight hundred dollars from Maggie Ross when she was living accept a thousand dollar gift now that she is dead?

Why is it that sometimes a man who indulges in social equality and racial amalgamation is not held to be a moral degenerate while these women, because they picked up a pickaninny, like some women pick up a Maltese cat or a poodle dog, are said to be guilty of a foul offense against Southern habits and traditions? A horrible situation! Do you know that if conditions as pictured prevailed at the Ross home that the community would have arose in angry protest? Mr. Stack says Mrs. Moore is the smartest woman he ever talked to, yet she was at the Ross home making clothes for that little pickaninny. She and Mrs. Taylor ate at the table with them at the Ross home, and Mrs. Moore permitted Mittie and Maggie to visit her in Charlotte. Horrible!

Those antebellum women had an affection for Bob Ross, a negro bound to them, the affection of a mistress toward a servant. You know he helped make that property. Even Dr. Ezzell admitted that he had the reputation of being the hardest-working negro on the Ross place. Isn't it natural that Maggie and Sallie should make some reparation for taking Bob Ross out of the protesting arms of his mother when he was a mere lad? Gentlemen, take Mrs. Tirzah Coan's view of the case. "If it was my cousin's pleasure," she said, "for her property to go to Bob and Mittie, I have no protest. I loved my cousin, and she loved me."

The eastern windows were dark. It was seven o'clock in the cloudy evening. The wind was blowing from the south. Judge Ray banged his gavel for recess. Early start Saturday morning, he announced: 9 A.M.

That same day, Walter Bickett addressed the fifty-third anniversary celebration of Hampton Normal and Agricultural Institute. He called the institute for black students in Hampton, Virginia, a foundation and shrine: "From it are constantly flowing streams that make waste places glad, and from every quarter of the continent weary pilgrims come here for a new birth of courage, of faith and love." He invoked the image of slavery to urge students to seek economic freedom:

Before the war if a negro wanted to leave his master's plantation, he had to get a permit. . . . This was a humiliating situation, but the negro who has to get an order from a white man before he can buy a sack of meal or a side of meat is almost as much as slave as the man who had to get a permit before he could leave his master's land. The borrower wears the yoke of the lender. Put this down: The negro as a race will not travel far until his credit in store or in bank is as good as that of the white man who lives at the other end of the street. . . .

The negro is entitled to equal and exact justice before the law. The white man must accord him that justice or be false to all those traditions that have made the Anglo-Saxon race the glory of the world. If there is anything that a white man despises it is another white man who tries to cheat a negro out of his wages or his property. One of the first cases that ever came to me as a lawyer was one in which a white man was trying to swindle an old negro out of his wages. Hot with indignation I went to the jury, preached for one-half hour on the text, "The laborer is worthy of his hire." The jury administered on that white man and gave the old negro every dollar that he claimed.

35

CHARGE AND VERDICT

Colored people when they come into the courts have exactly the same rights, guaranteed to them by the Constitution of the State of North Carolina and of the United States as other people, and juries should be careful to see that no injustice is done them by their verdicts on account of their color.

—JUDGE J. BIS RAY, 1921

April 16, 1921

The sky was still overcast but no rain was falling when Judge Ray opened court on Saturday. The dirt streets were dry but not dusty, and the smell of the moist earth freshened the warm air. Word had spread around Monroe and among the farmers coming to town that the testimony and the closing arguments had ended and the case would go to the jury that day. The crowd that crammed into the courtroom and down the steps appeared as festive as that on the first day of the trial, but an undertow of uncertainty, a sort of breath-holding for the conclusion of the spectacle—tinged with a vague sorrow that it should end at all—stirred deeply among them. Men among the hundred that had been excused from the jury came back, taut-jawed, to make sure the right verdict was returned. Freshly powdered ladies fanned demurely and sat straight in their best dresses, models of the Southern womanhood that Parker and Stack were trying to shield from the scandal of a crazy woman. The crowd crackled as it had not since the caveators rested, as if the spectators suddenly realized that the clear conclusion of their testimony was not yet the official verdict of the trial. No one could guess how long the decision would take. Judge Ray began reading his charge to the jury by defining the technical terms involved—"testator," "testatrix," "caveator," "propounder," "codicil," "probate," and "*devisavit vel non*"—"Did the textatrix devise or not?"

"The issue can only be tried by a jury, it being an issue of fact, and in passing upon the issue you, as a jury, are to limit your consideration exclusively to the evidence offered on the trial," he intoned from the bench. "You are to cut loose from any preconceived idea you may have had about the matter. You are not to allow any extraneous or collateral matter to influence you in your deliberations, but to determine from the evidence alone if the paper propounded be or not the last will and testament and the codicil of the late Maggie Ross. I wish you to forget for the time being any prejudices, if any you have ever had in the matter, and consider this matter as the law would have you consider it from the testimony as it comes from the witnesses."

He explained that the burden of proof with respect to the making and executing of the will was on the propounders—they must show, by preponderance of the evidence, that Maggie made the will.

If it were possible for you to make of each word spoken by each of the witnesses who testified in behalf of the propounders in favor of the probate of the will upon the contentions of the propounders, as affecting the making and execution of the paper and the sufficiency of the mind of Maggie Ross, deceased, giving to each word a definite weight and a relative weight to every other word, until you had gone through and considered all the testimony adduced at the instance of the propounders, until you got the sum-total of all its weight, going into the testimony produced at the instance of the caveators, which you find or might find tending to prove, or proving any contention made by the propounders and adding that to the sum-total of the evidence that you find favorable to the propounders' contentions, if such evidence you find, and placing it on one end of a scale for weighing, then taking the testimony adduced at the instance of the caveators, giving to every word a weight and a relative weight to every word, like you have for the propounders in the first instance and going into the testimony of the propounders, if any evidence you find wherein proving or tending to prove the caveators' contentions, and when you have given to it a definite weight, then place it in the other end of the scales, basing the testimony upon all the contentions of the parties as affecting the mental capacity of the said Maggie Ross, deceased, to make or not to make a will, and after observing the weight, if there is an equality of weight or an even weight of the testimony upon the question of mental capacity, then it would be your duty to answer the issue submitted to you negatively, as to the propounders, or No, for the evidence must preponderate in favor of the propounders, i.e., outweigh the evidence of the caveators, or the caveators are entitled to your verdict.

The crowd was already glazing at the drip of words from the judge's mouth. The jurors struggled to absorb it all as he explained in detail the legal requirements for the making of a will.

Besides the requisite formalities of the making of the will, a will is not valid unless the testator or testatrix not only intends of his or her own free will to make such a disposition but is capable of knowing what he or she is doing and of understanding to whom the property in the will is being given, its nature and kind, and in what proportion, who are the objects of the bounty and have natural claims upon such testator or testatrix, and who are being deprived as heirs or devisees under the will being made. The law requires that a person, in order to make a valid will, should be of sound mind and disposing memory. What is meant by soundness of mind in this connection is not that the mind should be in its full vigor and power, but that its faculties, its machinery, should be in working order, so to speak, with power to collect and retain the elements of the business to be performed for a sufficient time to perceive their obvious relations to each other.

He explained that the propounders bore the burden to prove that Maggie was of sound mind but that the law presumes every person to be of sound mind until the contrary is shown. "It is also a rule of law that though a person may possess sufficient mental capacity to make and execute a will, yet, if the making and executing a will by them be unduly influence by another, this would be a fraud upon the rights of those who, by relation of blood, would be entitled to receive such person's property under the law had they died intestate, i.e., without a will," he said, adding that the burden of proving undue influence lay on the caveators.

"Now undue influence in this connection is any means employed upon and which the testatrix, under the circumstances and conditions, was surrounded and which she could not well resist, which controlled the volition and induced such testatrix to do what she would not have otherwise done, and such may be accomplished by working upon or exaggerating any eccentricity the testatrix might possess. Undue influence to vitiate a will must have been actually exercised to produce the particular will at the very time of the execution of the particular paper in controversy as a will," Judge Ray said, bringing a strong objection from the caveators.

> To make a will, the maker must be a free agent, but all influences are not unlawful. Appeals to the affection, to gratitude for past services or pity for future destitution or the like are all legitimate and may fairly be urged upon the testatrix. On the other hand, pressure of whatever character, if so exercised as to overpower the volition without convincing the judgment, is a species of restraint under which no valid will can be made. In other words, the will must be the offspring of the testator's own volition and not the records of the wishes or desires of someone else; and in considering whether the testator's free volition has been overpowered or controlled, the jury must consider the age, physical and mental condition and all the circumstances surrounding the testatrix.

Judge Ray read pages of the caveators' contentions, focusing on her poor health, her protests of poverty, her belief in ghosts, her inability to make change, and especially her relationship with Bob and Mittie Bell:

> That she lived on terms of social equality with a negro girl, allowing said negro girl to eat at the same table with her, and to sleep in the same bed; that she went with the negro father of the said negro girl to Salisbury to visit her when she was a student in the negro school at that place, and spent the night in the negro school; that after the said negro girl had become pregnant with an illegitimate child and she had been told of this fact by a physician she allowed the negro girl to continue to live in her house and to give birth to the child in her own bedroom; the caveators contend that she aided and abetted in concealing the birth of said child, so that the nearest neighbors knew nothing about it; that she allowed the said negro woman to pull her nose and ears, to wear her clothes, underclothing and shoes and take other liberties with her; that she would nurse the children of the said negro woman and would allow the said woman to order her to clean her negro baby.

They claimed that Harriet Taylor and Margaret Moore were testifying against their own interests, given that they were beneficiaries of the will, while many of the propounders' witnesses were protecting their self-interest.

Caveators further contend that the will itself bears on its face evidence of the mental capacity of its maker, caveators contending that no persons with sufficient mental capacity would have willed the valuable property of Miss Maggie Ross, consisting of a large body of land in the heart of a white community, in such a way as to place it in the hands of negroes in such a way that it could not be disposed of by them, caveators contending that no persons with sufficient mental capacity to make a will would have affronted their names in such a way, caveators contending that the fact that the said will leaves fifty dollars every six months for five years to the same legatees and devisees to whom are willed the bulk of the large estate of Maggie Ross shows that she did not have sufficient mental capacity to understand the nature and the effect of the disposition of which she was making.

She devised the homeplace of her mother, which had come down from her grandfather, to two negroes who had no claims upon her bounty, and devised it to them in such a way with contingent demands as to tie it up on the hands of said negroes for years to come; she made special bequests to Mittie Bell Houston, her father, her mother, her husband, her grandmother and her daughter, caveators contending that these dispositions were unnatural, unjust and unreasonable, and were not such bequests as would have been made by a white woman living in a white community unless she had been unduly influenced to do so. Caveators contend that the various amounts devised to charitable institutions were placed in the will by a shrewd mind for the purpose of upholding the unnatural provisions of the will, caveators contending that said provisions were inserted for the purpose of enlisting the support of religious denominations and charitable institutions in upholding the will, so that those who had procured the executions thereof by undue influence would have the support and help of such institutions in upholding a will which was unnatural, unjust and shocking to the community where the property was situated.

The propounders, in addition to rehearsing the story of the will-signing, took a different legal tack in the pages they gave Judge Ray to read, forming a different story from the facts just as they had throughout the trial.

The propounders contend that the right to make a will is a right guaranteed to every person over the age of twenty-one and of sound mind and memory by the laws of the State of North Carolina, and that when such person complies with the requirements of the law as to the manner of executing his or her will, upon due proof thereof such will is entitled to probate as the last will and testament of the person so making it, regardless of the inequalities or unnaturalness of its provisions or bequests. The propounders further contend that the will which has been propounded is a natural, rather than an unnatural, disposition of her property, when all the surrounding circumstances are taken into consideration.

They contend that in early life, when they were poor, these old women were neglected by their kin and looked down upon by their neighbors when they were young; that they were illiterate, close and saving in money matters and unattractive in appearance; that at the time of the execution of their wills they had no nearer relatives living than second cousins; that the negro Bob Ross was taken by their mother or brother from his mother when he was about four years old and raised in their house, and was the servant of their only brother until his death in 1896; that until he married he never knew any other home; that they raised the girl, Mittie Bell, in their home and that she served them until she married; that neither of the Ross women were ever married, so had no children of their own to mother, and gratified their maternal instincts in this way; that a large part of their property was made by negroes and that they considered it a matter of right and justice that they should receive a part of this property when their use for it had ceased; that their kin-people had looked down upon them in the time of their adversity, although some of them fawned upon them in their prosperity, most of them who were living at the time of the execution of the will being more distantly related than second cousins, that they had no affection for such of them as needed help or reason for giving them their property, and in its disposition they remembered those that had helped them make it and who had been kind to them, although of another race and color.

The propounders attacked the hypothetical question for the alienists, mocked the theory of conspiracy among Dick Hudson, Bob, and Mittie Bell, and pointed out that strong-minded Sallie, not only supposedly weak-minded Maggie, had signed the same will.

Propounders further contend the alleged acts of social equality or familiarity between Miss Maggie Ross and her servants Bob and Mittie Bell also took place between Miss Sallie Ross and Bob and Mittie Bell, and as it is admitted by all the witnesses who have been on the stand that Miss Sallie Ross was a woman of sound mind, it necessarily shows that the familiarity of Miss Mag Ross with these negroes is no evidence of weak-mindedness on the part of Miss Maggie Ross.

Propounders further contend that the inference sought to be placed on the conduct of the Ross women towards Mittie Bell Houston when she became pregnant is not only unnatural and inhumane but unchristian in the highest degree, as they contend; that the evidence shows that Mittie Bell was practically adopted by the Rosses and raised by them in their home; they naturally felt not only the affection that the good mistress feels for her faithful servants, but also a certain moral responsibility for her proper training and upbringing and therefore, when they discovered her disgrace, their natural inclinations were not only to try to shield and protect her from the consequence of her condition for her own sake but also, the propounders contend the Ross women were actuated in their conduct, that if the knowledge of Mittie Bell's condition became common property that it would bring a certain amount of disgrace upon them.

The propounders contend further in this connection that if the Ross women had driven out this sixteen-year-old girl and sent her back to her father's as the caveators contend they should, thereby making her disgrace public property, that they would have failed in their duty, a duty which they owed to both Mittie Bell and her father, Bob Ross, when they took her and undertook to bring her up as a decent and respectable colored girl.

The propounders further contend that it is not the province of the jury to pass upon the question of the effect that a verdict sustaining this will might have upon the community in which this property devised to these colored people is located; that because these devisees are colored people should not prejudice your minds against them; that colored people when they come into the courts have exactly the same rights, guaranteed to them by the Constitution of the State of North Carolina and of the United States as other people, and that juries should be careful to see that no injustice is done them by their verdicts on account of their color; that the only question to be passed upon by this jury is *Is the will propounded the will of Maggie Ross*?

The clouds outside had broken, and the sun was rising higher and hotter among the white billows in the blue sky as the morning wore on. The listeners fanned listlessly. Judge Ray returned to his own words for the jury, detailing when the burden of proof was on the propounders, when on the caveators; describing how they should evaluate the testimony of eyewitnesses, of depositions, of alienist experts, of character witnesses, of interested and disinterested parties; outlining each issue on which the jury must answer "Yes" or "No." The judge, his monotone thick as the steamy air in the room, also read special instructions for the caveators and for the propounders. The caveators took exception to his charge that equal weight on the question of undue influence meant they should rule for the propounders, to his saying that the expert testimony counts for nothing if the jurors disbelieve the assumptions of the hypothetical question, to his reading the propounders' assertion that the codicil counted as a republication of the will, that the jury could consider Henry Adams's reputation, that any delusions Maggie might have had about ghosts or angels don't count unless they were influencing her at the making of the will, that Maggie's agreement with Sallie could make up for any feeble-mindedness she may have had.

"If you find from the evidence that Maggie Ross freely and voluntarily executed the paper purporting to be her will in manner and form prescribed by law and had sufficient mental capacity to understand the property she owned and its nature and extent, the natural objects of her bounty and the effects and consequences of making a will, then it would be your duty to answer the issue 'Yes,' even though you may find that Maggie Ross was old and infirm, feeble-minded and mentally weak, permitted familiarities by negroes and associated with them in preference to her neighbors and relatives, believed in ghosts and was superstitious," the propounders concluded.

Judge Ray completed his charge: "The Court submits to you but one issue which is given: *Is the paper writing propounded, and every part thereof, and the codicil attached thereto, the last will and testament of the said Maggie Ross, deceased*? Under the rules of law that I have laid down as to the preponderance of the testimony, it will be your duty to answer this issue 'Yes' or 'No' as you wind from the evidence it should be answered."

It was eleven forty-five when the jury shuffled out of their seats and through the door with a frosted-glass panel into their deliberating room. The charge, fifty-six pages long, had taken nearly three hours to read. Spectators, long ago numbed by the legal repetitions, fidgeted in their seats and wondered whether to go for lunch. Judge Ray had managed to quench the crowd's emotions as well as inform the jurors' deliberations. The clock in the tower above chimed twelve. Maybe this afternoon. Maybe not. The jury down in Georgia had taken eighteen hours a week ago after barely two days of testimony and a half-dozen witnesses. These twelve men had listened to two weeks of testimony, nearly a hundred witnesses. If it had taken Judge Ray so long to outline the issues, how could the jury even review them in less time, much less consider all they had heard since that long-ago midnight when they had all taken their seats? Even if, as many suspected, the conclusion was foregone.

Anyone who took a lunch hour missed the verdict. The clock was chiming twelve-thirty when the jurors returned to their seats, and the spectators buzzed with speculation about what such a quick decision might mean.

Judge Ray called the jury to stand.

"Is the paper writing propounded, and every part thereof, and the codicil attached thereto, the last will and testament of said Maggie Ross, deceased?"

"Yes."

36

REACTION

Perhaps no greater temptation has ever been placed before a jury to break a will, but it made bold to establish justice for negroes and write a triumph for the law.

—CHARLOTTE OBSERVER, 1921

Amid the roiling rumble in the courtroom, defiant for the moment of Judge Ray's gavel, the caveators' lawyers quickly moved to set aside the verdict, moved for a new trial for errors they said the court committed in admitting some testimony and rejecting others and in the charge to the jury. Overruled. Judge Ray signed the judgment over the caveators' objection. The caveators appealed to the state Supreme Court and filed a fifty-dollar appeal bond backed by Tip Helms and J. B. Coan. The lawyers agreed that the caveators would have until August first to serve their case on appeal and the propounders would have sixty days after that to serve a counter case or exceptions.

The jurors went home to face their families and neighbors. They had plenty of explaining to do. Of course, a southern jury just one week earlier had decided against a white man in a case that cost him his freedom, so they were not exactly alone. Besides, Mayor Sikes was a good man, and he was on the propounders' side. So was J. C. M. Vann, who was elected to succeed him as mayor with seven hundred twenty-four votes to his two opponents' total one hundred ninety-five—the very day of the verdict.

But some of their friends had been to the lynching of Tom Johnson and Joe Kiser across the Rocky River in Cabarrus County just twenty-three years ago. Everyone knew the story of Niggerhead Creek. White men in other sections were taking the little land that black people owned, and these white men were giving a white family's farm away. No one could imagine living next to a negro who owned eight hundred acres. In the eyes of many they were guilty, like Lincoln, of putting the bottom rail on the top, hoodwinked by a sharp Charlotte lawyer into robbing the governor's family of its rightful estate. Their world had lost the war to the Yankee army, the grandfather clause to the Yankee Supreme Court, and now so much soil—to a southern jury!

Adam Morgan told his relatives he had little choice: The reason why the white ladies willed their property to the two black people, he said, was that they were the only people who helped them. Their own people, the white cousins, turned their back to the ladies, near the whole damn list. By the time they got back to the jury room, they all knew it. Nobody wanted to be the first to say it—it took forty-five minutes for everybody to admit it—but they all knew it. The Ross cousins—it wasn't even really Ross land! It was Burleyson land, and the Ross side was evicted by Jonathan Burleyson's will even before the war. Susan wasn't even sleeping in the same cemetery with Nathan. It wasn't something Sallie and Maggie did when they were old—hell, it looked like what their mama meant when she went and got the lad in the first place. Bob Ross had been collecting their rents and ginning their cotton and laying off the road through their land long before they sat down, after Florence was born, on the anniversary of their mother's death, and signed their will.

But what about the bastard baby? Wasn't there plenty of reason to think the women were blackmailed? What about sleeping with them, eating with them, taking a lick off the same stick of candy? What about calling that girl their adopted granddaughter, or Tom Houston their son-in-law? What white people in their right mind would do that?

Well, turns out that John J. Parker and his team left the jury little way to think except that Maggie Ross considered Bob and Mittie Bell her family. For all their talk about "natural heirs," referring to cousins who never darkened the women's door, they showed that the natural relationship in this case crossed the color line. Miss Maggie called Tom Houston her son-in-law. Cansler was right about sharing and supporting and standing by the suffering: That's what families do—bear their mutual burdens, sympathize with tears, hold as one their woes, their fears, their hopes, their aims, their comforts, and their cares.

Bud Huey told his family he was highly in favor of giving the land to Bob and Mittie Bell: "They had taken care of those white women all their lives, and they deserved to have it."

The twice-weekly *Monroe Journal*, in its exhaustive covering of the closing arguments and verdict the following Tuesday, tallied the cost to the taxpayers at about five hundred seventy-five dollars in jury fees and other expenses, in addition to the court costs borne by the caveators. "Each of the twelve jurors received $45 for attendance during the fifteen days and mileage and expenses for the first day. Their effort to break the will will cost the caveators over a thousand dollars, it is estimated. There were about a hundred witnesses in attendance on an average of at least six days which, with mileage, will amount to $750; the clerk of court and sheriff's fees were in the neighborhood of $200; while it is believed that they had to pay those alienists who testified about $400. However, it is reported that attorneys for the caveators took the case on a contingent fee, and this being true, the cost will fall up on them. Attorneys for the propounders, a person in the position to know figures, will receive a total of $4500, at least $1500 of which will go to Mr. E. T. Cansler of Charlotte."

The *Journal* lampooned Cansler's use of *Pickwick Papers* in his closing arguments by noting a "startling similarity" between Dr. Pascal Abernethy's early appeal to be excused from the Ross jury and a chemist's appeal to be excused from the jury in Dickens's novel, which the paper quoted at length. "But fortunately, none of Dr. Abernethy's patrons' stock became stricken, and since the case is over we rather think he enjoyed the experience even if it was rather costly," the article concluded.

The *Charlotte News*, which had not covered the trial in progress, ran a brief front-page notice the day after the verdict—"ROSS WILL CASE

WON BY THE PROPOUNDERS"—so hastily written that it got Sallie's name wrong:

Monroe, April 16—The propounders of the will won the verdict in the celebrated Ross will case, which ended this afternoon, the 15th day of the trial. The jury, which was out only 45 minutes, brought in a verdict that the late Maggie and Mary Ross, spinsters, were of sufficiently sound mind to dispose of their estate when they made a will leaving about 1,400 acres of land to former negro servants.

The trial was before Judge J. Bis Ray in the superior court.

The estate that furnished the basis for the suit is estimated as being worth about $100,000. The makers of the will left their entire estate, with the exception of about $10,000 given to charity, to the negroes mentioned in the will. These were a negro man and his wife and child, who had long lived on the Ross place.

On April 21, the *Charlotte Observer* published its editorial reaction under the headline:

THE NEGRO, THE LAW AND RIGHT

About a year ago, The Observer made editorial suggestion that the Maggie Ross will, in which a white woman in Union County had bequeathed a fine estate to a family of negroes who had proved of faithful service to the white family during the lonesome days which had fallen upon it, and when it had apparently found itself forgotten by neighbor and kin, would afford excellent matter for editorial discussion by the papers of the North that have never been able to understand that the negro can be kindly treated in the South. Of course it was to be assumed by these papers that the will would be contested and broken by white relatives of the family and that they would better withhold comment until it was known if the will would stand. They may now proceed with free discussion of this interesting case, for the will has withstood the combined assaults of a battery of the best legal talent in the State, including a former governor, and a jury has decided that the estate, valued at $100,000, should be divided among the negro servants exactly in accordance with the bequest of the maker of the will. It was a notable case, and the general public might have been justified in a preconceived opinion that the will would be broken and the negroes would be cheated out of their rights by process in the court, but the jury, composed of white men, found in favor of the beneficiaries named by the white woman on every issue which had been submitted to it for decision. This in spite of the existence of much feeling and prejudice in the community. The verdict of the jury in this case affords ample demonstration of the fact that in North Carolina it is possible to establish justice even for a negro in a will. It was a legal battle lasting through 15 days and every point was hotly defended in behalf of the negroes. The outcome was that the will is to stand in every detail as written by Maggie Ross. The court respected the wishes of the dead woman even though the beneficiaries were negroes.... The lawyers attacked the sanity of the maker of the will and it was designated as "an unnatural will," but it was established to the satisfaction of the jury that the devisor wanted the family of negroes rewarded for faithful and loyal service when she had been otherwise left alone in life, and the jury decided that her wishes, natural or unnatural, should be carried out as she had requested. Perhaps no greater temptation has ever been placed before a jury to break a will, but it made bold to establish justice for negroes and write a triumph for the law.

Two weeks after the verdict, Ku Klux Klan organizer Ti-Bo-Tim of Charlotte wrote to twenty-six Monroe businessmen, announcing plans to start a branch in the town. "Your name has been given to me by a personal friend of yours, who stated that you were a real American and believed in our flag, the tenets of the Christian religion, good womanhood and white supremacy," his letter began. "The above order most positively stands for all these and also for the upholding, fulfilling and enforcement of the laws."

On May 10, Confederate Memorial Day, the *Journal* announced that the first attempt had failed for lack of interest, and the Klan would try again. On May 13, a front-page letter from a former *Journal* editor in Texas denounced the effort, which faded: "It is to be hoped that nobody in Monroe will be silly enough to join the so-called Ku Klux Klan," he wrote. "This is about the cheapest thing that has been sprung on an unsuspecting public.... Everybody knows that this scheme is a cheap appeal to thoughtless people to arouse ill will toward the negroes, or at least to trade on a supposed ill will that is thought to exist. It is an unpatriotic move in that it arouses old animosities, and painful experiences in the life of the past that it can do no good to resurrect. Men ought to be above such things at this time."

Meanwhile, not even the verdict in the Ross will trial could guarantee the resolution of the case. The cousins continued their fight.

37

NEW TRIAL

If a woman who is so feeble-minded that, alone and unassisted, she cannot furnish her attorney "details concerning her property, nor the persons or institutions to whom she wished to will same, nor directions as to the disposition of said property," then it can hardly be said that she is capable of making a will, disposing of a large estate, under the test as laid down in this and other jurisdictions.

—NORTH CAROLINA SUPREME COURT JUDGE WALKER PARKER STACY, 1921

February 18, 1924

A cold rain was falling on Monday, February 18, 1924, the gray clouds dripping just about enough to accumulate an inch all day. A few degrees cooler, and the northwesterly wind would be blowing snow. In Judge Thomas Shaw's Union County Superior Courtroom, twelve men swore their oaths, took their seats in the jury box, and faced their first case of the day. J. W. Tadlock, J. B. Hargett, J. B. Hartsell, Lonnie Wilson Tucker, Z. B. Presson, John Baxter Price, Jessie L. Helms, L. W. Ashcraft, W. M. Sell, T. B. Alexander, W. T. Medlin, and W. D. Hice had to decide whether to grant Ethel Knight a divorce from Walter Knight. The jury, finding that the couple had lived apart for five years, dissolved the bonds of matrimony.

Next case. In Re: Will of Maggie Ross.

In their appeal, the caveators accused Judge Ray of thirty-seven errors, beginning with his remark that the lawyers should not have taken George Sutton to their office "during recess of court and see what he will testify to" and ending with his signing of the judgment. They said he should not have admitted the wills of Sallie and Maggie, the letter from Henry Adams to the sisters, the reputation of Henry Adams, and large chunks of testimony from propounders' witnesses. They said he should have admitted testimony he struck from caveators' witnesses. They alleged ten errors in his charge to the jury.

The caveators filed a twenty-page brief with the Supreme Court. The propounders filed a thirty-two-page brief, defending the judge's rulings during the trial and pointing out that the mutual wills amounted to a contract between Sallie and Maggie, an issue that Judge Ray had excluded at the outset.

Judge Walker Parker Stacy agreed with the caveators' objection to part of the propounders' reasoning that Judge Ray had read to the jury concerning Maggie's dependence on Sallie. Their instructions said that even if jurors believed that "Miss Maggie Ross was feeble-minded and that alone and unassisted she could not have furnished her attorney" with details of the will, they could conclude that the sisters' joint session with H. B. Adams was sufficient: "Maggie Ross being present hearing such details and directions given, and by words or acts assenting to such details, directions and dispositions."

"There are several objections to this charge," Judge Stacy wrote.

> In the first place, it fails to observe the difference in time between the giving of the instructions to the attorney and the execution of the will. Ordinarily, the question of a few days might not be capitally important, but this would depend entirely upon the circumstances of the given case. It appears from the instant record that the testatrix was sixty-eight years of age at the time of the execution of her will; she was feeble-minded, in ill health, given to fits of weeping or crying, and was subject to spells of melancholia. There was further evidence tending to show that the testatrix was crying at the time she signed the will.
>
> The competency of the testatrix to make the will in question is to be determined as of the date of its execution, or of its republication as by a codicil and not when instructions for its preparation were given. Of course, the conduct of

the testatrix at the time of this conference is competent and relevant, as bearing upon the question of her testamentary capacity; but, notwithstanding her mental condition at that time, this would not necessarily establish her competency to execute the will at the subsequent date. The above special instruction, however, takes no note of this difference in time and really makes her capacity at the time of the conference, and not at the date of the signing, the test of her ability to execute the will. This is not in keeping with the law as heretofore declared.

Again, the giving of this special prayer was erroneous because it takes from the jury the question as to the due execution of the will. This was one of the grounds of the caveat, and the burden was on the propounders to establish the formal execution of the paper writing alleged to be the last will and testament of the said Maggie A. Ross.

But the overshadowing objection to this instruction is to the substance of the charge bearing upon the quantum of mind, or mental capacity, necessary to the making of a valid will. . . . The practical effect of this instruction was to say that although Maggie Ross was incapable of making a will, yet, if she assented to what her sister did, such conduct on her part would meet the requirements of the law and amount to a valid testamentary disposition of her property.

We do not think she could understandingly and competently assent to her sister's act when, at the same time, she was wanting in the requisite mental capacity to act for herself. We are not advertent to any authority holding that one person may make a will for another when the person for whom the will is to be made is wanting in testamentary capacity. In fact, the very statement of the proposition would seem to refute itself.

If the word "assent," appearing in its present context, is to be construed as giving such assent as the law requires, with sufficient capacity so to do, then the charge is self-contradictory; because the instruction starts with the assumption that the testatrix is without sufficient testamentary capacity. If she be without the necessary capacity of mind, then she could not legally assent to the act of another in disposing of her property by will. But in all events, the instruction was prejudicial to the rights of caveators, and we must hold it for reversible error.

If a woman who is so feeble-minded that, alone and unassisted, she cannot furnish her attorney "details concerning her property, nor the persons or institutions to whom she wished to will same, nor directions as to the disposition of said property," then it can hardly be said that she is capable of making a will, disposing of a large estate, under the test as laid down in this and other jurisdictions.

Judge Platt Dickinson Walker disagreed with his colleagues' analysis of the charge. "It is my opinion that there was no error in the selected instruction, when properly construed, but surely there was none if we read it in connection with those that preceded it. But even if there was any error in the instruction of the presiding judge selected by the court as the ground for a new trial, there was a

> codicil to the will which, in law, amounted to a republication of it, and there was no such objection to the charge as to the execution and validity of the codicil. For all that appears, she executed the same without any help or suggestion from others, and this cured any error in regard to the will, if there was any.

But Judge Walker, reluctantly accepting the authority of other courts on the question of evidence as to mental capacity, agreed with Judge Stacy and the court's order in the matter, issued on November 23, 1921: "New trial."

The propounders paid the Supreme Court costs, three hundred twenty-five dollars and ninety-five cents.

At the new trial, the jury that had divorced the Kikers sat for the evidence about the Maggie Ross will, for Judge Shaw's charge, for deliberation—all in minutes and hours, not days and weeks as the courtroom had witnessed nearly three years earlier. When they returned, they answered the same question.

"Is the paper writing propounded, and every part thereof, and the codicil attached thereto, and every part thereof, the last will and testament of Maggie Ross?"

They gave the same answer: "Yes."

Judge Shaw wrote the conclusion:

> It is upon motion adjudged and decreed that the paper writing propounded and every part thereof, and the codicil attached thereto, and every part thereof, is the last will and testament of Maggie Ross, deceased, and it is further ordered that the same be and it is hereby admitted to probate in solemn form.
>
> It is further ordered that the executors therein named pay all the costs of this proceeding out of funds coming into their hands belonging to said estate and that the order heretofore made by the clerk of this court directing the executors to proceed no further in the administration of said estate be, and forever is hereby, vacated.

PART IV

The Heritage

38

THE PEOPLE

We had a large community of colored people. All from Providence Road back this way was colored folks, and this was our church.

—LUCINDA HOUSTON, 1993

Mittie Bell Houston's baby Ervin had just turned three when Maggie died, and Florence, the oldest of her six children, was not yet thirteen. Through the years of trial, she and Tom were making a home in the house that the sisters had built for them after their wedding. No more trips to the big house between the churches: It was promised to Banks Presbyterian, and Reverend McIlwaine stayed there the summer after Maggie's funeral. The J. E. Efird Monument Company in Monroe inscribed Maggie Ross's name on her family's monument in the Banks Presbyterian cemetery and placed a footstone lettered M. A. R. at her grave on December 10, 1923. The work cost forty dollars. In March and April 1924, Banks Presbyterian Church, the Piedmont Industrial School (by then the Southern Industrial Institute), Marvin Methodist Church, Bonds Grove Methodist Church, the Western North Carolina Methodist Conference, the Home Missions Committee of the Presbyterian Synod of North Carolina, the Barium Springs Presbyterian Orphanage, Mittie Bell Houston, Bob Ross, Harriet Taylor, Margaret Moore, Will Garrison, R. A. Hudson, Sallie Hudson, Harry Hood, Dr. W. O. Nesbit, Henry Featherstone, Fannie Forbis,

Ed Yarbrough, Carl Yarbrough, and Margaret Jackson Crane Haney received their legacies from the Ross will. The individuals had inheritance tax deducted. The institutions' receipts were reduced by their share of the expenses of the legal contest. The Methodists, for example, received nine hundred dollars of their thousand-dollar bequest, and the industrial school received one thousand three hundred fifty of its fifteen hundred. Also in March 1924, the W. G. Thompson & Company shoe store in Charlotte got its twelve dollars and seventy-five cents for a pair of shoes Maggie had bought weeks before she died, Dr. J. B. Elliott of Fort Mill, South Carolina, got his fifteen dollars for his call two days before she died, and the Niven-Price Company in Waxhaw got its money for supplies that had been used to repair buildings on the land after Maggie died. Presbyterian Hospital received its one thousand dollars from the Ross will on April 8, 1924.

On February 26, 1924, R. B. Redwine and Dick Hudson won a partial victory in their fight to cut taxes on the inheritance. Judge Thomas J. Shaw ruled that the half the tax should be on the value of property at the death of Sallie Ross in 1909 and half on the value at the death of Maggie in 1920. He ordered the state to return $2,859.21. Legatees who paid inheritance tax received partial rebates on February 24, 1925. The cost of the trial, with propounders paying expenses, was settled in July 1925. The firm of Cansler and Cansler received $17,353.90, Parker and Craig $4,500, Walter B. Love $1,000. More than forty court decisions referred to "In re Ross' will" in the next sixty years.

Alice Massey, Bob's estranged wife, sued the estate for one hundred dollars, the amount given to her in the original will and cut out by the codicil. Judge T. D. Bryson ruled on June 10, 1925, that Alice should receive the money under Sallie's will, though not Maggie's, because the codicil could not affect Sallie's will. The executors paid Alice. When Jackson died, she married King Robinson and remained a close part of the growing family. Bob and Mittie Bell received the balance of their cash legacy, $2,967.57 each, on February 28, 1925. Florence Tucker Houston, who married Thomas Vinson, received her last payment from the estate, $61.63, on June 6, 1930.

The family grew fruitful and multiplied on the garden it was given, known as Rosstown. The dirt road that Frank Crane's crew had laid out was called Rosstown Road. Florence, known as "Tuck" to her descendants, had three children—Alice, who died; Thomas Erskin, known as "Tomcat," who had fifteen children; and Willie Earnest, who had five, of which Thomas, Peggy, Barbara, and Donny survived. Mittie's son Dennis Clyde "D. C.," Charlie "Paddycake," Robert Tom "Uncle Hop," Collins, and Ervin added dozens more. Collins moved to Charlotte, and some of his descendants lost touch with their Union County relatives. At his funeral, two men who had worked with each other for years realized for the first time that they were first cousins.

When Rosa Howie, Bob's mother, died in the 1940s, Mittie asked older white friends around the neighborhood to help her calculate her grandmother's age. Estimates ranged as high as 125. Youngsters who grew up with the dark-skinned, ever-bonneted, wide-eyed stern matriarch remembered her stashing sweets in her room and granting stale candy to favorite great-great-grandchildren.

Bob sired another son, Charlie Houston Ross, by a widowed neighbor—"He slipped around the door, I guess," the family explained. Bob had married Lois Marshall by 1920, when the census taker found them living with Thomas, 13; Margaret, 11; Emma, 8; Robert L., 5; Flosell, 3; and May Susie, 4 months. Bob gave his last name as Robinson, reflecting the family tradition of his father's name. Lois, Robert, and a baby named Watson, who was born in October 1921, all died of tuberculosis by the middle of 1924. By 1930, Bob was married to Etta, who brought Virginia, 16, and Wilson, 8, to the household, and he resumed the Ross surname.

Mittie and Tom's house remained the heart of the family for decades, with Marvin AME Zion Church as its soul. Two saplings Tom planted in the front yard grew into thick oaks. Umbrella trees, also known as chinaberries, graced the driveway, the side yard, and the back yard, where mature fruit trees yielded apples, plums, and fall pears. Mittie warned the children away from her prized damson tree in the front yard. Descendants who moved to Charlotte, Monroe, Waxhaw, and Mint Hill kept coming back on the weekends, spending Saturday night in the homeplace, going to church on Sunday, coming back to the house for reunion-style chicken dinners with cakes and pies cooked on a woodstove and tomatoes, okra, corn, and beans harvested from the kitchen garden. In the winter, pallets for the guests lined the wide hall, interspersed with the eight trunks Mittie had inherited from Maggie; in the summer, boys would sleep on the wraparound porch. At Christmas, a magnificent decorated tree presided in the hall. Generation after generation came to visit, to spend the night, to trick-or-treat. At the last family reunion, in the late 1950s, tables loaded with food lined both sides of the hall, and children played horseshoes outside. The home never had plumbing—water always came from the bucket at the well a short walk from the house, and an outhouse provided other necessary accommodations.

As the family grew, it suffered the pains of any large group—broken homes, scrapes with the law, children who died young, money troubles. Inherited land still required the backbreaking work of hauling sacks of barnyard-manure fertilizer in the spring and sacks of cotton in the fall. Crane's Store took eggs and corn for money, bartering snuff, tobacco, detergent, kerosene, salt, and matches. When electricity came in 1935, the bill was $1.50 a month. A quarter in the church collection plate was a widow's-mite sacrifice.

The inherited wealth did not last, as Ervin's daughter Rachel Houston might have predicted: "They say if you get something easy it slides right out of your hand." Tom and Mittie spent the money too freely, buying cars before most people could afford them, throwing lavish parties, driving back and forth to Charlotte. "They were eating things white folks couldn't afford to eat," said Rachel, who lived in Mittie's house when she was young.

For generations, the story of the family's heritage came to the young people in vague whispers and awkward asides from elders who wanted to forget their slavery-era roots and the embarrassing elements of their past. They said Bob was the first black man to win a court case in Union County, but they gave no details of the case or of his childhood apprenticeship or of his sending Mittie to live with the white women. He was working at Elmwood Cemetery in Charlotte when he died on September 20, 1948, but they brought his body to rest at Marvin AME Zion. When grandchildren and great-grandchildren found out that Mittie had been to Livingstone College but had not finished, she told them she had to come home because they put saltpeter in the food and water to dampen hormones and the chemical had affected her menstrual cycle.

But Mittie never stopped talking about Maggie and Sallie, when she was hanging out their washtub-scrubbed white chenille bedspreads, when she was scooping homemade ice cream into their pink-tinted and green-tinted glass sherbet dishes, when the sunlight was flashing rainbows from their mirrored pump organ, when she was cooking egg custard and pound cakes or canning peaches or plum jelly or beans or kraut as they had taught her. "That was her conversation," said Ervin's daughter Vivian. "She'd have something to say about Miss Maggie and Miss Sallie every day."

The grandchildren figure the antebellum women might have taught Mittie her medicinal as well as her culinary skills. "She would go out in the woods and she knew what kind of plants you could make a tea out of for different parts of your body," said Rachel Houston, who remembered Mittie's threading strips of bramble for a necklace around a baby's neck but doesn't remember why. "She used to make catnip tea. That was to keep the baby from hiving. Back then, you didn't go to doctors. The old people would use their remedies on you, and you would be healed. You drank the strong ginger ale to make the measles come out of you. We all had the measles. We all had the chicken pox at the same time." She'd seen deep splinters drawn out by fat meat tied over the wound with a broad leaf from a yard plant. She'd seen Mittie administer a bit of sugar and two or three drops of turpentine on a teaspoon to cure sugar worms: "If you ate a lot of sweets, a lot of candy, what they called sugar worms would be in your belly."

Mittie aged into a fearsome presence with large droopy eyes, deeply bowed legs and a cane constantly in her hand to help her through her severe arthritis. She was widowed on January 16, 1966. Later, she had

Tom and Mittie Houston and Family

a stroke and spent her last days in a nursing home. When she died on September 4, 1976, she had six children, thirty-seven grandchildren, ninety-eight great-grandchildren and thirty-two great-great-grandchildren. By the turn of the twenty-first century, a generation raised in the proud wake of *Roots* worked to gather a reunion of their far-flung family.

39

THE LAND

The white women raised my mama from the cradle,
and when they died, they left us this land.
—ROBERT HOUSTON, 1993

As the twenty-first century turned, bulldozers were reshaping the land of cotton, filling farm ponds, pushing over tenant houses, uprooting old oak trees, raising berms and hillocks in the high-dollar subdivisions spreading southeast from Charlotte. Acres worth fifty dollars when Bob and Mittie inherited them were selling at prices that soared above one hundred thousand dollars, and some of the houses on them above one million. When mansions started going up in Marvin around 1990, Mittie's son Robert Houston said they looked less like homes and more like "baby *ho*tels," as if they had run away from the big hotels in the city to grow up on fertile Union County soil. A single real estate transaction could surpass the sum of cotton crops across generations on the land.

The flower of southern farming had faded long before in Sandy Ridge Township, as corn and soybeans, beef and dairying supplanted cotton. Banks Stephens, who in the year that Maggie died left his tenant house and bought his own cotton farm near Weddington—with a tenant of his own and four head of mules—went on to buy the Delaney and George Sutton plantations. Before he was buried at Bonds Grove Methodist Church in 1932, he started a dairy herd partial to Jersey cows

Robert Houston at the Family Home, 1993

and sold milk to Foremost Dairies in Charlotte. A handful of families kept cropping cotton well into the second half of the twentieth century—Don Kerr from Marvin kept a cotton gin at Houston running into the 1980s—but the acres kept shrinking. In 1983, for the first time in two hundred years, cotton planting ceased across the county—not for lack of sales but in an effort to interrupt the life cycle of the boll weevil and eradicate the pest that had plagued farmers for most of the century. The success of the project brought back cotton briefly on the Ezzell and Kerr farms, but by then developers were already eyeing the fields as ripe for posh subdivisions and tempting farmers with bushels of greenbacks to reap the "last harvest" from their land. Charlotte was flourishing in a Sunbelt prosperity that created well-paying jobs in banking and technology and corporate headquarters, and executives recruited from the North and West favored palatial countryside escapes from the high-rises for themselves and their families. The wealth pushed down Providence Road, filling southeast Mecklenburg County so rapidly that in 1983 Weddington incorporated to avoid the risk of Charlotte's crossing Sixmile Creek, the county line, to annex more land. No one cared to stop the developers from buying and building, but the town could demand sufficiently large lots to preserve the rural air. Marvin, lacking a straight road like Providence linking it to the city, remained out of the path for another decade.

The Ross land that Maggie's will ordered sold to pay the legacies was marketed even before the new trial. The *Monroe Enquirer* published three hundred circulars and six notices of sale for the Ross lands, the *Monroe Journal* published five twenty-inch notices, and the *Charlotte Observer* published one in December 1923. About 1926, Frank Crane bought the tenant house that Maggie had made from the old Banks Presbyterian Church, removed the second story, and had it dragged down New Town Road by mules over rolling logs, a project that took six weeks. He set the building on a lot downhill from his house and fashioned it into a new store. In 1964, Dr. Rone's grandson Sam Ardrey bought the old house from Banks Presbyterian Church and moved it across Sixmile Creek to his farm in Mecklenburg County, leaving a vacant lot between the two churches at the heart of Marvin.

Most of the old Burleyson land had long gone out of the heirs' hands before cash became the chief farm crop in Marvin. County Surveyor R. W. Elliott surveyed the property for ten days in August 1924 for one hundred dollars and divided it between Bob and Mittie as the will directed. Each got 348.9 acres valued at $13,986, marked off with stake and stone, post oak, plum bush, and persimmon stump. Elliott submitted his plat on August 29. The court-appointed commission to oversee the partition, R. A. Hudson, J. D. Hemby, and A. W. Davis, submitted their report on September 2, and R. W. Lemmond, clerk of Superior Court, ordered it to be recorded on November 7.

By the terms of the will, Bob's share would go to Mittie upon his death. On February 20, 1926, he and Etta made a deal with Mittie and Tom. In exchange for five hundred dollars cash and clear title to one hundred eighty-five acres, the Rosses gave the Houstons the rest of his inheritance—four tracts that surveyed out to 182.4 acres—in a trust administered by R. B. Redwine. Bob now owned his land "discharged from any claim, right, title or interest in and to said land by the said

Mittie Belle Houston." He did not keep it long. On March 16, 1927, he put up the land for security on a three thousand dollar loan from T. M. Haywood payable in three years, with 6 percent interest payable every year. Bob could not pay, and trustee H. B. Adams sold the land at noon on October 25, 1930, at the post office door in Waxhaw. Haywood was the highest bidder at three thousand five hundred dollars.

The arrangement with Bob meant that Mittie was free to sell the land from his share of the estate, unlike her own land, which the will promised to her children. On March 1, 1926, she sold the 72-acre tract to J. M. Niven. On March 7, she sold the 19.9-acre tract and about 20 acres from the 35-acre tract to R. A. Hudson for $1,978. Then she decided not to sell any more and, for ten dollars, she received clear title to the land from the trust. In each transaction at the courthouse, officials took her aside and made sure that "she signed the same freely and voluntarily, without fear or compulsion of her said husband or any other person, and that she doth still voluntarily assent thereto."

On January 13, 1932, Mittie Bell and Tom petitioned to sell her life interest in the land to her children at ten dollars an acre. She had sold part of the inheritance and had one hundred ninety-four acres remaining. The clerk of Superior Court was holding the money from those sales, one thousand eight hundred four dollars and thirty-six cents, because it belonged to the children: Under the terms of the will, the land would have belonged to them at her death. Earl Ezzell estimated the value of the land at four thousand dollars, C. O. Howard three thousand two hundred fifty, R. A. Hudson three thousand eight hundred in affidavits to the Superior Court. Mittie was willing to accept a valuation of ten dollars an acre, or one thousand nine hundred forty dollars, about half the appraised value. Because of her age, the value of her life interest was calculated at one thousand one hundred forty-six dollars and six cents. The children would pay from the money that belonged to them from the previous sales. Gilliam Craig, John J. Parker's old law partner, was appointed guardian ad litem for Ervin, Collins, Robert, and Charlie, who were all younger than twenty-one. On February 29, 1932, O. L. Richardson, clerk of Superior Court, ordered J. C. M. Vann to be the commissioner to carry out the plan. Judge William T. Harding entered his judgment and decree at the March term of Superior Court. The survey on March 23, 1932, showed one hundred eighty-six and sixty-eight hundredths acres, reducing the value of the land to $1,866.08 and the values of Mittie's life interest to $1,104.56. Mittie got the money, and her children got the land.

On July 22, 1952, the children divided the land into six tracts of 32.75 acres each and gave Mittie the right to live on it until her death. Ervin, who was living in the house with Mittie, got that tract; Florence the tract to the west that crossed Rosstown Road; D. C., Collins, and Charlie the tracts to the east; and Robert the tract to the south that reached to New Town Road.

The following decades saw more land slip from the family, some sold for unpaid taxes, some sold for cash in hard times. Collins cashed in his heavily wooded tract first, selling the trees to a pulpwood company and then selling the land so that he could afford to move to a house in Charlotte. Robert sold his land on New Town Road so he could live closer to the homeplace. In 1955, Robert and Florence Vinson bought back from the Niven family the tract from Bob's share that Mittie sold to J. M. Niven, but in 1960 the Vinsons sold the land to Harry and Betty Short. The Shorts sold to developer William Nolan, who amassed eight hundred acres, much of it overlapping the Burleyson land, for his Providence Downs project—one-acre lots with homes from the upper five hundreds to more than one million, with streets named Calumet Farms Drive and Churchill Downs and Silver Charm emptying into Crane Road, as Rosstown Road was officially named after it was paved.

Once, Ervin Houston failed to pay the taxes and the grand house that Sallie and Maggie built for Mittie and Tom went up for auction. A cousin bought it and kept it in the family, but scarce money forced them to rent it out for a while. Ervin moved in with a neighbor, Clebo Ardrey; his daughter Vivian stayed with his sister Florence and his daughter Rachel with Florence's son Thomas Erskin Vinson. Eventually, they were able to move back into the house and remodel the inside, but the old wraparound porch was rotting beyond repair.

No one lived in the house after the early 1980s, and by the turn of the century it was crumbling to ruin. Rising land values were driving out the last of the family—no lynching was necessary, as in the old days, for wealthy whites to leave black landowners unable to pay their property taxes. Five or six small house lots clung to Crane Road, and even the homeplace was sold in 2004.

But by the early 1990s, the Marvin AME Zion Church that had started on Sallie and Maggie's land nearly a century earlier had outgrown its 200-seat brick sanctuary built in the 1940s. The church bought 5.8 acres for ten thousand dollars an acre in 1991 and started building a 400-seat, $482,000 sanctuary in 1993. It kept the old two-acre site where family tombstones dated back to baby Robert Waydie Ross's death in 1891. The new tract was part of the inheritance that Bob had lost in 1930, land that had changed hands a half-dozen times. After the turn of the century, the church had grown to some nine hundred souls—the sixth and seventh generations of Bob and Mittie's descendants, joined by scores of new members—and added a two million dollar sanctuary.

40

THE ABUNDANCE OF PEACE

But the humble shall inherit the land and delight themselves in the abundance of peace.

—PSALM 37:11

The *Statesville Landmark* celebrated the trial's conclusion as yet another example of Southern justice in an April 18, 1921, editorial headlined "Not Swayed by Prejudice." The column, like many other news reports, assumed that Bob and Mittie inherited all the Ross land, failing to distinguish between the eight hundred acres of Burleyson property and another seven hundred acres sold to pay legacies. The *Landmark* compounded the error by misreading 1,500 as 7,500, a mistake the *Monroe Journal* corrected to 1,500 when it excerpted the opinion.

The *Landmark* wrote:

> The jury's verdict in the Ross will case in Union county is one of many instances in which the gratifying fact stands out that white juries can and do disregard race prejudice. Maggie Ross, a white woman possessed of large estate, lived in retirement and it is alleged that she permitted her negro servants unusual privileges in her home. At her death it was found that she had willed the bulk of her estate to three negroes. Various bequests were made to churches, missions and charities (the orphanage at Barium Springs, $2,000), and small amounts were given to various white persons, but the bulk of the estate of 7,500 acres of valuable farming land and almost $35,000 cash was left to a negro man and his daughter

> and granddaughter. The white women had no near kin, but as soon as her will was made public second and third cousins and others farther removed, to the number of 109, entered suit to set aside the will on the ground that Maggie Ross was not mentally competent to make a will and that she was unduly influenced by the negroes who were beneficiaries. Many witnesses expressed the opinion that she was not mentally competent to make a will and when pinned down admitted that the opinion was based on the fact that she left her property to the negroes.
>
> That was a natural thought and that with the natural race feeling and the feeling that it was not best all 'round for so much valuable property to pass from the white race by gift into the hands of negroes, made a strong case to break the will. True the white beneficiaries employed counsel and gave their aid and influence against the effort to set aside the will, but most of these beneficiaries are outside of Union county. Their local influence would be small, while a jury of white Union county citizens would not be expected to look with favor on 7,500 acres of valuable Union county land passing into the hands of negroes, their heirs and assigns, for all time. But after a hard-fought contest of 15 days it took that Union county jury just 45 minutes to agree that Maggie Ross knew what she was doing when she made her will; that she wanted the negroes to have the property and she was entirely within her rights when she gave it to them. That is by no means an unusual verdict, either, from the point of race relationship. Not so many years ago a white jury, in Iredell Superior Court, took the word of an old colored man against that of two white men—men of property and standing as men of affairs in their community—in a matter involving the ownership of land. There are cases, of course, where passions are aroused, when race feeling sways judgment. But when the facts are set out in an atmosphere free from passion, in the clear light of justice, the negro will get his rights before the average Southern jury.

The "clear light of justice" shone sparingly in the middle decades of the twentieth century, although Union County commissioners eventually changed the name of Niggerhead Creek to Salem Creek. In 1930, a campaign by the fledgling NAACP helped thwart the nomination of Judge John J. Parker to the U.S. Supreme Court. President Herbert Hoover nominated the rare southern Republican, who had moved his law practice to Charlotte in 1922 and won appointment to the Fourth Circuit Court in 1925, to replace another southern Republican justice, Edward T. Stanford, on March 10, 1930. By the middle of April, opposition from labor unions and the NAACP threw the presumed-routine nomination into question. The NAACP used Parker's statement from the 1920 gubernatorial campaign about the negro's not wanting to be in politics to question whether he could justly rule on Fourteenth and Fifteenth Amendment questions: "Parker cannot approach similar questions with that dispassionate, unprejudiced and judicial frame of mind which would enable him to render a decision in accordance with the federal constitution. No man who entertains such ideas of utter disregard of integral parts of the federal constitution is fit to occupy a place on the bench of the United States Supreme Court." The Senate rejected the nomination 41–39 on May 7.

Parker stayed on the Fourth Circuit and participated in the Nuremberg Trials after World War II. In 1951, he sided with the segregated school system in Clarendon County, S.C., in a 2–1 ruling that was overturned by the 1954 Supreme Court decision ruling segregation illegal in public education. In 1955, in his third ruling on the *Briggs* case from Clarendon County, he established what become known as the "Parker Principle" used to resist integration across the South: "The Constitution . . . does not require integration. It merely forbids segregation. It does not forbid discrimination as occurs as the result of voluntary action. It merely forbids the use of governmental power to enforce segregation."

After the Ross will verdict, racial justice vanished in Monroe. In 1936, Monroe police officer Jesse A. Helms, Sr., a colleague of juror J. I. Fuller during the Ross trial, slammed a black woman to the sidewalk and dragged her to the downtown jail while white men laughed, black men hung their heads and backed away, and an eleven-year-old black boy named Robert Williams watched in horror. Williams grew up to be president of the Monroe NAACP in the 1950s, when the Klan had managed not only to organize in the town but also to hold large rallies and motorcades under the eye of sympathetic police.

In the summer of 1957, after a black child drowned in a Union County lake, black leaders appealed to the Monroe Parks and Recreation Commission to desegregate the public Monroe Country Club swimming pool. In 1958, police arrested two black boys, ages eight and ten, and charged them with kissing a white girl. The case exploded onto the national scene, and the boys were sentenced to the Morrison Training School for Negroes in Hoffman, North Carolina. The next year, a white jury in the Union County Courthouse took forty-five minutes to free a white man accused of raping a black sharecropper in spite of a white woman's testimony that she had seen the attack. Some jurors laughed at the black woman's story and accepted the defense's argument that the man was not guilty because he had been "drunk and having a little fun." After the verdict, Williams angrily told national newspaper reporters: "We must be willing to kill if necessary. . . . We cannot rely on the law. We get no justice under the present system. . . . Since the federal government will not bring a halt to lynching in the South and since the so-called courts lynch our people legally, if it's necessary to stop lynching with lynching, then we must be willing to resort to that method." That brought him more national attention, although he denied that he advocated lynching as such.

In March 1961, one month after the trailblazing sit-in at Woolworth's in Greensboro, Williams led a sit-in at Gamble's Drug Store in Monroe, then a boycott of lunch counters that wouldn't serve blacks. Within a year, one store had gone out of business and another removed the stools so everyone stood at the counter. In June 1961, for the fourth summer, black youths picketed the Monroe Country Club pool. Eventually, the city closed the pool, filled it with dirt, and planted a flower garden rather than allowing black children to swim in it. On a Sunday afternoon in August, a Freedom Ride march around the Union County Courthouse, with more than two thousand angry white people jeering and threatening, erupted in fistfighting, gang attacks, and gunfire that went on in the streets far after dark. Williams fled the country.

In the midst of the years of strife, on May 13, 1960, the *Monroe Journal* reprinted the entire Last Will and Testament of Sallie A. Ross, almost forty years after the paper published the freshly discovered document. The eighty-one column inches of text ran under the headline "Interesting County Document: Miss Ross Willed Estate to Negroes." The editors' note explained: "Mrs. S. B. Parker of Waxhaw R-1, whose family used to live on one of the places involved, brings in a copy of the May 28, 1920 issue of The Journal which contained the celebrated Ross will. She requests that it be published again for two reasons: 1. Many younger people will read it for the first time and 2. Her copy has been passed around so much it's about worn out."

If Mrs. Parker and the *Journal* editor intended to promote racial harmony in Monroe with the record of the Ross relationship, they failed. It would be nearly two decades before the first black person won election to the Monroe City Council, nearly three decades before the name of Niggerhead Creek was changed to Salem Creek. But in Marvin, seventeen miles to the southwest, the harmony was unbroken across the decades. "Respect links races in Marvin: Sisters' affectionate act over a century ago still bearing fruit," reported the *Charlotte Observer* in 1993:

"The key to their peace is mutual respect, say blacks and whites who grew up together in a social order where each person's work was valued for its contribution to the common good. 'We'd work all together in the cotton field—hoeing cotton, picking cotton,' explained Luella Fetherson at last year's celebration while she hugged her neighbor, Jewell Carter, whom she rarely sees. 'When she was little and my children were little, she'd come out and play with mine,' Carter said. 'It's been 50 years ago.'"

Black and white children romped together and ate dinner at whatever house they found themselves when mealtime came. They went to separate churches for freedom of cultural expression, as Banks Presbyterian organist Lavinia Kell explained to a black friend: "You go to church and stay all day and come home carrying your shoes. I get my religion and come home." Otherwise, only officially segregated schools kept them apart. Philanthropist Julius Rosenwald built a school with real glass windows for black children in the 1920s.

Most of life was integrated, Mittie's granddaughter Alvenia Houston Morrison told the *Observer* in 1993: "It was wonderful, wonderful. I was raised with the white kids, so I played with them. I didn't have any prejudice and they didn't have any. We got along so well. We always played together. The whites got buses before the blacks, but we all walked that road together."

Blacks and whites depended on each other on the farm, as Bob and Mittie's descendants worked their acres and other black families bought their own land. James Robert Houston, a cousin of Tom's, and his wife,

Lucinda, were tenant farmers for the first twenty-one years of their marriage. They saw an advertisement for 3 percent loans from the Farm Security Administration and arranged to buy a sixty-one acre farm from Ben Price, a white man from Waxhaw. Earl Ezzell, Houston's neighbor and friend who worked at the county agent's office in Monroe, encouraged the move. Houston borrowed $3,665 in 1939, when his net worth was about $1,000. By 1946, he had paid off the farm—all from raising cotton, chickens, and cattle—and increased his net worth to $7,550.

"This family is an outstanding influence in the 'Ross Town' community, having been responsible for a very successful organization of a community group of colored people," the *Journal* reported on February 22, 1946. "We have also secured many applicants for farm ownership by the influence of this family. The comparison between the social and commercial position of this family now and at the time of acceptance of the program is quite marked. They have expressed the opinion that they have more and healthier food to eat, better clothes to wear, more freedom in planning and a feeling of security which they never realized as a tenant family."

As the economy shifted away from farming, Marvin lost the centers that brought people together—the store, the grain mill, the blacksmith shop—and contact among the families concentrated on church-based festivals and community-wide worship at Thanksgiving and other special times. Marvin AME Zion grew by the hundreds while Banks Presbyterian and Marvin United Methodist dwindled in membership, but the churches kept up their fellowship. Marvin AME Zion leased its old building to Freedom Baptist Church, a white congregation, and members started scheduling frequent gatherings.

Newcomers marveled at the relationships. Gordon Suhre, a native of Virginia Beach who became mayor when Marvin incorporated in 1994, was unprepared when a Justice Department official called to ask about black and Hispanic populations in the village. "My reply to the woman: 'I really don't know—does it make a difference?' " he said. "We've never had any problems." Suhre, who joined the foot-tapping worship and feasted on homemade apple pie when he was invited to Marvin AME

Zion, made historic preservation of a strip of New Town Road a priority when he won reelection in 2003. He opened the village office in a brick house between Banks Presbyterian Church and the vacant lot where the Rosses once lived and proposed gaining historic designation for the churches, the cemeteries, Frank Crane's house, and the former Crane Store, the original Banks Presbyterian Church that Maggie Ross once used as a tenant house.

Outsiders and old-timers agreed that Marvin was worth preserving. "When we were building this place, black folks visited," Lauri Pistolis, who established a horse farm with her husband Dennis in the mid-1990s, told the *Charlotte Observer* in a September 14, 1997, story headlined "Marvin's Crane Road church, farms are study in racial harmony." "They watch out for us, help take care of us. Some white people might have been concerned, driving down this road and seeing a lot of black residents. That would have been a mistake. This is a great area to live." Michael Stitt, whose family no longer lived in Marvin but still worshipped at Marvin AME Zion, told the *Observer*: "A lot of things are changing. People are moving out this way, moving out from Charlotte. But I hope it doesn't change. We're all children of God. Here, we all get along together."

Mildred Keiser, who went to school with Mittie's descendants, said the whole community enjoyed the peace and mutual respect that the Ross family established: "I grew up here not knowing there was anybody named Jim Crow. When my relatives died, the white people put on their suits and came to our house. I thought black people and white people helped each other."

WHITE ROSS GENEALOGY

- Martin Ross m. Peggy Brown
  - William
  - Arden
    - m. Martha (Patsy) Irby
      - Amon
      - William
      - Ellison
      - Martin
      - James
        - m. Martha Ernest
          - James
          - William
          - Frances
      - Margaret
        - m. Henry Neilly
      - Frances
        - m. Benjamin Trott
  - Nathan
    - m. Susan Burleyson
      - Jackson
      - Dennis
      - Sarah
      - Margaret
  - Samuel
    - m. Sarah Yarbrough
      - Jonathan
        - m. Sarah Starnes/Molly Grier
      - Hugh
        - m. Sarah A. Helms
      - Hilliard
        - m. Lucy Richardson/Lucy Ashcraft
          - John T. Ross
          - Sarah E. Ross
            - m. Henry A. Helms
          - Milbry Ross
          - Samuel E. Ross
          - George W. Ross

m. Susan Bonds
Mary Bell
Ben
Robert
Edward
Thomas
Charles
Benjamin
Frances Collins
Joe Ross
Jasper Ross
Newton A. Ross
Peter P. Ross
m. Sarah Elizabeth Parker
Edward O. Ross
m. Rebecca Dees
Laura Ross
m. Ransom Helm
Virginia Ross
m. Adam Helm
Izetta Ross
Lillian Ross
m. Claude C. Broom
Thomas R. Ross
m. Helene Dry
Patricia E. Ross
m. Mrs. Alice Langtry Hyde
Henry G. Ross
m. Alice Castor
Curtis H. Ross
m. Alice Richardson
Julia Mae Ross
Sarah Ross
Melber Ross
(Martha Ann Ross)
Ezekiel
m. Mary Margaret (Polly) Deese
Franklin K. Ross
James E. Ross
m. Emma R. McLendon
Sarah M. Ross
m. John W. Morris

Lizzie Morris
m. Manford Newton Manus
John Manus
Janie Lee Manus
m. Parce Henry Deese, Sr.
Henry (Harry) Adam Manus
Bradley Manus
Franklin Manus
Carl Manus
m. Laura McCoy
Elizabeth A. Ross
m. N. A. Hinson
William Ross
m. Dealie Cook
Bud Ross
Pearl Ross
Effie Ross
May Ross
Brack Ross
Angeline Ross
m. John Cook
Florence Alice Cleo Ross Cook
m. William Arthur Lindsay, Sr.
T. Pink Ross
m. Dovie Cook
Henry A. Ross
Raymond B. Ross
Ernest Ross
Ida Ross
Carl Ross
Mary Ross
Lula Ross
Bunyon Ross
Lovin Ross
Bright Ross
Johnnie Ross
Grady Ross
Nay Ross
Roy Ross
Coy Ross
Willie Ross
Joe Ross

Lucinda
m. Coleman Lee
Louise Lee
Martha Lee
Mary Lee
Ida Lee
Louisa Jane
m. Bryant Washington Deese
James Manford Deese
Edmund Green Dees
m. Martha Hagler
John Robert Dees
m. Martha Secrest
Edwin Green Dees
Bahama Lea "B. L." Dees
Mary Dees
Raymond Shute Dees
Alvin Robert Dees
Arthur Thomas Dees
Joseph C. Dees
Cloye Dees
Parce Henry Dees, Sr.
m. Janie L. Manus, above
Carrie Dees Killough
Julia Dees Killough
Lucinda Dees
Sarah E. Deese
m. Bollivar Thompson
Penelope Dees
John Wesley Dees
Jemima
m. Jesse Parker (first cousin)
Mrs. Sarah Ross
Mrs. Matt Broom
John Parker
Charlie Parker
Hugh Ross
m. Euridice Jordan
William
James Ross
m. (2) Susan Cuthbertson
Margaret Ross

  - m. Sarah Helms
    - Lessie Ross
      - m. Williford Crook
- Marina "Riney" Ross
  - m. Matthew Parker
    - Thomas H. Parker
    - Jesse L. Parker
  - m. Jemima (first cousin)
    - Louisa
    - Susanna
    - Rebecca
      - m. Gilbert Franklin Crowell
        - Harriet Jerusha Crowell
          - m. John Houston Rogers
            - William Thomas Rogers
            - Claudious Bernard Rogers
            - Simon Luther Rogers
            - Cyrus Marion Rogers
            - Grover Elmore Rogers
            - Ernest Eugene "Joe" Rogers
            - Wiley Davis Rogers
            - John Grady Rogers
            - Flossey Jerusha Rogers
              - m. Charles Lee Haywood
            - Mary Ida Rogers
              - m. William Houston Pierce
    - Jemima Elizabeth
      - m. Gabriel Helms
        - J. Tip Helms
- Ellen Ross
  - m. Wylie Parker
    - Burwell Parker
    - Wilson Parker
    - Stephen Parker
    - James Parker
    - Thomas Parker
    - Emeline Parker
    - Elizabeth Parker
- Rebecca Ross
  - m. John W. Helms
- Annie Brown Ross
  - m. William O. Beckett

- Elizabeth Ross
  - m. James Bickett, Jr.
    - Sample Bickett
      - m. Mrs. Gipson
    - Thomas W. Bickett
      - m. Miss Covington
        - Gov T. Walter Bickett
    - Teresa Bickett
      - m. Abel Funderburk
    - Louisa Bickett
      - m. George Funderburk
    - Harriett Bickett
      - m. William Windle
    - Mary Jane Bickett
      - m. James Debonan
        - Edwin Debonan
      - m. Mr. Smith
        - Estelle Smith
          - m. Mr. Horn
            - W. W. Horn

BLACK ROSS GENEALOGY

- Rosa Ross
  - —— Robinson
    - Bob Ross
      - m. Alice Featherstone
        - Waydie Ross
        - Mittie Bell Ross
          - m. Thomas Houston
            - Florence Houston (Oct. 19, 1907–June 30, 1992)
              - m. Robert Vinson
                - Willie Ernest Vinson
                  - m. Nancy Jane Miller
                    - Thomas Billy Vinson
                      - m. Patricia Evelyn
                        - Kimberly Vinson
                          - m. Ivey
                        - Patrice Vinson
                          - m. Bryson
                        - Thomas Vinson, Jr.
                        - Tiffany Vinson
                - Peggy Vinson
                      - m. T. C. Stinson
                        - Thomas Chuck Stinson
                        - Heidi Stinson
                          - m. Williamson
                    - Barbara Davis Vinson
                      - m. Garfield Davis
                        - Cassandra Renee Bell Davis
                        - Sean Davis
                    - Donnie Drake Vinson
                        - Chevonda Johnson
                        - Jewel Vinson
                    - Cassandra Vinson
                - Thomas Erskin Vinson
                  - m. Maggie Ruth
                    - Thomas Ray Vinson
                    - Rayford Dennis Vinson
                    - Kent Vinson

- Robert Ned Houston
  - m. Amanda Yarbrough
    - Thomas Houston

Carolin Vinson
Shirley Ruth Vinson
Randy Vinson
Robert Vinson
Brouce Vinson
Glend Vinson
Andy Vinson
Claud Vinson
Alice Vinson
Wonda Kay Vinson
Laperal Vinson
Douglas Vinson
Dennis Clyde Houston (Nov. 22, 1909–March 7, 1993)
m. Catherine Ivey
Charlie Houston (Oct. 2, 1911–Feb. 12, 1985)
m. Georgia Massey
Charles
Robert Tom Houston (April 8, 1913–Oct. 7, 1995)
m. Janie I. Ivey
Collins Houston, Sr. (June 13, 1914–Jan. 10, 2000)
m. Hattie Lee Kirkpatrick
Ervin Houston (April 7, 1917–Feb. 12, 1979)
m. Maggie Belle Sims
Rachel Houston
Vivian Houston
m. Lois Marshel
m. Etta
m. Samuel Howie

SOURCES

All of the weather-related material in the book comes from the Voluntary Observers' Meteorological Record at the Monroe station, where the Moore family has kept records since 1898.

The *Monroe Journal* that covered the trial was a twice-weekly newspaper, published on Tuesdays and Fridays. The *Charlotte Observer* was a morning daily that had a report almost every day. The *Charlotte News* was an afternoon daily that covered only the verdict.

The transcript, certified by the clerk of the Superior Court of Union County on Oct. 14, 1921, is not a question-and-answer transcript except on rare occasions (e.g., pp. 135, 149, 184) but appears as speeches, sometimes very lengthy and disconnected, by each witness. It appears that the transcriber embedded the questions in the answers. "Do you have an opinion as to her mental condition?" "Yes" becomes "I have an opinion as to her mental condition" (or "Yes, I have an opinion as to her mental condition," with no question recorded, as on p. 169). Frank Crane is represented as saying that he had not seen the cousins (listing each by name) at Maggie's house, but then he says "I don't know the most of the names that were called to me," showing that in fact the names were read to him and he responded. I have reconstructed the exchanges accordingly. Some material that does not appear in the transcript is preserved in newspaper accounts. The transcript was apparently prepared for the state Supreme Court. One copy is on file in the Supreme Court library and another in the Heritage Room of Union County. It has a table of contents by witness.

Legal documents are available at the Union County Courthouse or the N.C. Division of archives. They include In Re Ross' Will (Supreme Court of North Carolina, Nov. 23, 1921, 109 S.E. 365); Minute Docket (Union Superior Court, 1924, p. 338); Union County Superior Court Minutes (C.097.30010 Vol. 14, p. 58, 61, 66, 79–95); "In Re Will of Maggie A. Ross" (N.C. State Archives microfilm); Union County Superior Court Minutes (C.097.30011 Vol. 15, p. 339, 372–73); "In Re Will of Maggie A. Ross" (N.C. State Archives microfilm); Union County Estates NC CR.097.508.186 Sallie Ross 1909 and Maggie Ross 1920 (Folder No. 1, N.C. State Archives); Union County Estates NC CR.097.508.186 Sallie Ross 1909 and Maggie Ross 1920 (Folder No. 2, N.C. State Archives). Jonathan Burleyson's and Maggie Ross's wills are in the Union County Courthouse.

General histories that contribute to understanding of the area and its history are John M. Redwine, *Union County, North Carolina, 1842–1953* (Monroe: Cory Press, 1953); Suzanna S. Pickens, *Sweet Union: An Architectural and Historical Survey of Union County, North Carolina* (Monroe: Union County Board of Commissioners, Monroe-Union County Historic Properties Commission, and Union County Historical Society,

1990); and LeGette Blythe and Charles Raven Brockmann, *Hornets' Nest: The Story of Charlotte and Mecklenburg County* (Charlotte: McNally, 1961).

In the Prologue, the courtroom material and most facts about Maggie are from the transcript. The description of Maggie's wealth is from the *Monroe Journal*. Information about Parker is from William C. Burris, *Duty and the Law: Judge John J. Parker and the Constitution* (Bessemer, Ala.: Colonial Press, 1987) and Kenneth W. Goings, *The NAACP Comes of Age: The Defeat of Judge John J. Parker* (Bloomington: Indiana University Press, 1990).

In Chapter 1, the history of Marvin is from a 1960s account and from reminisces of Jennie Helms, including "A Letter from Miss Jennie Helms" (*Monroe Enquirer*, Sept. 17, 1964), "The Marvin Community" (*Monroe Enquirer*, Nov. 30, 1964), "Visiting Marvin with Miss Jennie Helms" (*Monroe Journal*, Dec. 4, 1964), and an unpublished description of her family's country store. Church-specific information is from M. Catherine Squires, "History of Marvin Church" (unpublished), Rev. W. E. McIlwaine, "Historical Sketch of Banks Church" (unpublished), and Bill F. Howie, Footprints of Faith: Methodism in Union County (self-published, c. 1990). All of this material is in the collection of the Heritage Room of Union County. Other material is from Louise Barber Matthews, *History of the Providence Presbyterian Church, 1767–1967* (Charlotte: Brooks Litho, 1967). Material about E. M. Marvin is from the Oklahoma Historical Society, Chronicles of Oklahoma 4 (no. 3), September 1926. Information about the J. J. Rone House is from an interview with Sam Ardrey in the house and from Dan L. Morrill, "J. J. Rone House," Sept. 6, 1983, prepared for the Charlotte-Mecklenburg Historic Landmarks Commission. Descriptions of Dr. Rone's reason for leaving and the neighbors' response to the Rosses are from interviews with Joe Kerr and Lavinia Kell. The deed to Marvin AME Zion Church is in the Union County Register of Deeds. Other material is from the transcript. Sallie Ross's obituary is preserved as a newspaper clipping in the Heritage Room of Union County.

In Chapter 2, The Niggerhead Creek and the John Medlin stories are widely published in Union County newspapers and histories. One version of the Medlin story is in Virginia A. S. Kendrick, *Looking Back at Monroe's History* (Monroe: City of Monroe, 1995). Other lynching stories appeared in the *Monroe Journal*, sometimes reprinted from other papers, and the *Charlotte Observer*. The lynching of Anthony P. Crawford was documented in an Associated Press series in 2001. Other items are identified by the newspapers from which they came.

In Chapter 3, the history of Fusion is from Hugh Talmage Lefler and Albert Ray Newsome, *North Carolina: The History of a Southern State* (Chapel Hill: University of North Carolina Press, 1973). Other items are identified in the text by the publication from which they came.

In Chapter 4, the descriptions of John J. Parker are from Burris, *Duty and the Law*. Other material about his campaign is from the *Monroe Journal*. The description of A. M. Stack is from Amos M. Stack and Roland Beasley, Sr., *Sketches of Monroe and Union County* (Charlotte: News and Times Print, 1902). The description of Judge Bis

Ray is from J. W. Pless, "Memorial of Judge J. Bis Ray" (Twenty-Seventh Annual Session, N.C. Bar Association, pp. 161–65). Descriptions of his courtroom activity are from the *Monroe Journal*. Descriptions of J. O. B. Huey, A. E. Morgan, and Holmes Morris are from private correspondence with their descendants, Gladys Huey Cox, Emma Morgan Hinson, and Holmes Morris, Jr., and from Virginia A. S. Kendrick, *The Heritage of Union County* (Monroe: The Carolinas Genealogical Society, 1993), which is also the source for information on Henry Pigg. Descriptions of E. T. Cansler are from personal interviews with his granddaughter Betty Thomas and great-grandson Robert Thomas. Descriptions of other lawyers are from Kendrick and from the *Monroe Journal*.

In Chapter 5, descriptions of the family history and land purchases are from genealogical and census records, Jonathan's Burleyson's will, and deeds in the Union County Register of Deeds. The description of Samuel Hoey Walkup is from Kendrick, *Heritage of Union County*. Dennis Ross's Confederate service is on file in the U.S. Department of Archives. The apprenticeship law is in William H. Battle, *Battle's Revisal of the Public Statutes of North Carolina* (Raleigh: Edwards, Broughton & Co., 1873, pp. 81–82). The court order is in the transcript.

In Chapter 6, the description of the Battle of Kinston is from Ted Sampley, "The First Battle of Kinston," *Olde Kinston Gazette*, Sept. 2001. The description of Job Squier Crane is in Kendrick, *Heritage of Union County*. Land purchases are from deeds in the Union county Register of Deeds. The death of Dennis Ross is from the diary of Confederate Capt. W. E. Ardrey, transcript, and the *Charlotte Observer*. Henry Grady's column on cotton was reprinted in the *Monroe Journal*. Purchases at Crane Store are recorded in the store's ledgers, in possession of Crane's descendants. Other information is from the transcript.

In Chapter 7, some descriptions of Mittie are from interviews with her descendants, including Rachel Massey and Vivian Houston, and descendants of Frank Crane, Margaret Crane Butler, and Cornelia Crane Plyler. Other information comes from family genealogy, the transcript, and the *Monroe Journal*'s coverage of the trial.

In Chapter 8, the descriptions of Sallie and Maggie are from the transcript, except their joining Banks Presbyterian Church, which is in the church's records. The obituary of Dr. William A. McIlwaine is in the *Monroe Journal*. The cost of living is from Viriginia A. S. Kendrick, *Looking Back at Monroe's History*.

In Chapter 9, the descriptions of life in Marvin and of Frank Crane are from interviews with his descendants. The April Fool's joke is from the *Monroe Journal*. The description of Crane's Store is from Jennie Helms. Examples of news discussed in the store are from the *Journal*.

In Chapter 10, descriptions of Steve Walkup and Amos McIlwaine are from interviews with the descendants of Frank Crane and from the writings of Jennie Helms. Descriptions of R. A. Hudson are from Kendrick, *Heritage of Union County* and from the *Monroe Journal*. Other information is from the transcript.

In Chapter 11, descriptions of R. B. Redwine and H. B. Adams are from Stack and Beasley, *Sketches of Monroe and Union County*. The story of Barium Springs is from

Alan Keith-Lucas, *Meeting the Needs of the Times: A History of Barium Springs Home for Children, 1891–1991* (Welcome, N.C.: Wooden Printing Company, 1990). Other information is from the transcript, the will, and the estate file.

In Chapter 12, information about Maggie's death is from the *Monroe Journal.* Details of her burial are from the estate file. Information about the Ross family is from genealogy. The description of Walter Bickett's 1909 trial is from Daniel J. Sharfstein, "Passing Fancy," *Legal Affaris.* Sept.–Oct. 2003. Other information about Bickett is from R. B. House, ed, *Public Letters and Papers of Thomas Walter Bickett: Governor of North Carolina, 1917–1921* (Raleigh: Edwards & Broughton Printing Company, 1923). Other information about Maggie is from the transcript and the estate file. The caveators' brief is on file. The published citation is from the *Journal.* The record of the caveators' activity is in the estate file.

In Chapter 13, information about the jury seating is from the *Monroe Journal.* The delay in the trial's beginning is from court minutes. The *Greensboro News* article was reprinted in the *Journal.* The caveators' bill of particulars, printed in the *Journal,* has been relieved of its legal jargon, especially the use of "said" as an adjective. The receipt for Bud Huey's hotel room is in the estate file.

In Chapter 14, the description of the courthouse is from the Union County Courthouse self-guided tour (1986) and from Wayne K. Durrill, *The Union County Courthouses, 1843–1981* (Charlotte: Herb Eaton Historical Publications, 1986). The actions of the court are from the *Monroe Journal,* the *Charlotte Observer,* and the transcript.

In Chapter 15, information is from the transcript and the *Monroe Journal,* which gives the exchange about charitable giving absent from the transcript.

In Chapter 16, information is from the transcript and the *Monroe Journal* .

In Chapter 17, information about Steve Walkup is from the *Monroe Journal.* Information about Baxter Clegg Ashcraft is from Kendrick, *Heritage of Union County.* Testimony is from the transcript.

In Chapter 18, testimony is from the transcript. The caveators' names have been corrected in accordance with a list in the estate file.

In Chapter 19, testimony is from the transcript.

In Chapter 20, testimony is from the transcript. The description of Margaret Moore's behavior on the witness stand is based on the closing argument remark that she tried to "vamp" the jury.

In Chapter 21, testimony is from the transcript. Information about Henry Banks Stevens is from Kendrick, *Heritage of Union County.* Description of George Washington Ross is based on an interview with a descendant.

In Chapter 22, testimony is from the transcript.

In Chapter 23, testimony is from the transcript. The description of Dr. S. H. Ezzell is from Kendrick, *Heritage of Union County.*

In Chapter 24, testimony is from the transcript. The hypothetical question addressed to the alienists has been relieved of its legal jargon ("said" as an adjective). The discussion about the difference between mental inferiority and moral depravity, absent from the transcript, is mentioned in the *Charlotte Observer*. The story of Ed Alexander and Ralph Connor is from the *Monroe Journal*.

In Chapter 25, testimony is from the transcript. The decision not to call the fourth alienist is from the *Charlotte Observer*. Information about Rev. Bobby McIlwaine's preaching is from the *Monroe Journal*.

In Chapter 26, information about the Williams case is from the *Charlotte News*, the *Charlotte Observer*, and the *Monroe Journal* as indicated. This case is the subject of Gregory A. Freeman, *Lay This Body Down: The 1921 Murders of Eleven Plantation Slaves* (Chicago: Chicago Review Press, 1999). The *Observer*'s summary of the Ross case was reprinted in the *Journal*.

In Chapter 27, testimony is from the transcript. Information about Parker's potential judgeship is from the *Monroe Journal*.

In Chapter 28, testimony is from the transcript.

In Chapter 29, testimony is from the transcript.

In Chapter 30, testimony is from the transcript. The description of Capt. W. C. Heath is from T. B. Laney, *Biographies by T. B. Laney*, in possession of the Heritage Room. The Application for Apprentice is in the transcript.

In Chapter 31, testimony is from the transcript.

In Chapter 32, closing arguments are from the *Monroe Journal*. The description of John Sikes is from the Magazine Section of the *Journal*, Oct. 23, 1925.

In Chapter 33, closing arguments are from the *Monroe Journal*.

In Chapter 34, closing arguments are from the *Monroe Journal*. The text of *Pickwick Papers* is from Charles Dickens's book, chosen as directed by the *Journal*'s description. Walter Bickett's speech at Hampton Normal and Agricultural Institute is in R. B. House, *Public Letters and Papers*.

In Chapter 35, the charge is excerpted from the transcript. The verdict is from the transcript.

In Chapter 36, the courtroom activity is from the transcript. The election results are from the *Monroe Journal*. Information about what Adam Morgan and Bud Huey told their families is from private correspondence with Emma Morgan Hinson and Gladys Huey Cox. Other reports are from the *Journal*, the *Charlotte News*, and the *Charlotte Observer* as indicated. Information about unsuccessful Klan activity is from the *Journal*.

In Chapter 37, the jury list in Thomas Shaw's court, the verdict in the Knight divorce case and the verdict in the Ross case are in court minutes. Propounders and caveators' briefs and the state Supreme Court ruling are on file in the Supreme Court library.

In Chapter 38, information about execution of the will's terms is from the Account and Inventory, R. A. Hudson and R. B. Redwine, executors of the Last Will and Testament of Miss Maggie Ross (N.C. Archives), and estate files. Information about the growth of the family is from genealogy records and from the bulletin at Mittie Houston's funeral. Personal information about family members is from interviews with descendants and from *Union Observer* and *Charlotte Observer* stories.

In Chapter 39, information about Banks Stephens and about Frank Crane's moving the former tenant house is from Kendrick, *Heritage of Union County*. Information about land sales is from the estate file. Information about Sam Ardrey's moving the house is from an interview. Information about division of the land is from the estate file and from deeds and plats in the Union County Register of Deeds. Information about the family's use of the land is from interviews. Information about development in general in the Marvin area is from *Union Observer* stories. Information about the growth of Marvin AME Zion Church is from *Union Observer* stories and interviews with Rev. Henrico White.

In Chapter 40, the *Statesville Landmark*'s editorial is from the newspaper, reprinted in the *Monroe Journal*. Information about John J. Parker's Supreme Court nomination is from Goings, NAACP *Comes of Age*. Information about Parker's later career is from Burris, *Duty and the Law*. Information about racial tensions in Monroe is from Timothy B. Tyson, *Radio Free Dixie: Robert F. Williams and the Roots of Black Power* (Chapel Hill: The University of North Carolina Press, 1999). The reprint of the Ross will is in the *Monroe Journal*. Information about the success of the James Robert Houston family is from the *Journal*. Information about harmonious race relations in Marvin is from the *Charlotte Observer*, the *Union Observer*, and interviews.

INDEX

References to illustrations appear in *italics.*